Oxford ESOL Handbook

AB

·dor· ·itne· colleg

Also published in
Oxford Handbooks for Language Teachers

Teaching American English Pronunciation
Peter Avery and Susan Ehrlich

Success in English Teaching
Paul Davies and Eric Pearse

Doing Second Language Research
James Dean Brown and Theodore S. Rodgers

Teaching Business English
Mark Ellis and Christine Johnson

Intercultural Business Communication
Robert Gibson

Teaching and Learning in the Language Classroom
Tricia Hedge

Teaching Second Language Reading
Thom Hudson

Teaching English Overseas: An Introduction
Sandra Lee McKay

Teaching English as an International Language
Sandra Lee McKay

How Languages are Learned 3rd edition
Patsy M. Lightbown and Nina Spada

Communication in the Language Classroom
Tony Lynch

Teaching Young Language Learners
Annamaria Pinter

Doing Task-based Teaching
Jane Willis and Dave Willis

Explaining English Grammar
George Yule

Oxford ESOL Handbook

Philida Schellekens

in collaboration with
Krystyna Vargas

OXFORD
UNIVERSITY PRESS

OXFORD
UNIVERSITY PRESS

Great Clarendon Street, Oxford OX2 6DP

Oxford University Press is a department of the University of Oxford.
It furthers the University's objective of excellence in research, scholarship,
and education by publishing worldwide in

Oxford New York

Auckland Cape Town Dar es Salaam Hong Kong Karachi
Kuala Lumpur Madrid Melbourne Mexico City Nairobi
New Delhi Shanghai Taipei Toronto

With offices in

Argentina Austria Brazil Chile Czech Republic France Greece
Guatemala Hungary Italy Japan Poland Portugal Singapore
South Korea Switzerland Thailand Turkey Ukraine Vietnam

OXFORD and OXFORD ENGLISH are registered trade marks of
Oxford University Press in the UK and in certain other countries

© Oxford University Press 2007

The moral rights of the author have been asserted

Database right Oxford University Press (maker)

First published 2007
2012 2011 2010 2009 2008
10 9 8 7 6 5 4 3 2

ISBN: 978 0 19 442281 9

Printed in China

CONTENTS

ACKNOWLEDGEMENTS

This book has evolved out of my experience as a language learner and teacher in the Netherlands, Australia, and England, and latterly as an associate inspector in adult and further education. I would like to thank those students and colleagues with whom I have worked over the years and whose enthusiasm for language learning has made my time in education such an interesting and fulfilling experience. It is impossible to refer to them all here but I would like to mention two inspiring colleagues, Pat Hackett and Chris Juodvalkis, who made the beginning of my teaching career at Canberra TAFE in Australia such a formative experience.

I would like to give special thanks to Krystyna Vargas for her contribution to this book, both for her input and careful feedback. I am grateful to the students and staff at Greenwich Community College and the College of North West London for permission to use their work. I thank David Mallows, Jo-Ann Delaney, John Field, Karen Dudley, Tania Horak, and Dale Vargas for their valuable feedback on earlier drafts. Thanks also to my editor Julia Sallabank for her guidance and encouragement.

The authors and publishers are grateful to those who have given permission to reproduce the following extracts and adaptations of copyright material:

Shelley Bennett for permission to reproduce a quotation from an interview about teaching Outreach classes.

Birmingham and Solihull Learning and Skills Council for permission to reproduce an extract from *Full on English* in chapter 7.

Canberra Institute of Technology Adult Migrant English Program/ELEMENTS Employment and Study.

Career Psychology Ltd. for permission to reproduce a personality test.

The Department for Education and Skills for permission to reproduce an extract from p.120 of the ESOL Core Curriculum, and an extract from the Skills for Life Materials Pack ESOL Entry 1, p. 2 (Crown copyright).

Habia for permission to reproduce an extract from the National Occupational Standards for Hairdressing, Level 1 – salon reception duties.

Mercury South London Press for permission to reproduce an article.

The National Research and Development Centre for Adult Literacy and Numeracy for permission to use extracts from *ESOL Case Studies* in chapter 7.

NIACE for permission to reproduce a sample exercise from their Citizenship materials pack, pp. 116–117.

Oxford University Press and John Field for permission to reproduce an extract from 'Lexical Segmentation' by John Field from *ELT Journal* 2003 57/4.

The Qualifications and Curriculum Authority for permission to reproduce two samples from the National Literacy Tests from the QCA website (ref: communication L1/2.1/P4).

Skills for Logistics for permission to reproduce an extract from the National Occupational Standards for Dealing with Payment Transactions in Chapter 7.

Taylor and Francis for permission to reproduce an extract from 'The Human Heart' by Umashankar Joshi from p.183 of *The Languages of the World* by K. Katzner (Routledge, 2002).

Michael Vaughan-Rees for permission to use an extract from *Rhymes and Rhythm*, a poem-based course for English pronunciation and listening comprehension.

Peter Watcyn-Jones for permission to adapt a diagram from *Pair Work* (Penguin Books, 1981). Copyright © Peter Watcyn-Jones 1981.

Professor Alison Wray and Dr. Huw Bell for permission to reproduce the cartoon 'After you'.

Andy Smith for permission to use the 'iceberg' drawing.

Although every effort has been made to trace and contact copyright holders before publication, this has not been possible in some cases. We apologize for any apparent infringement of copyright and if notified, the publisher will be pleased to rectify any errors or omissions at the earliest opportunity.

Illustrations by: Sophie Grillet pp. 37, 176; Ann Johns p 150.

INTRODUCTION

This handbook is about the English language needs of migrants and refugees who have come to settle in English-speaking countries. Some learners may be able to speak English well and need very little support; others have substantial language needs. The sheer variety of skills and needs, countries of origin, and individual characteristics makes this an exciting field in which to work. At the same time its complexity can be bewildering, and often creates major challenges. On the other hand, what all these learners share is a desire to learn English and it is on this aspect that the book concentrates primarily. Many examples, case studies, and exercises are presented here to enable you, the reader, to explore what the learner does with the language, why that might be, and what teachers can do to promote development of language skills. To achieve this the teacher needs to be able to create opportunities for learning which are based on observation and language analysis. This includes nurturing the learners' awareness of how they are using the language and what they can do to develop their skills further. While there is reference to recent research and discussion of specific techniques which have proved to be effective in the classroom, the goal of this book is not necessarily to promote these above others. This is not least because fashions in language teaching change, sometimes rapidly, as new insights come to light which enhance our understanding of learning. It can also happen that what works with one learner or group of learners may not be suitable for others. Even more important, however, is the objective which underpins this book to promote thinking about learning. Teachers who reflect on the language use of their learners are more likely to provide that special learning opportunity that moves them along. In this respect, teaching is a constant cycle of observation and problem-solving.

This book promotes the use of activities which reflect situations in which learners will need to use English in their daily lives. This includes helping them to function in their new environment, from being able to say hello to their neighbours and learning to write in English, to achieving their long-term goals of finding a job or attending a course of study.

The teaching practice described here is set in the context of state-funded provision in the UK and undoubtedly some aspects reflect its structure and culture of language teaching. At the same time, the primary focus is on the perspective and experience of the learner. As teachers who have worked abroad or have shared their experiences with colleagues working in other countries will know, there are common elements to the learning of a new language and the settlement in a new country. It will be very pleasing if the profiles of the learners and their experiences are sufficiently universal to make this book suitable for an international audience.

This leaves the question as to who this book is aimed at. It is most likely to be of interest to qualified and practising teachers as well as those who are new to teaching migrants and refugees, for example, trainee teachers and teachers of English as a Foreign Language or first language literacy.

Guidance on using the book

Teachers of migrants and refugees work in a great variety of organizations and contexts. Many are based in large colleges of further and adult education, others work for small training providers and voluntary organizations where they may be the only person engaged in the management and delivery of English for Speakers of Other Languages (this term will be defined in the next chapter). This handbook tries to address the wide range of contexts that teachers find themselves working in, as well as the variety of issues that they may need to deal with. Different sections are likely to appeal to different types of teachers. The book is organized into eight chapters and the outline below gives an indication of which ones are most likely to be useful to the reader.

Chapter 1 gives a potted history of the development of teaching English to migrants and refugees, with a particular focus on the UK. This chapter will be of interest to readers who are very new to English language teaching or who are not yet familiar with the UK framework. It will also be useful to readers in other English-speaking countries as it provides guidance on equivalences of levels of qualifications as well as an overview of the contexts in which the needs of learners are met in England, Wales, Northern Ireland, and Scotland.

Chapter 2 provides information on the learners' backgrounds: the reasons why they left their country of origin, their education and skills profiles, and their motivation to learn English. The impact of these aspects on classroom delivery is looked at, especially the need for sensitivity and awareness of psychological factors. This chapter is likely to be most relevant to teachers who are new to working with migrants and refugees. They may be on their first teacher training course or have come from other disciplines, such as English as a Foreign Language or literacy teaching to people whose first language is English.

Chapter 3 describes the major characteristics of teaching English to migrants and refugees. This includes a comparison of language teaching and the teaching of literacy to people whose first language is English, which will be especially relevant to teachers working in the UK. The four language skills are also addressed and their uneven development, which is often referred to as 'spiky profiles'.

Chapter 4 is called 'Language analysis and language teaching'. This covers major aspects of teaching and learning, such as grammar, tenses, word order, and vocabulary learning. These topics will be of interest to all teachers. The same applies to Chapter 5 on the four skills of speaking, listening, reading, and writing.

Chapter 6 deals with the management of learning. The assessment of the learners' skills is covered as well as lesson planning, dealing with individual needs, giving feedback on language use, and the evaluation of lessons. This chapter is likely to reflect most strongly the context of language teaching in the UK. However, the actual practice of assessment, giving feedback, etc. should be of general interest.

The focus of Chapter 7 is on the delivery of language support—language teaching which is related to mainstream vocational courses, for example, carpentry, nursing, or hairdressing.

And last, Chapter 8 is about reflective practice which encourages practising teachers to think about their assumptions of teaching and learning. It also identifies ways in which classroom research can enhance the effectiveness of teaching.

1 KEY CONCEPTS OF LANGUAGE LEARNING AND TEACHING

A definition of ESOL

Before we start on the main subject of this book, it is important to define the term ESOL. It stands for English for Speakers of Other Languages and is used in the United Kingdom (UK) to describe English language provision for learners who have come to settle permanently in this country and who attend government-funded provision. We will use the term ESOL in this sense in this book.

However, ESOL does not just have one meaning. Howatt (2004), tracing the history of English language teaching, states that ESOL was originally coined in the 1960s as an umbrella term covering all types of English language learning. Then in the late 1980s, ESOL was adopted in the UK in the sense in which we use it now, and in preference to the term English as a Second Language (ESL). The change was made because it was felt that ESL did not acknowledge any other languages that the learners might speak in addition to their first language. It is worth bearing in mind these two uses of the term ESOL when you access literature on the subject of English language teaching and learning. For example, you will find that both ESOL and ESL are used to describe provision for migrants and refugees, with the latter predominantly being used in countries such as the United States, Canada, and Australia. Figure 1.1 gives a schematic overview of the dual use of the term ESOL as well as some other terminology which will be used in this book.

In addition to the term ESOL, which appears twice, once as the generic, umbrella term and once as it is used in the UK, the diagram contains the abbreviation EFL. This stands for English as a Foreign Language and applies to people who learn English in their country of origin or attend a language school while temporarily based in an English-speaking country.

If in the past EFL and ESOL were seen as two separate fields, more recently teachers have begun to recognize that the two fields have more in common than was originally thought. For example, areas such as the application of language learning theory and teaching techniques are of interest to both.

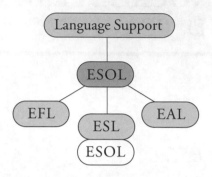

Figure 1.1: An overview of ESOL terminology

Teaching literacy, one of the great strengths of ESOL, has begun to influence EFL in recent years, too. However, what continues to create significant differences between EFL and ESOL is the context in which people learn English. EFL tends to concentrate on language for business and study as well as for leisure, travel, and fun activities (especially where young learners are concerned). By contrast, ESOL aims to help adults learn the language for everyday use, such as attending a doctor's appointment, filling in benefit forms, finding a job, etc.

The diagram also contains the term 'language support'. This covers language learning which is related to vocational courses, for example, hairdressing or engineering. Language learning may be completely integrated into the curriculum or may be attached to the vocational course as a separate block of learning. We will use 'language support' as a broad term which colleagues working in EFL and foreign language teaching would recognize as covering Content and Language Integrated Learning (CLIL) or English for Specific Purposes (ESP).

This leaves the term English as an Additional Language (EAL). Whereas ESOL provision is for adult learners who are 16 and older, EAL is used in the UK to describe provision for young learners who are up to 16 years old and in primary and secondary school.

Terminology to refer to the learners

In this book people whose first language is not English and who attend English language classes will be referred to as 'language learners' or 'learners'. In addition, where comparisons are made between categories of learners, for example, speakers of other languages and people whose first language is English, the former may be referred to as 'second language speakers'. This is for the pragmatic reason that this term is easier to understand than the alternative 'other language speakers'. This does not imply that any other language skills that the learners have are ignored. The term is used in the sense that the learners may have more than one other or second language, of which English is one.

Overview of ESOL delivery in the UK

While many of the aspects raised in this book can be expected to apply to English language teaching classrooms across the world, this book has been shaped in particular by the delivery of ESOL teaching. For those who work outside the UK or are new to ESOL teaching, a brief outline is provided below. If you want to find out more, the websites listed in Further Reading provide full information.

The UK consists of four countries: England, Scotland, Wales, and Northern Ireland, all of which have their own national strategies for basic skills, covering numeracy, literacy, and ESOL. If we take England first, the introduction of the Skills for Life strategy in 2001 created major opportunities for the expansion of provision for adult learners. One set of national standards was developed to cover the literacy and communication skills of both native English and second language speakers. These standards are underpinned by separate curricula for literacy and ESOL. Table 1.1 gives an overview of the five levels of the national literacy standards in the first column, with (in brackets) the ages at which first language speakers are expected to achieve these levels of performance. Scotland has its own set of qualifications, which you will find in the second column. For readers who are not familiar with either set of levels, two more sets of descriptors have been added. The third column contains broad level descriptors which are commonly used to describe the language levels of coursebooks and language provision. The last column contains the Council of Europe language levels. The table below should be seen as providing a broad rather than precise alignment of standards and levels. In particular, there is some uncertainty about the accuracy of the placement of the national literacy standards against the Council of Europe levels, as aligned in the Department for Education and Skills document *Pathways to Proficiency* (2003).

Learners working to the National Literacy Standards can achieve external accreditation in three modes: Communication (consisting of Speaking and Listening), Reading, and Writing. ESOL provision in England consists largely of courses at Entry 1 to 3 but, increasingly, more advanced level courses are also offered. Most of the provision is delivered in adult and further education colleges but vocational training providers, the voluntary

National literacy standards used in England, Wales, and Northern Ireland	Revised ESOL Framework used in Scotland	Commonly used level descriptors in ELT	Council of Europe levels
Level 2 (equivalent to achievement at age 16)	Higher	Advanced	C2 C1
Level 1 (equivalent to achievement at age 11)	Intermediate 2	Upper-intermediate	B2
Entry 3 (equivalent to achievement at age 9)	Intermediate 1	Intermediate	B1
Entry 2	Access 3	Pre-intermediate	A2
Entry 1	Access 2	Elementary / Beginner	A1

Table 1.1: National literacy standards for England

sector, and the prison service also offer courses. While general English is offered mostly, some providers have introduced progression routes to mainstream vocational courses, such as carpentry, bookkeeping, and childcare.

We now turn to the provision for language teaching in Northern Ireland, Wales, and Scotland. Northern Ireland has adopted the Skills for Life model without significant modification. In Wales, the Welsh Assembly launched its basic skills strategy entitled *Words Talk – Numbers Count* in 2005. This differs from Skills for Life in that it covers both Welsh and English as target languages and it encompasses the needs of young learners as well as adults. The strategy also contains a section on helping speakers of other languages.

The fourth country is Scotland, which has a model that differs substantially from the Skills for Life strategy. This is at least in part because, historically, Scotland has always structured its education system differently from the other countries. The National Qualifications in ESOL are available at five levels, starting at Access level. The most advanced level is called Higher, which prepares the learner for entry to university. This means that, under the Scottish model, learners have access to a much higher level of English than in the other countries in the UK.

Further reading

The websites below provide full and up-to-date information on government strategies for language, literacy, and numeracy.

England   http://www.dfes.gov.uk/readwriteplus
Scotland   http://www.sqa.org.uk/sqa
Wales   http://www.elwa.ac.uk
Northern Ireland   http://www.essentialskillsni.com

Department for Education and **Skills.** 2003. *Pathways to Proficiency: The Alignment of Language Proficiency Scales for Assessing Competence in English Language.* London: DfES Publications.

This publication provides an overview of the various frameworks that are used in England and Wales to accredit the skills of language learners, such as the National Literacy Standards, the Common European Framework, and the National Language Standards. While this is a useful document and the only one of its kind, there is some uncertainty about the accuracy of the alignment across the standards.

2 THE LEARNERS

Central to this book are people who have come to live in an English-speaking country, such as the United Kingdom, and who want to learn English. In this chapter we shall look at their range of backgrounds, skills, and needs.

The learners' backgrounds

Every English-speaking country will have its own community profile, but it is likely that language learners come from all over the world. In the UK they are often categorized into four groups, for both funding and educational purposes. While these categories describe the largest groups in the UK as they were at the time of writing, they are subject to constant change due to political and economic factors.

- Refugees who have fled national or international conflict. People from Iraq, Sri Lanka, and Somalia make up the largest groups, but conflicts in countries such as Burundi, Democratic Republic of Congo, and Zimbabwe have also caused many to flee.
- New Commonwealth citizens, many of whom came in the 1970s and 1980s for economic reasons from countries such as India, Bangladesh, and Pakistan. Many of the new arrivals come for reasons of family reunion, most often because they have married a partner already living in the UK.
- European Union (EU) citizens who are entitled to free ESOL classes.
- People from countries outside the EU, for example, from Japan, Korea, or Argentina. They are normally not entitled to free ESOL provision, unless they have settled permanently in the UK.

Impact of status on educational entitlement

Most commonly people emigrate to find safety, employment, or to join their family or partner. These reasons affect not just their chances of permanent settlement, but also their entitlement to government-funded learning. This is because the status of the learners is an important factor in deciding whether they have access to provision. Guidance on entitlement is provided by government departments and can change, sometimes dramatically. For details on how to access up-to-date advice, see the list of websites at the end of this book.

Organizations vary in their approach to checking eligibility. While many have dedicated staff responsible for carrying out documentation checks, others expect their language tutors to be involved in the process. In the case of the latter, you should have a clear definition of your role, access to guidance on the entitlement to provision, and a contact point to get advice on individual cases.

English language and other skills

As Figure 2.1 shows, the range of the learners' English language, education, and professional skills is amazingly wide.

Migrants' skills	
No English language ←→ Highly proficient	
No formal education ←→ Highly qualified	
Few transferable skills ←→ Professional skills and experience	

Figure 2.1: The range of migrants' skills

All people arrive with their own set of skills, ranging from full proficiency to substantial learning needs. At the same time, long-term trends in settlement can be observed. For example, the level of language skills of new arrivals has changed over time. Most of the economic migrants from New Commonwealth countries such as Bangladesh and Pakistan had little or no English when they came to the UK in the 1970s to work as unskilled labour in factories and workshops. This situation is changing. While language teachers still find that a substantial minority of learners has no English at all, English is being taught all over the world and it is increasingly likely that people have learnt the language in their country of origin. For example, a group of newly married women from Pakistan reported that they had been on an English language course 'How to be a bride in Birmingham' prior to their moving to the UK (Schellekens 2001). Others, for example, people from countries such as Sri Lanka or China, will have learnt about English grammar but have had little opportunity to speak the language.

New arrivals show an equally wide range of educational and skills levels which is reflected in research commissioned by the Home Office (Kempton *et al* 2002). This found that 'the foreign-born population is concentrated at both the low and high end of the skills distribution.' Nineteen per cent of the foreign-born population were found to hold a degree, compared to 15 per cent among the UK-born population. At the other end of the spectrum, 19 per cent of the foreign-born population had no qualifications, compared to 16 per cent of the UK-born population.

Even if people appear to have low skills levels, we find much untapped potential among them because many have never had the opportunity to access education. For example, the civil war in Somalia stopped many young people from attending school and university. Although at first sight their lack of acquired skills makes these learners look unpromising, many have the potential to do well. One of the rewards of teaching ESOL students is to watch them succeed once they access education.

The learners' backgrounds, education, skills, and the reasons why they left their country of origin create a complex picture. It is not static either, as new people arrive all the time. It is a real challenge for teachers to deliver suitable provision for this wide spectrum of needs, from learners who have had little schooling and have never learnt to read and write in their own language to fully qualified engineers or doctors.

TASK

What learner needs should teachers take into account when planning a language course?

The more you know about your learners, the better you can plan for their learning. To teach effectively, you need to take into account not just language needs, but also prior experience and educational background. For example, people may have been educated beyond secondary school level, in which case they are likely to have acquired study skills which are transferable to their new learning environment. On the other hand, if the learners have had little prior education, study skills will need to be planned for to enable them to carry out language learning tasks. Since you are likely to have learners with a variety of skills and needs in the same class, this also means that you will need to work out how to meet individual needs. We shall come back to these aspects in Chapter 6.

The learners' motivation to learn English

Learners enrol on language classes for a variety of reasons, ranging from wanting to use English in their everyday lives, to finding employment and undertaking further study. The introduction of the UK government's Nationality, Immigration, and Asylum Act 2002 has added another reason to learn English. The act 'requires UK residents seeking British citizenship to show a sufficient knowledge of English, Welsh, or Scottish Gaelic and to have a sufficient knowledge about Life in the United Kingdom' (Home Office 2003).

One of my studies (2001) throws further light on the motivation of English language learners. Two main reasons for learning English were identified.

People who had been in the country for less than two years prioritized communicating in everyday life: 'If you live in England, you must speak English.' By contrast, those who had been in the UK for longer than two years hardly referred to the need for general communication skills. They strongly identified finding employment and / or study as their main reason for learning English. It should be noted that men and women were equally interested in learning for work and study purposes regardless of ethnic minority background.

TASK

What role should the learners' own learning goals play in the planning of learning?

In the past, the language skills of the learners functioned as the main starting point for planning learning. However, more recently, it has been acknowledged that the context in which the learners want to use their new language is equally important. For example, some learners prioritize communicating with their neighbours or their doctor; others have it as their long-term goal to practise in their field of expertise, such as teaching, medicine, or carpentry. When planning a scheme of work for your class, clearly the context in which the learners want to use English is relevant and motivates the learner.

Learning language outside the classroom

Language learning in the classroom is a central theme in this book. However, it is also important to consider how much learners can benefit from learning language outside the classroom.

TASK

People who come to live in an English-speaking country have a variety of options to learn English. Some may feel that they are able to learn the language from day-to-day contact; others think that getting a job will help develop their English. Why may this not be the case?

My study (2001) showed that many learners had little or no contact with native English speakers and that it was confined to transactional relationships with the doctor, landlady, or their own or child's teachers. The learners' sense of social isolation was often palpable. Teachers of English need to be aware that refugees and migrants may not speak much or even any English in their daily lives.

A second indicator, economic participation, shows that unemployment and under-employment (where people with professional skills work long-term as cleaners, waiters, and minicab drivers, for example) are widespread. It appears that many employed second language speakers get stuck in a vicious circle: they can only get work where low level English is required and this in turn stops them from developing their language. That is why learning in the classroom is often the only way for them to extend their language, such as using more formal English or learning to write in the work context.

Psychological aspects

One dimension which is unique to ESOL teaching is the pastoral care that asylum seekers and refugees need. Many have experienced trauma and loss in their country of origin. When they arrive in the UK, they then often face isolation and loss of status. The extract below from Luna speaks for itself. She is a French speaker from Burundi where she read economics at university and has been in the UK for ten months.

> I'm coming from Burundi, part of East Central Africa where there is a war between society, between people from Burundi. There are two ethnic [groups] which are fighting between them because of power. So I try to escape and come up to here [UK] but it's so sad when I remember my sisters. I don't know where they are. Some are killed. My parents were killed in '93 when they killed our president who were elected officially. But he was Hutu. And the Hutu are majority in my country. But the government is held by Tutsis which are the minority … . We didn't choose really to come here to be living on social service. Only we can't get the job we need. We can't get the school we need … . Otherwise if there was a choice we would like to go back to our country if it was peaceful. But most of the people [in UK] they can't understand why we are here.

The impact of a forced move together with anxiety over family members left behind or missing can only be imagined.

The second shock is often that people face low socio-economic status and loss of status once they arrive in the UK. This can affect, in particular, those who had high status in their country of origin. Thirdly, many refugees and migrants encounter racism which makes it even harder to find their place in society.

Culture shock

Kalvero Oberg (1960) was the first to identify the concept of culture shock. In essence, he identified the following four stages of settlement:

- Initial euphoria: you are excited because you have just arrived and look forward to your new life in your new country.
- Irritation and hostility: you become aware of differences between your own culture and that of your new environment and may reject many

aspects of your host country. You may complain a lot and feel inadequate all at once.

- Adjustment: you get used to your new environment and are starting to understand what is going on around you. You may also begin to reflect on your own culture and identity.
- Adaptation: you can function in two cultures. You may well find that you prefer some of the customs of your new country. You understand that there are different ways to live and that no way is really better than another, just different.

Since many learners in English language classes can be expected to experience culture shock, it is a good idea to look out for symptoms. These are similar to those of depression, for example, people may feel sad, lonely, and not in control. Some feel annoyed much of the time and become unwilling to interact with others; others have trouble sleeping. You may well recognize these stages and feelings of culture shock if you have lived abroad yourself. However feelings and attitudes are expressed, essentially people feel lost and inadequate and in a sense they are right: they have lost the environment in which their identity was well-established and in which they knew how to operate. They now need to re-establish themselves, which can be particularly hard for people who have had to flee their own country and yearn for the time when they were happy there.

TASK

How can you use the concept of culture shock to help language learners cope with the process of settling in their new country?

It is important to be alert to your learners' emotional state. Sometimes people can come across as aggressive or lethargic. Is that because they are suffering from culture shock? If you think that it is, it may be worth raising this subject either with individual learners or in the whole group. Many people are relieved to know that their experience is not unique and that life will get better as they move into Oberg's stage of adjustment. Others realize that they have got stuck in one stage of culture shock and that they need to assess how they can move on.

It is often assumed that asylum seekers and refugees suffer greater culture shock than other migrants. In reality, this is not always the case. Some refugees realize early on that they have no option of going back to their country of origin. This can make it easier to adjust to their new country of residence. Other migrants by contrast can feel much less settled as it is possible for them to return to their country of origin.

Being sensitive to the backgrounds of the learners

In this section we will look at three case studies which are set in different teaching contexts. The first is a situation where a new, traumatized learner arrives in class. The second case study is based on a get-to-know-you activity with a new class. The third looks at common interview questions to assess the learner's language level on enrolment. We shall use these case studies to explore how ESOL teachers can respond sensitively to the needs of their learners.

CASE STUDY 1

A new student arrives in your class. He has just escaped to the UK. He had been held in prison for a long time and was tortured there, when suddenly and inexplicably he was released. His family were scared that he would be arrested again and managed to bundle him out of the country. He arrives in your class, keen to learn English but also very traumatized. He is overwhelmed by everything that has happened to him and clearly needs to talk about it. This affects his classmates, some of whom you know have gone through a similar experience. What do you do?

This case study is based on an actual situation which was difficult to handle because there was a conflict between the needs of the new learner and the rest of the group. It was clear from their reaction to the new student that they found it hard to cope with his anguish because it brought back memories of what had happened to them.

This was a difficult situation which required not just sensitive handling in the classroom but also external help. If you find yourself in a similar situation, the first step should be to find out what advice and guidance is available through your organization and other local counselling services such as general practitioners. There is also the Medical Foundation for the Care of Victims of Torture which offers medical, psychological, and psychiatric consultation and treatment. For details, please see the end of this chapter.

There is also the more general question of what support ESOL teachers can and should give to learners who are in distress. Many learners have little contact with English speakers and often their teacher is the only sympathetic person they can talk to. In addition, learners may have a different understanding of the role and status of the teacher and expect him or her to be able to intervene on their behalf, for example, to get access to services. In turn, teachers want to help their students but may lack the skills to give effective support. They may find themselves in psychological difficulty if they are faced with overwhelming trauma. It is important to bear in mind that the teacher's role is first and foremost to help the learners to learn

English and to be aware that other professionals may be in a better position to deal with the learners' personal problems.

CASE STUDY 2

Here is an activity which I adapted from *Pair Work* by Peter Watcyn-Jones (Penguin English 1981) when I was a very new ESOL teacher. It was used as an introductory exercise to get the students in an intermediate level class talking to each other. Do you think this exercise is successful?

> Read the sentences below and write down your answers.
>
> Next to number 1, write down your name.
> In the circle, write down the year you started to learn English.
> In the rectangle, write the name of your favourite teacher.
> Next to number 2, write down something that once made you very frightened.
> Next to number 3, write down what you really love doing.
>
> 1 _____
>
> 2 _____
> 3 _____

This is a nice introductory exercise which gives the learners a first opportunity to work and talk together. In some countries people have little opportunity to practise language in class. Instead, they are taught about language by the teacher, often in the first language rather than in English. So this exercise is useful in two ways: it breaks the ice and signposts a potentially new way of learning. But one of the questions is problematic. It asks the learners to write down something that once made them very frightened. This is perfectly all right in an EFL class, for which this exercise was designed and where you might expect an answer such as: *I once saw a spider under the bed,* or *I read a scary story which frightened me.* But this question is not appropriate for refugees who are likely to have experienced truly frightening events. It is not a good idea to use prompts of this type in the ESOL classroom, especially with a class you do not yet know. Teachers may want to use EFL materials in the ESOL classroom, or texts taken from the web or print media, as they can provide interesting and relevant resources. It is important, however, to read through them carefully beforehand to see that they are suitable for use.

CASE STUDY 3

It is common practice to hold an initial interview to assess the language needs of new learners. These are often conducted using standard prompts to guide the discussion. Which of these four questions is it not appropriate to ask students of ESOL?

- Where do you live?
- What kind of job would you like?
- What is your favourite TV programme?
- Where are your family?

In many cultures, it is common for people to ask each other questions about their families as part of the getting-to-know-you phase. However, the last question can distress asylum seekers and refugees. What if their relatives are missing or dead? That is why many teachers of ESOL do not broach the subject of family life with their students. They wait until the learners mention their family circumstances themselves.

Tolerance and discrimination

Learners may report to their English language teachers that they suffered discrimination because they are foreign; and those who are not white that they suffered racism. Many countries have legal safeguards which give a degree of protection, for example, in the UK, the Race Relations Act of 1976 made it unlawful to discriminate on racial grounds in relation to employment, training and education, and the provision of goods, facilities, and services. The Amendment Act of 2000 extended the Act further to include public authorities, outlawing race discrimination in functions not previously covered.

However, racism persists, not least because it is often hard to prove. For example, a learner who has applied for a job and has been rejected may receive feedback that another candidate matched the job specification better than her. It may be the case that she was rejected because of her race, not because of her ability, but equally it may not. If teachers are asked for guidance on cases such as this, it is important to handle these sensitively. Make sure that you do not inadvertently give wrong or misleading advice and, if necessary, arrange for professional advice to be provided, either through your organization or other local advisory services.

Managing diversity in the classroom

Where you do have the responsibility to make sure that learners do not suffer discrimination is in your own organization, and more specifically, during lessons. This can be complex, especially when people who come from homogeneous societies face the diversity of racial and cultural backgrounds that are commonly found in English-speaking countries. This can require a major adjustment but many learners develop a tolerant attitude to people from other races in the classroom environment. For example, a white, Eastern European woman who became firm friends with a Somali classmate reflected that one of her important learning experiences had been to overcome her own racist attitude.

TASK

If you already teach English, you will undoubtedly have students in your class from countries or ethnic minorities which have been engaged in conflict. Here are some examples:

• Iraqis and Iranians
• Kosovans, Croats, Serbs, and Albanians from the former Republic of Yugoslavia
• Tutsis and Hutus from Rwanda.

How would you manage learners from these conflict areas?

On the whole, learners are very respectful of each other. Many say that they left their home country to escape conflict and violence. The last thing they want is trouble again. At the same time, it is good to be prepared in case you find that problems arise. Teachers are often expected to produce a class profile which can reveal important information about the learners' backgrounds, including conflict areas. Organizations also produce rules of conduct which they expect you to use in class. A perfect opportunity is to introduce these during induction, an introductory session during which the learners are given information on their course. Since concepts such as rules of conduct are culturally defined, the students may need time to work through them to understand their own and their peers' assumptions and to come to a common understanding of what they mean in an English-speaking environment. If despite these preparatory activities a conflict arises during the lesson, you have the option to deal with it in class or talk to the learner afterwards.

More complex is the way in which individuals from the same ethnic minority group may respond to living in the UK. For example, there may be two young Somali women in your class, one of whom has adopted a liberal attitude, and the other a more traditional one. They are likely to differ in their opinions on practical as well as moral aspects.

TASK

What would you do if during a discussion a heated exchange develops about access to education for girls and boys?

You would want to encourage students during lessons to use English freely and for a real purpose, such as exploring different points of view. However, if you judge that the discussion is getting too heated, you can always interrupt the discussion with a language point, for example, the pronunciation of words, question formation, or turn-taking in the discussion. Once you have given feedback on aspects such as these, the learners can return to the topic and usually become more moderate in their exchange. And if a serious conflict arises, you may have to resolve it outside the classroom, if necessary with the help of your manager.

The culture of learning

Many learners find that they are not just learning a new language, they are getting to grips with a new learning culture. Education systems can be surprisingly different and, within that, traditions of language learning. For example, in countries such as China, classroom sizes of up to 70 students and a focus on reading and writing rather than speaking and listening create a style of teaching which allows for little oral work by the students themselves.

TASK

What might the learners' classroom experience be in their country of origin and how might it differ from the learning culture in countries such as the UK?

If you have ever been a learner or teacher in another country, what was it like? Was the approach to learning different from what you were used to?

Teachers need to be aware that their learners' understanding and experience of the process of language learning may be very different from the English language classroom with its emphasis on student participation. There is evidence that cultural differences can form obstacles to language learning. For example, an in-house study of language learners in a London college by Hully Wolderufael (1998) showed that they had been used to formal teaching in their country of origin. They expected concrete and regular feedback on their performance. The study showed that they did not rate the quality of their learning experience in London highly. They saw the college attitude as 'laid-back', the classes as unfocused, and the teachers as not 'addressing the desperation [the students] feel to master the language and get on with life.' Their comments indicate a culture clash between two very different educational systems. Learners with such perceptions are sometimes described pejoratively as 'traditional learners', but perhaps this judgement is a little harsh. Leaving aside the question of whether one type of delivery is more effective than another, teachers should be aware that learners may need to be gradually introduced to new styles of learning. For example, teachers may provide structured activities at the beginning of the course, such as written prompts to create a dialogue. Once the learners get used to this practice, they can be introduced to free language practice such as role-play.

Further reading

Department for Education and Skills. 2003. *Working with Refugees and Asylum Seekers: Support Materials for ESOL Providers.* London: DfES Publications.

http://www.torturecare.org.uk
This website run by the Medical Foundation for the Care of Victims of Torture provides information on its services and referral system.

If you want to find out more about the countries of origin of your students, the following websites give useful background information.
http://www.fco.gov.uk
http://www.economist.com/countries
http://www.worldbank.org

3 THE CONTEXT OF ESOL TEACHING

In the previous chapter we looked at the learners, their characteristics, and backgrounds. Now we turn to explore some of the major characteristics of ESOL teaching and its sister discipline of teaching literacy to first language speakers. This chapter will be particularly useful for people who are in the early stages of learning to teach and those who are thinking of transferring from other fields such as EFL and literacy teaching.

The main characteristics of the ESOL class

Considering the variety of the learners' backgrounds, languages, and other skills, it will not come as a surprise that diversity is one of the main defining characteristics of the ESOL classroom. A single class may have fifteen learners in it, all with distinct knowledge and skills and quite possibly all speaking different languages. In addition, learners may want to use English for a variety of purposes, for example, to attend a doctor's appointment or a job interview, or to learn to say hello to a neighbour. It is the task of the teacher to create relevant opportunities for language learning while at the same time bearing in mind the individual needs of the learner. This requires not only a good understanding of how the English language works, but also the ability to manage a complex range of needs. In Chapter 4, for example, we explore how teachers can teach vocabulary to buy and prepare food. They may find that some learners already know the meaning of words, but that for others, the vocabulary is completely new. All may need help with pronunciation, but with different sounds. Some learners may have few literacy skills so for them to learn to read and write the word 'shop' is a huge undertaking. Planning and managing these needs is clearly a more complex task than teaching EFL in non-English-speaking countries where foreign language teachers tend to deal with learners who share the same language background. For example, if you teach English in Madrid, you are likely to teach people who all speak Spanish and who have had similar educational experiences.

ESOL teachers also face constantly changing patterns of student enrolment. These are influenced by international, political, and economic factors such as, at the time of writing, the influx of Eastern European workers to meet the demand for labour in the UK, or the arrival of people from Zimbabwe seeking asylum. As a result, teachers need to make continuous adjustments to lesson plans, materials, and activities. These factors create a demanding, but at the same time exciting, environment in which to teach.

In the next chapters we will look at how teachers can manage what can be a bewildering variety of learning needs. Here we want to point out two important principles which can help teachers and learners achieve effective learning. The first is the teacher's ability to **observe** how the learners handle the language, both what they can do and cannot yet do. The second is the concept of **noticing** which Richard Schmidt (1990, 2001) formulated on the basis of his own experiences as a language learner. He became aware, as he learnt Portuguese, that there were moments when he noticed language features for the first time. In his view this process of noticing was the first step towards learning. Taking Schmidt's principle into the classroom, teachers can promote learning by creating opportunities for the learners to notice how they are using English. These two processes of teacher observation and learner noticing are especially relevant in a mixed-level ESOL class, because they enable teachers and students to focus on individual and independent learning. You will find examples to show how this can be done throughout this book.

ESOL and literacy teaching

It is important to review ESOL in relation to literacy teaching as these fields are closely aligned in the Skills for Life strategy. By literacy teaching, we mean provision for people whose first language is English and who have problems with reading and writing. As far as it is known, the policy of treating ESOL as part of literacy is unique to England. It is undoubtedly true that both groups of learners want to improve their English language skills and teachers of ESOL and literacy do see similarities, for example, the need to spell accurately. At the same time, teachers also observe important differences between people with literacy and ESOL needs. Here are two examples to explore these.

CASE STUDY 1

Two teachers plan to use the same reading task in an ESOL and a literacy class respectively. Both teachers need to give oral instructions on how the learners should carry out the task. How would you expect their approaches to differ?

In the case of the literacy teachers who teach first language speakers, provided that they do not use complex or technical language, they can safely assume that their oral instructions will not present any problems for their learners. However, the same instructions are likely to create major difficulties for language learners. It often happens that, when these learners hear spoken English, they hear a stream of sound which they cannot break down into words, even if they know them as individual items. As a consequence, they are unable to understand the instructions. The language teacher needs to be alert to this and match the language of instructions to the learners' level of understanding, for example, by simplifying the language, slowing down, and by pronouncing words individually. She may have to supplement these strategies by repeating the instructions, explaining the meaning of new words, and by checking back that the learners have understood. Since most students find it hard to understand instructions at a normal speed of speaking, the teacher will also need to build the development of listening skills into the curriculum. Techniques to help the learners improve their ability to identify individual words in a stream of sound are dealt with in Chapter 5.

CASE STUDY 2

A teacher is marking an assignment written by students on a business course, of which two samples of writing are provided below. Both students word-processed and spell-checked the assignments.

Student A

This company has many aims and objectives like most company's have. You can tell it's a small business but all it's staff are trained to the right standard so they can do their work in the best possible manor.

Student B

The owner have invested his money into the business, he is expecting a progress.

Customers are the stakeholders. They expect good customers service in case the goods is damaged they expect them to be replace by other goods.

These pieces were written by students with literacy and language needs. Can you tell which was written by which? What learning needs can you identify?

Student A has English as his first language. The structure of his writing is good, even if it is a little informal, and he uses accurate language, apart from some spelling mistakes in words such as the plural of *company*, the use of *it's*, and *manor* instead of *manner*. The second piece was written by a student whose first language is not English. Her spelling is accurate but she has problems with the agreement between the subject and the verb, as in *the owner have*, and *the goods is damaged*. The strengths and weaknesses of the work of these two students indicate that they will need different types of support. Student A needs to work on his spelling and formal writing; and Student B needs to work on aspects of English grammar. Meeting such different needs is of particular concern to teachers who have both types of learners in their class.

As the examples above show, students who do not have English as their first language need to develop skills which first language speakers already have, such as listening and accuracy of grammar. But both literacy and language learners may also have common learning needs, of which accurate spelling is an obvious example. Add to that the complex processes which are involved in the production of language, many of which cannot be observed directly, as illustrated by the analogy of an iceberg in Figure 3.1. So it is perhaps not surprising that standards writers and teachers have found it hard to define what distinguishes the language use of first and second language speakers.

Figure 3.1: Observable and unobservable language abilities

Unless first language speakers have a physical or mental impairment, they can be expected to speak and understand English fluently and accurately. What they lack is the ability to use English in a variety of contexts, such as in formal situations. They may also have difficulty in reading fluently or in expressing themselves in writing. They need to extend their existing skills which are represented by the part of the iceberg that we can see above the waterline.

By contrast, second language speakers need to acquire a whole set of new skills: the system of the language that native English speakers have already mastered, for example, grammar, pronunciation, and intonation. In our image of the iceberg, these aspects are hidden under the waterline because the ability to use the language, or LANGUAGE COMPETENCE, underpins the development of the four skills. At the same time the four skills and language competence are interdependent, just as the parts above and below the waterline form part of the same structure. The challenge for teachers of ESOL is not only to cover the skills of reading, writing, speaking, and listening. A major focus is the development of language competence, which does not always get sufficient attention in the Skills for Life documentation. We shall return to this aspect in the next chapter.

The four language skills

As we have seen in the iceberg diagram above, the English language is processed through speaking, listening, reading, and writing. We can distinguish these skills in two ways: in the first place, by whether they appear in spoken or written format; and secondly, by whether the information is produced or received. These two categories are shown in Table 3.1.

Format	Productive skills	Receptive skills
Oral skills	Speaking	Listening
Written skills	Writing	Reading

Table 3.1: Categories of language skills

TASK

Do learners of English develop these skills at the same pace?
Which of the four language skills are most likely to develop first?

The development of the four skills of speaking, listening, reading, and writing is normally by no means uniform. Typically, people's receptive skills of listening and reading will be more developed than their productive skills of speaking and writing, because learners cannot say or write what they have not heard or read before. Secondly, the vast majority of people have better oral than written skills because they communicate through spoken English much more than they read and write. Writing is the hardest skill for many learners (as well as for most native English speakers) and the least developed. The term 'spiky profile' is often used to describe this uneven development of the four skills. New language teachers often express surprise at their learners' wide range in skills levels but, in fact, spiky profiles are the norm.

TASK

Since the four skills normally develop at different rates, they need to be assessed separately. Here are some examples of language achievement. Are these profiles typical?

Aydan is frustrated that she has learnt only a few phrases in English since she came to live in London. Now that both her children go to school, she is able to come to class. She can read a little in her first language, Turkish, but is by no means fluent.

The result of Aydan's language assessment is:
Listening skills at Entry 1
Speaking skills at pre-Entry 1
Reading skills at pre-Entry 1
Writing skills at pre-Entry 1

Ali speaks English fluently but he makes many mistakes. This makes it difficult to understand him. He did not go to school in his own country.

The result of Ali's language assessment is:
Listening skills on the border of Level 1–2
Speaking skills at Level 1
Reading skills at Entry 2
Writing skills at Entry 1

Lee is from China and wants to take an Higher National Diploma in Engineering, an employment-related foundation degree. Lee learnt English at school where he was taught to read and write in English rather than speak. His pronunciation is very difficult to follow.

The result of Lee's language assessment is:

Listening skills at Entry 3
Speaking skills at Entry 2
Reading skills at Level 2
Writing skills at Level 1

First of all, we should stress that all learners are different and that the typical learner does not exist. Our three learners all have spiky profiles, which is a normal feature of language development. Aydan and Ali have listening as the most developed skill and writing the least. However, Lee's profile is quite different. His speaking and listening skills are much less developed compared to Aydan and Ali's. This is because, in China, the focus of English exams is on reading and writing skills, not on speaking and listening. Lee had little opportunity to practise speaking and listening in English, which is reflected in his language profile. These differences in skills profiles show that initial language assessment is essential. We will explore the four skills further in Chapter 5; and assessment in Chapter 6.

You may have noticed that the listening and speaking skills of all three learners were assessed as at different levels. Teachers should know that, while during initial and on-course assessment, individual scores can be recorded, under the Skills for Life strategy, speaking and listening are awarded one mark when your students take an externally accredited exam at the end of the course.

Further reading

http://www.dfes.gov.uk/readwriteplus
The Department for Education and Skills website allows easy access to documentation on the Skills for Life strategy, publications, and resources. It also provides information on how to order paper copies through DfES Publications. Here are some key publications:

Department for Education and Skills. 2001. *The Adult ESOL Core Curriculum.* London: DfES publications. Available online at http://www.dfes.gov.uk/curriculum_esol

Department for Education and Skills. 2000. *National Standards for Adult Literacy and Numeracy.* London: DfES publications.

Department for Education and Skills. 2004. *ESOL Exemplars for Speaking and Listening, Reading, Writing.* London: DfES publications.
This publication provides a useful overview of the expected levels of achievement from Entry 1 to Level 2.

Windsor, V. and **C. Healey** 2006. *Developing ESOL, Supporting Achievement.* Leicester: NIACE.
This publication provides an introduction to ESOL teaching and learning.

4 LANGUAGE ANALYSIS AND LANGUAGE TEACHING

When people communicate with each other, they use many aspects of language to convey what they want to say. This chapter explores some of these key concepts, such as grammar and vocabulary. Here is a brief exchange between two learners to set the scene.

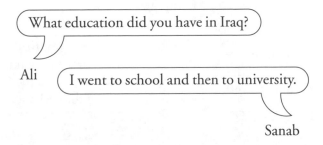

Ali — What education did you have in Iraq?

I went to school and then to university. — Sanab

Although this is a relatively simple exchange, Sanab and Ali are using many features of English to get their message across. They use **nouns** such as: *education* and *school*. They use the **past tense**: *did (you) have* and *went* to indicate that the action happened in the past. As the exchange involves speaking, the students must be able to say the words in such a way that they are understood by the listener. For example, Ali would be expected to use the correct **question form** and **intonation** when he asks: *What education did you have?* People who speak English as their first language may not know – and indeed do not need to know – the rules and conventions that underpin a simple exchange like this. This is because children acquire their first language without any need to learn explicit rules. However, when you work as a language teacher, it is important to know how English works.

So far, Ali and Sanab's language has been largely described in terms of vocabulary and grammar. While these two aspects have traditionally dominated language teaching, there are others which are particularly relevant for people who have settled in English-speaking countries. For example, there is the question of how language is used to express the purpose, or FUNCTION, of the communication, in the case of Sanab and Ali, asking for and providing information. In addition, speakers often express their attitude and intention through their choice of language, a concept which is called PRAGMATICS.

As the description of this brief exchange shows, there are many ways of analysing language. The aspects which will be addressed in this chapter are represented in the Figure 4.1.

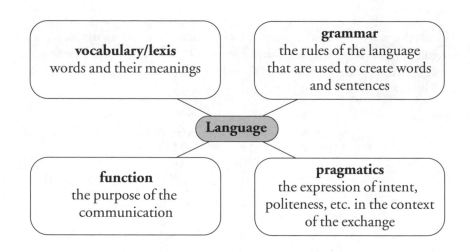

Figure 4.1: Ways of analysing language

Grammar

GRAMMAR is the term that teachers and learners use to refer to the way that language is organized. It refers to the collection of rules which are used to create words and sentences. To second language speakers, these rules can appear to be random and completely bewildering. Newly qualified teachers may also have their own perceptions: to them the word grammar may conjure up an association with rules which they had to learn when they were studying another language. Grammar is undoubtedly about rules, primarily a tool for the teacher to observe and describe language. Knowing about grammar is not just useful in the classroom, it is equally valuable when planning lessons and selecting materials, for example, when analysing a video clip of the news to see if it is of a suitable level for a particular group of learners.

Grammar covers a wide range of aspects and you will find here a selection of areas to which learners and teachers commonly pay attention. These are:

verb tenses in English, *active and passive voice*, and English *word order.* These areas are used to demonstrate a teaching approach that works well: taking as the starting point the language that the learners produce and understand, and using these to create activities that help the learners develop their ability to communicate.

In addition to the grammar points which will be covered in this book, the Glossary on page 210 contains an overview of the most commonly used terminology and you will also find a list of books and resources at the end of this chapter. These include some student's books, not only because they make good classroom resources, but also because they provide a good introduction to language analysis. For example, you may find that learners ask if it is better to say: *I shall* or *I will.* If you do not know the answer, you can consult these resources to find the answer.

Teaching the simple present

In this section Sameena, a student in an Entry 1 class, describes the school system in her country of origin.

CASE STUDY

The text below is a transcript of Sameena talking about the school system in her country of origin. While she managed to convey the general meaning of the message, we can see that there are two learning points on verb use for her to consider. What might those be?

> **Sameena** childrens starting … school at seven. They leaving at 18. They taking exams and going to university.

Sameena's teacher observes that, judging by the use of the verb endings in *starting* and *taking,* her student is trying to use the present continuous tense. This tense is normally used to describe an action which is taking place at the moment and is of short duration. However, Sameena is describing a general state of affairs here, so she would be expected to use language such as: *Children start … leave … take exams … and go to university.* This tense is called the present simple. We use it to describe habits and general truths, such as *She usually catches the 37 bus* or *Most people are right-handed.*

The second point to notice is that Sameena does not use the present continuous tense accurately: she has missed out the verb *are* in all three sentences. Beginner learners, such as Sameena, often appear not to notice words like *is, are,* and *have.* To help them with this aspect, they will need to work on distinguishing between *they're taking* and *they take,* for which also see the section on listening skills in Chapter 5.

The teacher decides to work on the simple present tense, not least because she has observed that Sameena is not the only learner in her class who struggles with it. She has designed two activities for the next lesson. She knows that the learners are able to read and write simple English sentences.

STEP 1   The students are given a text describing the educational system in the UK. The task is to complete the text, putting the missing verbs in the blank spaces.

> In the UK, children _____ school at the age of five. First, they _____ to primary school. At the age of 12, they _____ to secondary school. Most pupils _____ until they are 18, but some _____ school at 16.
>
> stay   start   move   go   leave

STEP 2   The teacher checks in the whole group that the learners have completed the task correctly.

STEP 3   The learners now move on to consider the educational system in their country of origin. The teacher has provided a text frame consisting of four sentences. These are similar but not identical to the text they read earlier.

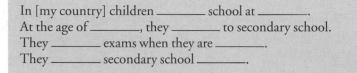

> In [my country] children _____ school at _____.
> At the age of _____, they _____ to secondary school.
> They _____ exams when they are _____.
> They _____ secondary school _____.

The learners work in small groups. They use the text frame as a speaking prompt to explain to each other how the education system works in their own country. The teacher listens to the learners' spoken language and, if they do not use the simple present accurately, helps them produce the right language, such as *go to school, take exams,* etc. She then asks them to describe the education systems to the whole group, again inviting the learners to notice how English works.

The learners then use the text frame to produce a description in writing. The more advanced students are encouraged to add more sentences.

STEP 4   In the next session, the teacher gives the learners their marked written work and shares some examples of writing with the whole group to recap on the previous lesson.

TASK

Why do you think that the teacher structured the lesson like this?

These tasks allowed the learners to start with a simple gap-fill activity and gradually build up to more challenging levels where they increasingly used language independently. They used all four skills, starting with reading the text, after which they practised the language they learnt by discussion in groups. They ended by using a set framework to write their own description. The teacher monitored their language throughout and helped the learners notice and produce the present tense. Since many learners find it difficult to produce written work, the model text used in step 3 worked well. The fact that the teacher asked the learners to write about their personal experience is also significant, as many find it motivating to write about aspects that relate directly to their own lives.

STEP 5 A month later Sameena is writing about the college where she is learning English. This is what she writes:

> *The college is in north west London. It is a big college. It has three sites. Many students come from many different countries.*

Sameena's writing indicates that she has made real progress in handling the simple present, which the teacher notes on her individual learning plan. She makes a note to monitor over time whether Sameena remains accurate in her use of the present tense when giving factual information, describing places, etc. However, not all learners in the class have made the same progress, so the teacher decides to plan additional work for them. While she works with these learners, she sets the others a discussion task based on a short reading passage.

STEP 5 The teacher puts those learners who need further work in one group. She asks them to tell each other about the country where they grew up. When they have finished talking, the teacher helps them write down some of the words that they have used to discuss their countries of origin. Here are the words that Adalarasan from Sri Lanka wrote down and which he uses to guide his writing.

Sri Lanka	an island

near India

speak	Tamil	Singhalese

many rivers	beautiful beaches

Adalarasan uses these prompts to write the following text:

> Sri Lanka is island. It near India. People speak Tamil and Singhalese. Many beautiful beaches.

Once the learners have finished their writing, the teacher asks them to check each other's work. This allows them to compare both the use of the present tense and the structure of their descriptions. In the case of Adalarasan, he uses the present tense correctly in two sentences but needs help with *It is near India.* The teacher could provide support with this by finding a similar sentence written by one of Adalasaran's peers and by asking him to compare the two sentences.

In these lessons the teacher provided a series of activities on the same topic. This is because there is evidence of a relationship between the frequency with which learners encounter new language and their learning of it. Teachers cannot predict how many times a learner needs to come across a particular aspect, but we know that returning to it over time increases the chances that learning will take place. We will come back to this in Chapter 6.

Teaching the past tense and present perfect

Sometimes teachers question the relevance of spending time on aspects of grammar, such as tenses. However, it is not just a classroom activity: learners often need to use grammar for real communication. They may find themselves in high-stakes situations, where the tense carries meaning, as this example shows.

CASE STUDY

A class of Entry 3 learners was working on the concept of time and how it is expressed in English. When the teacher explained that *I worked in a factory* had a different meaning to *I have worked in a factory*, one of the learners, a care worker, looked worried and said: 'So when I am at work and see in the logbook '*The patient has been restless*', I need to go up and check because she is not better?' Until that moment the learner had thought that '*was restless*' and '*has been restless*' meant the same. She suddenly realized not just that the meaning of the two sentences was different but also that there was a professional implication.

An example such as this makes it clear why it is important that the learners know how to use tenses accurately, in this case the difference between the present perfect *have worked* and the simple past *worked.* The present perfect can be used to indicate that something has started in the past and is still relevant, whereas the use of the past tense shows that the action is finished. The present perfect is a feature of English that most learners find difficult to understand and apply consistently. Here are some ideas to help them reflect on the structure of the tense and its meaning.

STEP 1 Give learners these two sentences:

I last saw her two months ago.
I have lived in London for two months.

Ask them what *saw* and *have lived* tell the reader about when the action started and finished.

STEP 2 Ask the learners to match the two time lines below to the two sentences above and invite them to describe how these two sentences differ in the way they express time.

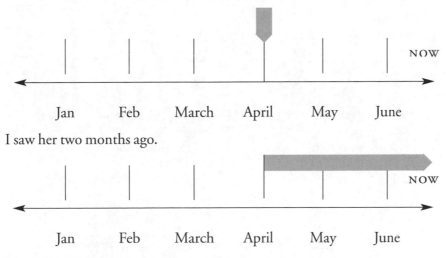

I saw her two months ago.

I have lived in London for two months.

Many learners find it helpful to see a visual representation of time. They also report that it helps them remember how the two tenses work.

STEP 3 The next activity also focuses on noticing the past simple and the present perfect but extends to adverbial phrases of time.

Give the learners a set of cards which contain half a sentence. Ask the learners to match the cards to form meaningful sentences.

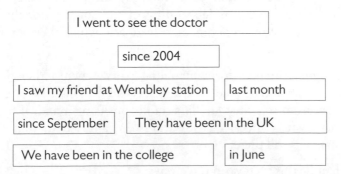

STEP 4 Many learners need help over time to understand how the present perfect and the past tense are used to express time in English. They also need reinforcement, for example, when they say *I am on this course for three months*. In addition, learners like doing exercises such as the one below. Why do you think that they find it useful?

Write the past or present perfect tense of the words in brackets.

1 Shakespeare (write) _____ a lot of plays.
2 Do you see that man over there? He (write)_____ a lot of plays.
3 John's father died last week. _____ you ever (meet) _____ him?
4 I never (meet) _____ the present Prime Minister.
5 She (come) _____ in a moment ago.
6 She just (come) _____ in.
7 He (not play) _____ tennis since 1968.
8 I (not see) _____ Helen from 1965 to 1968.
9 Why you (not go) _____ to bed yet?
10 You (be) _____ very tired last night. Why you (not go) _____ to bed early?
11 It's five o'clock – time to go home! I (not do) _____ much work this morning, but I (do) _____ a lot this afternoon.
12 A Where's Monica? I (not seen) _____ her since Monday.
    B That's funny, she (be) _____ around yesterday.
13 Paul is in Canada now. He (be) _____ there for three years. When he was a child, he (be) _____ there for a short time.
14 Girlfriend to (soon-to-be ex-)boyfriend: 'How long you (wait) _____ for me last night? Not very long, I hope.'
15 Anna (save) _____ £20 this month. That's a lot less than last month when she (save) _____ £50.
16 I'm trying to give up smoking. Yesterday I (smoke) _____ only six cigarettes and so far I (smoke) _____ only three today.

Adult Migrant English Program, Canberra Institute of Technology

The teacher chose the exercise because its pattern of contrasting sentences helps the learners notice how the two tenses are used. The learners like doing this exercise because it allows them to apply their logical thinking skills. They test their emerging understanding of the concepts of the past and present perfect tense and get immediate feedback, which they can then apply in subsequent sentences.

The first eight sentences form matching pairs, where either the past or present perfect should be used. The next six sentences have a mixture of both tenses, apart from sentence 14. This stands on its own and, if the learners choose 'have you waited', many learners are amused to think that this implies that he is still there.

You can handle this exercise in three ways:

• Before you start the exercise, you can use the time lines in step 2 to refresh people's memory on how the two tenses work.
• You can ask the learners to do the exercise without any prior explanation to see how well they are able to use the language independently. You can of

course introduce the time lines at a later stage if the learners need a visual reminder.

- If you think that the learners are likely to experience difficulties, ask them to do the first four sentences and check the answers. This provides an opportunity for the learners to engage actively with the material, which reinforces learning.

STEP 5 Most learners find that they increasingly produce correct answers as they work through the exercise. However, some may not feel totally confident at the end. If this is the case, reintroduce the same exercise a few weeks later. It is likely that they will work faster and get more, if not all, answers right. This is motivating for the learners and a good opportunity to consolidate learning.

Passive and active voice

CASE STUDY

The teacher of an ESOL Entry 3 class knows that a local news story has attracted much attention in the local newspaper and radio. It is about the closure of a factory in the area, with 200 redundancies. The teacher is asking the learners questions to find out how much they know about this and whether some of their relatives might have been affected.

Read the discussion below. Which aspect of grammar do the learners find difficult?

TEACHER	Did you hear the news last week about the factory and the redundancies?
LEARNER A	Yes, 200 people made redundant.
LEARNER B	Factory closed.
LEARNER C	People transferred to another branch.

This transcript shows that the learners missed out parts of the verbs: *were made redundant*, *was closed*, and *were transferred*. This omission of verbs may lead to ambiguity, as there is a difference in meaning between *People transferred* and *People were transferred*. The former suggests that they transferred voluntarily, while the latter implies that they did not have a choice in the matter. When the person performing the action is given, as in: *The owner closed down the factory*, we say that the sentence is in the **active voice**, with *the owner* as the **agent**.

When we focus on the process rather than the agent, we use the **passive voice** as in: *The factory was closed (by the owner)*. Teachers need to be able to explain not just how the active and passive voice work but also that users of English have a choice as to which they apply. For example, they may opt to focus on the description of process, as tends to happen in formal and technical writing, or focus on the action and the agent, which we see mostly in spoken English, informal language use, adverts, etc.

However, there is an additional challenge. The passive is often used in formal documents, which language learners are likely to encounter from the moment they meet officialdom, for example, to gain access to housing and benefits. Here are two examples:

> *Forms can also be completed online.*
> *Passports should be shown on application.*

Although there is no obvious indication in these sentences, they are, in fact, instructions. Many learners miss this altogether. This causes frustration, not just for the learners, but also for the staff who deal with their cases. The problem is that, while new arrivals are confronted with passive constructions as soon as they arrive, these are only introduced much later on in the language learning sequence. For example, the passive is introduced in the ESOL core curriculum from Level 1 onwards, which it can take a beginner learner three years or more to reach. This is an example where the immediate needs of the learner need to be met in another way. Since the learners need to be able to recognize the passive rather than use it actively, teachers can present the learners with examples that they come across in everyday life, for example *Children can now be enrolled for the crèche* or *Books should be returned by Friday*. Because sentences such as these are likely to contain an instruction, learners should also know that it is a good idea to ask for clarification if they cannot understand them.

When the learners' language skills are more advanced, the teacher can then introduce the passive voice as a productive structure for use in the learners' own writing.

Using technical language in the classroom

When managing learner language and teaching, teachers often use terminology to describe features of the English language. This is called META-LANGUAGE. Knowing how language works is a useful skill which forms part of the teacher's tool kit. It can be compared to the car mechanic who knows the parts of the engine and what they do to power the car. But does the customer need to have the same knowledge of component parts that the engineer has?

Figure 4.2: Language as part of the teacher's tool kit

The same question can be asked of the language learner. Although opinions have varied in the past, a consensus has emerged among teachers and teacher trainers in the UK that knowledge of the English language is an important skill for teachers of ESOL. However, that does not necessarily mean that they must use this knowledge and the terminology explicitly in the classroom. This is because the learners' primary objective is to use the language, not necessarily to learn about language. At the same time, teachers should consider the various attitudes that the learners have towards the use of meta-language. Most learners develop a degree of knowledge about English as they attend language courses and find it useful to guide their learning. A minority do not find it helpful and may even be intimidated by it. Therefore, it is important for teachers to judge when and how to use grammatical terminology to help the learners to develop their language skills.

Word order in English

In this section we look at the order in which words appear in sentences and noun phrases in English. We compare these against examples of word order in other languages and suggest some activities to help the learners develop this aspect of the language.

Word order in sentences

TASK

What should the word order be in this sentence?

I a shirt bought yesterday.

Fluent English speakers know automatically that this word order is not right and that it should be *I bought a shirt yesterday.* This is because the English language relies heavily on word order to express relationships between words. For example, the meaning of *the dog bit the cat* is different from *the cat bit the dog* because the order of the words is different. English uses the order of Subject–Verb–Object (SVO) to indicate 'who does what' as in the example:

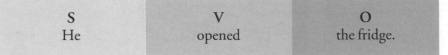

S	V	O
He	opened	the fridge.

While many languages favour SVO order, most allow more flexibility in sentence structure than English. This is because these languages have a second way to indicate the relationship between the components of the sentence: they can add markers to individual words to indicate their function. This allows other languages to move words around in the sentence, a feature which is often used to emphasize an important word, for example, *Her handbag she lost* (not her shopping bag).

The SVO rule is on the face of it easy to understand but, as classroom experience shows, not all learners find it easy to apply it consistently. One factor which may play a part is the word order of the learners' first languages.

TASK

Here are two examples of sentences in Hindi and Turkish which are accompanied by a word-for-word translation into English. How does their word order differ from English?

Hindi	Turkish	English
मैं कल कालेज नहीं आ सकता।	Yarin koleje gelemem	I can't come to college tomorrow
I tomorrow college not come can	*Tomorrow college to come can't (I)*	
मैं काम 6 बजे छोडा।	<u>Saat 6'da işten ayrıldım.</u>	I left work at six o'clock
I work six o'clock left	*O'clock six at work from left (I)*	

These sentences show substantial variation in word order. The English has Subject–Verb–Object order, as we would expect, but the Hindi and Turkish examples show quite different patterns. In Hindi the order is Subject–Object–Verb, and in Turkish Object–Verb with the subject *I* not expressed as a separate word. But the time markers *tomorrow* and *six o'clock* are also placed differently. In Turkish they are placed at the beginning of the sentence, in Hindi they are squeezed in the middle, whereas in English they appear at the end of the sentence. This is another important rule in English:

adverbs of time (and place) normally follow the Subject–Verb–Object sequence, for example, *I will see you tomorrow at six.*

If the order of the Hindi and Turkish sentences seems complex and confusing to an English speaker, Hindi and Turkish speakers must feel the same when they come across English word order. Learners have said that getting used to English word order is like learning to use your left hand when you have always used your right one.

Word order in noun phrases

Word order is not just used to express the relationship between sentence components; it is also applied in phrases. This is most easily demonstrated by a comparison between the English phrase *a nice big car* and their equivalents in Arabic and Portuguese:

Arabic	Portuguese
سيارة كبيرة وجميلة	un carro lindo e grande
car big and nice	*a car nice and big*

A comparison between these phrases shows that, while in English the adjectives always come before the noun, this is not the case in the other two languages. Secondly, in Arabic the sequence of the adjectives is reversed as in *big and nice.* Incidentally, in English this cannot be done because adjectives expressing opinion come before descriptive adjectives, for example, *a nasty old man, a great new bag.*

The examples from English, Hindi, Turkish, Arabic, and Portuguese show that they handle word order differently. But can we relate errors made in the new language directly to the patterns of the first language? ESOL teachers report particular problems for speakers of Hindi, Farsi, Arabic, and Chinese languages. They may assume from their experience of working with students that there is a great deal of transfer from the first language. Yet, while teachers may attribute errors to the influence of the first language, research findings show that we cannot be certain that this is always the case. We shall explore this aspect further in Chapter 6.

We will now take the topic of sentence structure to see what teachers can do to help the learners notice word order patterns. Here is a sequence of learner and teacher activities.

CASE STUDY

The teacher of a mixed ability class observes that some of the learners are struggling with sentence structure, both in their spoken and written English. This is what she does:

STEP 1   The teacher notes examples of the language the learners produce, both in terms of what they can do well and where they struggle. She uses this information for two purposes. She uses her notes to reflect on the learners' language and to plan future lessons. Her notes also give her a benchmark of learner language, which she notes in the individual learning plan (for which see also Chapter 6).

STEP 2   The teacher makes up cards like the ones below, using the language she noted in Step 1. The cards are colour-coded, so that all the 'subject' words are blue, for example, and all the 'object' words are green.

Subject	Verb	Object	Place	Time
I	left	work		at six o'clock
I	like to eat	chocolate ice cream		after dinner
He	took	his exam		yesterday
My children	play	computer games	in their bedroom	all the time
My new dress	arrives			tomorrow
I'll	see	you	at the station	at seven o'clock

The learners use the cards to create sentences. The colours provide a visual reminder of where the word categories go. Some learners memorize these colours and use them long after they have done this exercise. For example, teachers hear them comment, while proofreading their written work: *Oh, that's a green word and I put it in the wrong place.*

Once the learners are comfortable putting the words in the correct sequence, the teacher gives them coloured pens and asks them to create sentences of their own.

STEP 3   The teacher extends this activity by exploring with the learners what the language patterns are in their own languages. She writes on cards *I will see you at seven o'clock* using the appropriate colours, and asks the learners to use the coloured pens to produce the equivalent in their own language. If we use Hindi as an example, this would be:

I	you	seven o'clock	will see

Some learners like to move the cards around from the word order in their own language to English to confirm the differences between English and their own languages.

The teacher uses this exercise to see if the learners' word order in English is influenced by the word order of their first language. She also asks the learners whether they think their first language plays a part.

STEP 4 Once the teacher has done this exercise with the learners, she observes how they use English word order over time. She comments on the learners' word order in their spoken and written language, if necessary using coloured pens to reinforce the right sequence and the coloured cards to reinforce learning.

The teacher includes word order in the progress review with her students and records progress in the individual learning plan.

TASK

Here are two examples of written language to practise your observation and planning skills. How would you help these learners improve their word order skills?

Ibrahim, an Albanian speaker from Kosovo, writes:

> I pen bought yesterday.

You can ask Ibrahim to use the coloured pens to underline the Subject Verb Object parts in this sentence. If you think that this is too difficult, you can make up cards with the words written in the right colours. Once he has sorted the words into the right order, ask him to write the correct version out to memorize the sequence.

Maria, a Czech speaker, writes:

> During the lesson if are the window open is the class very noisy and I can not concentrate.

Although the writer manages to convey the meaning, the sentence is hard to understand because Maria has reversed the subject and verbs in this sentence. You could draw arrows as a visual prompt to show Maria that she needs to reverse the verb and subject.

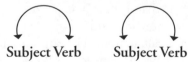

Subject Verb   **Subject Verb**

This guidance allows her to repair the sentence to:

> If the windows are open during lessons the class(room) is very noisy and I cannot concentrate.

Vocabulary

In this section we focus on two major aspects of vocabulary learning: how learners use words as individual items and as strings of words which belong together. We consider the impact on learning of the learners' communicative needs outside the classroom. We look at word-building skills and investigate the reasons why the learners create word strings such as *I am very keen applying this job.*

The learners' perspective on vocabulary

TASK

Learners often find it a challenge to use the right words when they speak and write in English, as the following two examples show. Here are two students, one a Tamil speaker from Sri Lanka and the other a Polish speaker, describing the city where they live. Which words cause them difficulty and why?

> Traffic is big problem. I think the roads width are quite small.
> It has old slim streets.

While the reader can understand what these sentences mean, the students have not quite found the right words to describe the streets in their city. For example, the Sri Lankan student describes the width of the roads as *small* rather than *narrow,* which would normally be expected here. The Polish student has chosen the word *slim* which in English we use to describe people and objects, such as a book or a woman, but not streets. As to why they described the roads as *slim* and *small*, this may be related to the interface between their first and second languages. For example, Polish has several words to describe slimness, narrowness, thinness, etc. but their meanings do not overlap neatly with their English equivalents. When students start to learn a new language, they may assume that there is a linear relationship between words in their own and their new language. They expect that it is sufficient to learn equivalent words and it can be a real surprise to realize that there is not always an exact match. The attempt to align words across languages is very likely to have influenced our Polish student's decision to use the combination *slim streets.*

Students may find that acquiring the meaning of words is even more of a challenge when the equivalent to a particular meaning does not exist in their own language. For example, many languages only have one verb for *borrow* and *lend*, with different prepositions to indicate who gives what to whom. Learners may also find that words look the same or very similar but that the meaning in their own language differs from English. These are often called 'false friends'. We find examples of these even in varieties of English, for example, *gas* in American English means *petrol* and in British English *a fuel that is used for heating and cooking*. If you have learnt a new language yourself, you may well recognize the confusion that many learners experience when trying to get to grips with vocabulary.

As the two examples above show, the learners' language use provides good opportunities to explore vocabulary. When a learner uses a word which is not quite right in the context, this allows you to focus on shades of meaning. For example, one of your students may write about his religion *in my belief you must … .* The students can explore the meaning of words such as *religion* and *belief.* More generally, teachers can make the learners aware of the principle that words which exist in their language may not have a direct equivalent in English.

Teaching vocabulary

The starting point for planning lessons should be the communicative needs of the learners and the situations and contexts in which they are likely to need to use English. It is a good idea to check what their priorities are. For example, if they want to learn the language for cooking food, they will need to know the names of ingredients such as *onions, peppers*, and *garlic;* or words to describe how to prepare food: *cut, fry,* or *mix;* and words to manage quantities: a *teaspoon, half a pound*, or *a pinch*. It is also important to find out what students already know, as it is very likely that they will have learnt at least some of the vocabulary outside the classroom. This allows the teacher to build on the learners' existing skills and to activate vocabulary which they recognize but cannot yet use actively.

A useful first activity would be to ask the learners to brainstorm what words they know and to create mind-maps to organize vocabulary, as shown in Figure 4.3.

There are multiple benefits to getting the students to work together like this. In the first place, they can learn and confirm language by pooling their existing knowledge. They also use meaningful language to explore and negotiate.

While the learners are working together, the teacher is free to circulate and to work out from the discussions and the emerging mind-maps what

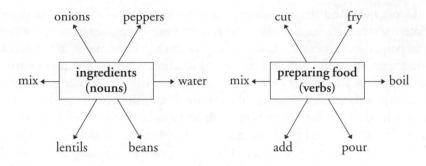

Figure 4.3: Mind-maps to organize vocabulary

vocabulary the learners already know. Useful language recorded in one or more groups can be disseminated to the others, either by asking learners to go and check language with other groups, or in the feedback session with the whole group.

Teachers can also extend and recycle language by one or more of the following activities:

- Use pictures of vegetables or real objects (which are sometimes referred to as REALIA) such as *peppers, cutlery,* or *a bowl* to present new language
- Demonstrate actions, for example, *cutting, pouring,* or *mixing*
- Explain the meaning of words, for example, of *disappointed,* e.g. give an example of a friend who cooked dinner for her son's birthday and was *disappointed* when it was burnt.
- Give or elicit SYNONYMS (words which mean the same), for example, *disappointed = unhappy, not pleased*
- Give or elicit ANTONYMS (words which mean the opposite) such as *disappointed ≠ relieved, pleased*
- Explore shades of meaning, for example, in words such as *disappointed, shocked, dismayed,* and *astonished*
- Practise vocabulary in a dialogue or role-play. Students could tell a partner about their favourite food and how to make it. Or they could role play feeling *pleased* or *disappointed* with a birthday present.

Teachers will have no problem encouraging students to learn vocabulary; indeed they tend to be pre-occupied with it. This is true across the spectrum, from complete beginners to more advanced students. Wilkins' quote (1972) 'without grammar very little can be conveyed; without vocabulary nothing can be conveyed' applies particularly to newly-arrived migrants and refugees, who find themselves in situations where they have to communicate in English whether they are ready to do so or not. Using individual words without any sentence structure is often a survival mechanism on which people rely, at least in the early stages of settlement. Handling vocabulary remains a preoccupation at more advanced levels, too, especially when learners expand into new domains, such as when their children go to school and they need to attend parent–teacher meetings; or when they want to attend further education and need to extend their ability to use formal language. However, publications on language teaching and government guidance, including the ESOL core curriculum, have paid little attention to vocabulary. Yet as Hedge (2001) says, its neglect sits uncomfortably with the significance which the learners place on it.

Here is a task to explore how you might teach vocabulary, this time taking a text on personality testing as a starting point.

TASK

How might you use this text on personality traits to teach vocabulary? Design a lesson plan, predict what vocabulary is likely to be new to the students, and plan how you will teach it.

What are you like?
Selection of questions adapted from a personality test used by recruiters

1 Do you have a small but close circle of friends?
2 Do you prefer to take your time over a task?
3 Do you enjoy meeting new people?
4 Are you usually punctual for meetings?
5 Do you find it easy to make friends with new people?
6 Do you enjoy solving practical problems?
7 Do you like taking the lead in group discussions?
8 Do you prefer to do a routine job?
9 When upset, do you prefer to be left alone?
10 Do you like looking at complicated patterns on buildings, paintings, etc?
11 Would you say you are strongly opinionated?
12 Do you tend to act immediately on your desires at the time?
13 Are you happy with the way you look?
14 Do you normally notice things which other people ignore?
15 Do you feel good about yourself?
16 Do your friends think of you as quite a dependable person?
17 Would you say that you know people from a variety of backgrounds?
18 Are you a good timekeeper?
19 Would you help a friend out even though it was inconvenient?
20 Would you prefer a quiet night in or go to a big party?

Adapted from Career Psychology Consultancy

Here is how you can use the text:

STEP 1 To help weaker students, you can make up cards with explanations of difficult words. You will need to do this before the lesson.

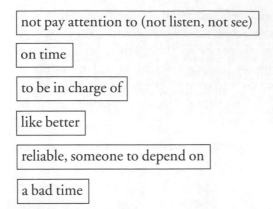

not pay attention to (not listen, not see)

on time

to be in charge of

like better

reliable, someone to depend on

a bad time

STEP 2 To start this activity in class, explain that employers may use tests such as these in the recruitment process. Put the students in small groups, making sure that the weaker ones work together. Ask the students to read the questions on their own and see if they can answer them.

STEP 3 Language learners often want to know the meaning of unfamiliar words as soon as they encounter them. This can be disruptive while others are still reading the text. At this stage of the task, ask the students to underline words they do not know. Once they have finished reading, ask them to work out meaning in their small groups. Encourage them to use their dictionaries and compare the meanings they find. If the weaker students get stuck on individual words, give them the cards as extra support.

STEP 4 Ask the students to move back into the whole group and check which questions they felt applied to them and why. The students are likely to want to confirm the meaning of new words. If they ask for the meaning of words which occur on the cards which you made earlier, ask the students with the vocabulary cards to explain what they mean.

STEP 5 Give the students the answers to the personality test and check that they understand terms such as *sociability*.

How did you do?

Sociability: 1, 5, 9, 17, 20
Attention to detail: 2, 6, 8, 10, 14
Self-confidence: 3, 7, 11, 13, 15
Reliability: 4, 12, 16, 18, 19

If you answered 'yes' to three or more questions in each section, an employer is likely to assess that you have the positive characteristic being measured.

Ask the students to check their answers against the four categories and to discuss in their groups what their strongest characteristics are. If the more advanced students finish this task before the others, you could ask them if they agree with each other's statements about themselves, for example if, in their opinion, student X really is sociable.

STEP 6 Tell the group that they are going to write a brief description of themselves, using the language and concepts they have learnt so far. They can pool ideas on how to do this in their small groups. You can use these to draw up a framework for writing, if you feel the learners need it. Once the learners have written their piece, you can ask them to hand in their work so that you can provide feedback on it in the next lesson.

STEP 7 At the end of the lesson, you can ask the students to list new words that they have learnt and encourage them to write these down, if they have not done so already.

TASK Some follow-up questions

1 Students really like this type of activity. Why do you think it works well?
2 Why do you think the weakest students were asked to work together?
3 Why is it a good idea to ask the students with the vocabulary cards to explain the meanings of new words?
4 Why are there so many different stages to this activity?

This activity works well because the text is fun and broken up in short sentences rather than a heavy block of text. More importantly, learners are fascinated to find out what the test tells them about themselves. Many see real value in having the opportunity to familiarize themselves with the vocabulary for describing their personality because they may well need this type of language when they apply for jobs.

On the second question, putting the weaker students together allows the teacher to give them extra attention, explain the vocabulary, and give them the vocabulary cards to help them learn new words. While working with the weaker students, she will need to keep an eye on the other groups, as it is quite possible that help is needed there, too. At the same time, the learners are a great resource because those who already know the meaning of words can explain them to the others.

The third question was why the weaker students with the vocabulary cards are asked to explain the meanings of words. They are often reticent during whole group discussion and having the answers on the cards creates a low-risk opportunity to participate. This builds their confidence.

As to why there are so many stages to this activity, research shows that learners need to encounter a new word many times before they know its meaning. Paul Nation's (2001) overview of several studies on vocabulary learning shows that most new vocabulary is learnt after six or seven occurrences, but that it may need as many as twenty. The recycling of vocabulary during the various stages gives the learners many opportunities to see or hear words that are new to them. Every time new vocabulary is used, the memory of it is reinforced and the likelihood of recall is increased. This approach can be extended across lessons, too, when teachers create a 'recycling' environment, reintroducing words in subsequent lessons. For example, the teacher could select examples of the students' written work and put these on a transparency or PowerPoint presentation during the next lesson.

On a more general point, students should also know that reading has been identified as a particularly useful source for learning new vocabulary and embedding the meaning of words they have encountered previously. For further discussion on reading, see also Chapter 5.

Adapting vocabulary to the level of the students

This personality test has been used successfully with Entry 3 and Level 1 students. You could use it with lower levels, if you wish, by replacing the more difficult words in the text with the words on the vocabulary cards given to the weaker students. In fact, the test you see in front of you has itself been adapted. Here are three of the sentences as they appeared in the original version.

1   Do you have a small but '*close knit*' circle of friends?
10 Do you like looking at *intricately designed* buildings?
12 Do you tend to act *impulsively* on your desires at the time?

The words in italics were changed because it is unlikely that the students would need to understand words like *intricately designed* or *impulsively* and they are probably not going to encounter them often enough for them to become part of their vocabulary store. A second consideration is whether introducing this vocabulary would be a productive use of lesson time. When you look at lesson materials, such as course books, or the Skills for Life and Citizenship materials, it is a good idea to look at them critically and to consider whether the vocabulary they contain is relevant to the learners.

Word-building skills

So far we have looked at the learning of individual words. We now explore how the students combine elements to create new words and categories of words.

TASK

These three examples show students using English, some of it in unexpected ways.

> It was a big hapious moment

Student 1 describing an Indian festival:

> I have a small balcony but it can be dangers if they play there.

Student 2, a mother of two children, giving reasons why she dislikes her flat

> The north of Iraq is very beautiful because there are many mountains and wallwaters.

Student 3 writing about her country of origin

These students have created new word combinations by fusing elements, some of which do not go together in English. What may have prompted them to do so?

Although at first sight the language of students 1 and 2 appears to have nothing in common, both are trying to use the adjectival ending *-ous*. Student 1 has created the word *hapious* which does not exist in English. It appears that she has transferred the ending *-ous* which is commonly found in adjectives such as *curious*, and *nervous* to the adjective *happy*. When students apply an existing rule beyond the context in which it is normally used, we say that they have OVER-GENERALIZED it. Children often do the same in the early stages of language learning, for example, when they call all animals *dogs* or all men *daddy*. While this may appear to be a negative feature, over-generalization can be a positive sign. It shows that the student is aware of the rule, which is an important first step to applying it correctly.

Student 2 also tries to use the ending *-ous* but in her case the spelling *dangers* is not correct. This is likely to have happened because she is familiar with the spoken form of *dangerous* and is writing what she thinks she hears.

Student 3 uses the appealing but non-existent word *wallwaters*. Instead, English requires the word *fall* to combine with *water* to produce the word *waterfall*. This learner may have realized that in English it is possible to form a new word out of two or more existing words, a process which is called COMPOUNDING.

These three examples demonstrate that the learners are making use of patterns of language, even if the resulting language is not always accurate. It is well worth building on these patterns by working out with the learners what they already know, for example, how student 1 created the word *hapious*. Many students enjoy analysing their own language and often demonstrate that they have insight into the reasons why they produced a particular feature. This process can in itself provide the opportunity for the learners to refine their understanding of how English works.

Here are some ideas on how to advise the learners whose language we analysed earlier.

Student 1

With the use of *hapious* above, you could alert student 1 to the fact that it is possible in English to take some words and add new parts to its front and / or back; but not with others. A particle added to the front is called a PREFIX; and to the back a SUFFIX, both are added to the ROOT of the word. These prefixes and suffixes give the English language tremendous flexibility. Students' vocabulary can be expanded to a very great extent if they can develop the ability to combine various parts effectively. For example, they may already know the word *employment,* for which the root is the verb *employ.* This has a variety of other possible endings: *employer, employee,* and *employable,* or it can have a prefix added at the front: *unemployment.* Some students find it useful to build up lists of words which are made up of a combination of prefix-root-suffix sequences. Rinvolucri's (1985) domino game is a good exercise to enable the learners to discover and practise the rules of prefixes and suffixes. You will find other references to resources at the end of this chapter.

Student 2

This student had problems with writing the word *dangerous.* She needs the opportunity to help her hear the difference between the pronunciation of *dangers* and *dangerous* and to improve her spelling. Dictation can provide a useful technique here to assess whether the learner can make the aural distinction and produce the right spelling. You will find an example of such a dictation activity in Chapter 5.

Student 3

This student who wrote *wallwater* can be reassured that many words are made up of two words, for example, *wall heater.* In many ways, these behave like single words and need to be learnt and remembered as one unit. It is useful for the teacher to know that the most prolific combinations of compounding are noun + noun, for example, *ticket office, door handle,* or the more recent combination *memory stick.* However, other combinations also occur:

babysit   noun + verb
double park adjective + verb
download   adverb + verb

Collocations and word strings

Many learners like to learn vocabulary. It gives them a sense of control, a space where they can 'pin down' aspects of the language before they are exposed to what can be the bewildering experience of making sense of spoken and written English. However, words do not appear alone, they have a habit of appearing together in set combinations. For example, if we look again at the expression *slim streets* which the Polish student used in her writing on page 42, it is clear that these words do not go together. Words which habitually belong together are called COLLOCATIONS. Learners benefit from developing a sense of what word combinations go together, for example:

narrow { street
         opening
         escape

slim   { woman
         waist
         chance

Essentially these collocations have to be learnt, which is time-consuming. Paul Nation (2001) recommends a variety of techniques, of which the following are particularly useful:

- Encourage the deliberate learning of chunks, for example, by writing them on cards with their translation on the back
- Provide the learners with opportunities for reinforcing the use of collocations across the four skills of speaking, listening, reading, and writing
- Encourage the learners to embed collocations by reading and listening to English as much as possible.

In addition to collocations, we also find longer chunks of language, which as Lewis (1993) notes are extremely common in the English language. These are often referred to as 'formulaic sequences' or 'word strings', the term we shall use in this book. Word strings feature heavily in everyday communication, for example, in situations such as greeting, thanking, interrupting, and apologizing: *Nice to see you, That's very kind of you, Thanks a lot, Excuse me, I am sorry but I can't*. Recent research by Wray (2002) provides insight into why so much of the language is made up of word strings:

1 Humans can only hold a limited amount of information in their short-term memory. It is thought that language users produce expressions such as *How are you today? Nice to see you. It seems to me that …* as one unit

rather than a series of individual words. This is more efficient than if all words have to be individually produced and makes it easier for the speaker to be fluent.

2 Not only does the speaker benefit from the use of familiar language, the listener does, too. It is easier to understand a speaker who uses chunks of language which the listener knows already. Hearing familiar language reduces the likelihood of misunderstandings and allows the listener to concentrate on the message.

3 Discourse markers, such as *first of all* and *finally*, map the structure of the text and make it easier to produce and follow content.

4 Language is used to express identity and membership of a group. Take for example the use of Black Caribbean and Asian vocabulary and pronunciation among teenagers in the UK to distinguish themselves from the older generation.

It appears that first language speakers learn an amazing number of word strings from childhood onwards. They are able to recognize and reproduce these automatically and without any doubt about accuracy. However, when we observe the language produced by second language speakers, we find that they often have great difficulty in achieving the same accuracy and automatic recall. Figure 4.4 shows an example of this given by Wray in her plenary lecture at the IATEFL conference in 2005.

HELEN   MATT

Figure 4.4: 'After you' cartoon by permission of Alison Wray and Huw Bell

When she showed this picture of a man holding the door open for a woman and asked first language speakers what he was likely to say, they mostly replied *after you* or *ladies first*. By contrast, most second language speakers said that the man would have said: *lady first*. The irony is that the second language speakers were more logical in their choice of language since there is only one woman in the picture. Yet, first language speakers would never say *lady first* because that word string is not stored in their memory.

Do you agree with the comment: 'Anybody knows what the learners mean by language such as *lady first*. What does it matter that they make minor mistakes like these?'

It is undoubtedly right that a few mistakes should not interfere with communication. However, as we have seen earlier, language is not just used to communicate information but also to express identity and membership of a group. The ability to express belonging is of particular relevance for people who are settling permanently in English-speaking countries, for example, when greeting neighbours, or when applying for a job, where the ability to 'fit in' is seen as a major criterion for selection.

Secondly, the use of inaccurate language can create a disorientating effect which causes the listener to spend time processing the language in order to make sense of it. This slows down the information flow and creates the potential for misunderstandings as well as a sense of alienation, where the speaker literally does not speak the same language as the listener. So ESOL teachers may be right that language learners get their message across, but they often do so at a cost to communication, potentially hampering the exchange and alienating the listener.

Using the concept of word strings in the classroom

We have already seen that adult language learners are keen on learning vocabulary. However, they tend to home in on individual words, especially those that have meaning. As Wray observes, they ignore equally important information, namely the surrounding words. Since word strings occur so frequently and learners often struggle to produce them accurately, this aspect is well worth paying attention to in the classroom. Teachers need to make sure that learners notice words strings and learn them as chunks. Here are some examples of how this can be done.

ACTIVITY 1 Writing

Working with an individual student on noticing word strings

These sentences were written by Arkan as part of a job application. How good is his use of word strings? How can you help him improve his letter?

I am very keen for applying this job.

I am writing this letter in regard of the vacancy available.

I wish to do diploma with some working experience.

Arkan's choice of vocabulary is good in many respects. He is able to use words such as *keen, apply*, and *vacancy*. However, he is struggling to use these words in accurate strings, for example, *I am very keen for applying this job* and *in regard of.* He is not alone in finding it difficult to do this. It appears to be the production of chunks of language such as *I am very keen to apply for this job because …* that causes learners many problems, even if their other skills, such as their use of grammar and vocabulary, are at an advanced level.

There are various ways in which you can help this student improve his use of word strings. You can ask him to read the text again and see if he is able to improve his own writing, if you think that he is aware of the language but not yet secure in using it consistently. For example, he could underline the words he is not sure about or correct them. If you think that he is not yet aware of the correct word string, for example, *I am very keen for applying this job*, you can give him an exercise such as Unit 24 from *Recycling Your English* (West 1996) to practise this aspect. Once the student has done this exercise, you can then ask him to see if he can use the new language he has learnt to improve on his own writing.

Other word strings that Arkan will have to learn include *with regard to, work experience*, and *take a diploma.* Paul Nation (2001) recommends their deliberate learning. Arkan can do this by adding these strings to his vocabulary list, set of cards, etc., and by studying them at regular intervals until they have become part of his active vocabulary.

ACTIVITY 2   Reading and writing
Working with a group of students on noticing word strings

While chatting to the students during the coffee break, a teacher learns that many learners in her Entry 3 class are smokers. When she comes across an article on quitting smoking in the local newspaper, she decides to use it as a reading exercise.

How can the teacher use the article, the beginning of which is reproduced here, to reinforce the use of word strings through reading and writing?

> *Dear Abby…*
>
> My husband has been nagging me for ages to give up smoking. He says it's expensive, messy, and that it's aging my skin prematurely. I would like to quit but I can't. What should I do?

This is what you can do:

STEP 1   When the learners have read the article, they are likely to ask the meaning of new vocabulary. For example, they may ask what *nag* means. Explain the meaning of the word, using the whole phrase: *If you nag someone, it means that you* … . You could then ask a learner with children: *Can you think of an example when you nag your kids?* And the whole group: *Who else might you nag?*

STEP 2 Ask the learners in pairs to think about the advantages and disadvantages of smoking. In the whole group, ask them to present some of their arguments, reinforcing good use of language and helping them improve their use of word strings where necessary.

STEP 3 Ask the learners to write how they feel about smoking. When marking their written work, draw attention to their use of words by providing the correct word strings or underlining the words that are not quite right. (See also Chapter 5 on how to help the learners structure their writing.)

STEP 4 In the next lesson put some samples of the learners' written work on the board or interactive whiteboard.

> Some people have an allergy with smoke.
> When we smoke some people do not like to sit near us.
> From smoking your skin becomes earlier old.

STEP 5 Ask the learners to work out in small groups whether these word strings are accurate and, if not, how they could improve them. Quite often they produce a correct word string between them such as *Some people are allergic to smoke.*

Refer the learners to the original article for examples of accurate language use, for example, *Smoking ages your skin prematurely.*

Make sure that you put on the board not just language which needs improving but also well-phrased sentences, such as the second example above *When we smoke some people do not like to sit near us.* This provides a good model and reminds the class that they are perfectly capable of producing accurate language.

ACTIVITY 3 Speaking
Working with a group of students on noticing word strings

Set the class a speaking task. With an Entry 1 or 2 class, this could be a role-play on food shopping. With an Entry 3 group or higher, you could set up a group discussion on a topic of interest, such as what the students think of their children's education in the UK.

How could you use the language they produce during the discussion to help the learners notice their use of word strings?

STEP 1 Listen to the students talking to each other. As in the previous exercise, note examples of word strings that need improvement and those that are fine. If you can find examples of language that the learners used to struggle with but now can do, so much the better. This allows you to show the learners that they really are improving.

STEP 2 Put the strings you selected on the board and ask the students to decide if the phrases are OK and improve them if they are not.

ACTIVITY 4 Speaking

Learning to use everyday language with E1 and E2 learners

Ask the learners to think in pairs what they would say in situations when, for example:

- they meet someone for the first time
- they meet their neighbour
- they do not understand what someone said to them.

How would you use this to teach word strings?

This is how you can use this activity:

STEP 1 Ask the learners to give examples of the language they would use. Feed back on the word strings that they already use well and where they need to improve.

STEP 2 Encourage the learners to learn stock phrases such as *How are you today?* and *Thanks a lot.*

Explain that it is a useful skill for the learners to be able to use language to express hesitation and lack of understanding, such as: *I am sorry, I don't understand* or *Can you say that again?* While you are teaching these phrases, make sure you also pay attention to the intonation.

STEP 3 Ask the learners to write new word strings down and to look at these at regular intervals. If learners have problems remembering a particular phrase, saying it aloud can help them remember it.

STEP 4 At the beginning of the next session, ask if anyone has used their new language outside the classroom and how it went. Ask also which phrases they remember from the previous lesson.

Reflecting on vocabulary learning

As Hedge (2001) points out, vocabulary learning has been neglected in the literature on English language teaching and learning. The ESOL core curriculum, which is used as a guide to teaching in England, Northern Ireland, and Wales, similarly pays little attention to vocabulary. This sits uncomfortably with the priorities of the learners themselves. Teachers can meet the needs of their learners by creating opportunities for learning vocabulary, but these should not just be viewed as individual items. Learners benefit from noticing how groups of words habitually go together. This is for two reasons which are particularly important to people who have settled in an English-speaking country: to express meaning as well as membership of the group.

Language in context

The functional approach

The purpose of the interaction and context in which communication takes place form an important aspect of communication. Here are three examples:

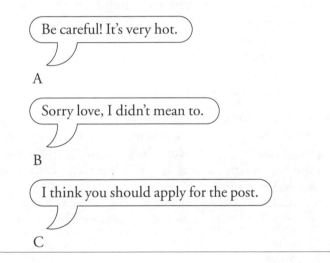

Be careful! It's very hot.

A

Sorry love, I didn't mean to.

B

I think you should apply for the post.

C

TASK

What might be the situations in these examples and who might be the speakers?

Here are some possible speakers and settings, but you can no doubt think of others:

A A mother warning her child in the kitchen
B A husband apologizing after saying something hurtful to his wife
C A manager advising one of her members of staff looking for promotion

The purpose of communication, such as warning, apologizing, and advising in the examples above, is called their *function*. Functions can be expressed through language as well as non-verbal communication and are often closely tied to the situation in which they are used. Taking the function of giving advice, we can give the same message but shade its meaning. Compare the advice given above with the more colloquial: *I'd go for the job, if I were you.*

TASK Choosing a focal point for teaching

When planning learning activities, should you use functions as a starting point or would it be better to focus on grammatical forms, vocabulary, and intonation?

While in the past teaching function and form have been seen as opposite approaches, they are not mutually exclusive. On the contrary, they provide two useful perspectives from which to address the language needs of the learners. Since learners of ESOL have to handle functions outside the classroom, even if they have limited language skills, the functional approach is a good starting point. It enables teachers to find out for what purpose and in which situations learners want to use English in their daily lives. It may be that they need to request a form to get housing benefit or that they need to learn how to ask for a bus ticket. This information can be used to focus on the type of language that will help the learners perform these actions, for example, *Town centre, please* for an Entry 1 student or *I'd like a ticket for the town centre* for more advanced learners.

Teaching functions and language structures
Here is an extract from a lesson plan for an Entry 2 class to show how language and function can be combined. At this level the learners would be able to use simple language to describe people and their appearance, on which this exercise builds.

Functions	Learner speaking tasks	Vocabulary	Grammar
Describing people's appearance Exploring meaning and negotiating agreement			
Activity 1 Use pictures to learn new and activate existing language for describing people	Talk in pairs about the age and appearance of the people in pictures provided	• age, appearance, clothes, etc. • antonyms *tall / short, curly / straight* • colours: *dark / light blue*	Present simple *She is … She has …* Present continuous *She is wearing* The accurate use of these tenses

Functions tasks	Learner speaking	Vocabulary	Grammar
	Tutor observation: Check that the learners are able to use these aspects before going on to the next activity, especially *he is wearing a blue T-shirt*; *she has short hair.* Pay attention to pronunciation of words such as: *clothes, wearing, dark*, and *curly*		
Activity 2 Use language for • describing people • exploration and guessing • confirming, agreeing / disagreeing	Sit back to back with a partner. Describe from memory what your partner looks like and what clothes he or she is wearing. Check with each other if you have remembered correctly.	Vocabulary for exploration: • *perhaps, maybe, I think / Is it possible that you are wearing … ?* • *Do I remember this right?* Vocabulary to agree / disagree • *Yes, that's right* • *Actually, I am not very tall …* • *No, I am not wearing that today. That was yesterday!*	Questions and statements in present simple and continuous: *Are you wearing, Do you have?*
	Tutor observation: Observe language used during exercise, identifying points for learning and examples of good language use. Discuss these with the whole group to reinforce learning, putting examples of language on the board.		

In the description of these two activities in the lesson plan, language and functions are well matched.

Functions and the level of language

When teachers plan to teach functions, it is worth considering the level at which these might be presented.

TASK

Which three functions would be taught at Entry 1 and which at Level 1?

a compare people, places, objects
for example, the educational system in the UK and the learners' country of origin

b give personal information to see the doctor
for example, registering name, address, place of birth, and making an appointment

c explain and give reasons
for example, why diet and exercise are important for health

d tell the time
for example, read and say the times on a clock

e greet people
for example, greet the teacher or a new classmate

f make recommendations
for example, how to make our cities cleaner

At first sight, it may seem obvious that the functions described under *b, d,* and *e* would be taught at Entry 1; and the functions under *a, c,* and *f* at Level 1. However, the match between functions and language levels is not always as straightforward as it might appear. While a function such as *telling the time* generates well-defined, predictable language, other functions are not so easy to define in terms of language level. For example, on page 29 we saw that a learner at Entry 1 gave a very brief description of the education system in her country. We could set the same task to a learner who is at Level 1, or indeed a postgraduate student. They would all perform the same function but their written texts would look very different, both in terms of language use and content. In the same way, many functions can be handled at different language levels. Take for example, *giving personal information* and *making an appointment* in the list above. A student at Entry 1 might be able to say his name and address but to make an appointment effectively, learners need to have far more language skills than just being able to pass on their personal details.

Function features prominently in the National Literacy Standards and the ESOL core curriculum. For example, we find the level descriptor: *Engage in discussion* at Entry 2 (DfES 2001: 120). This is exemplified by aspects such as:

1b Take part in more formal interaction
a introduce self
b give personal information
c state problems, wishes, etc.
d apologize with some elaboration

When planning lessons and schemes of work, the teacher will need to interpret functions such as those described above, because they can be expressed at multiple language levels. Here is an example of a teacher who teaches learners at Entry 1, Entry 3, and Level 2. She might work on the function of *expressing possibility* across these three levels:

Express possibility		
current	future	hypothetical
Entry 1	Entry 3	Level 2
I can see you now.	*I will be able to see you this afternoon.*	*I would have been able to see you, but …*

Pragmatic competence and register

When people interact with each other, they do not just want to achieve the function of the communication, such as *greet someone* or *ask for help*. They will also want to get their message across in language that is right for the audience and the context. Here is an example of how we deduce information about the status of relationships between speakers:

> Oh hi, my train's late. I'm not going to get in till after ten.

This is the start of a typical mobile phone conversation between people who know each other well. We know this from the use of *hi*, which in the UK indicates a close relationship between the speaker and listener, the use of the informal *get in*, and the assumed knowledge on the part of the listener of where the speaker is and what he or she is doing. People operating in their own language produce language that fits the purpose and context of the interaction. This skill is called *pragmatic competence*. However, second language speakers have a much harder time matching the language to the message. The following scenario illustrates this point.

CASE STUDY

A language class has just started and the teacher is about to check last week's homework. Mohamed, one of the students, was not there the week before and says:

> Give me paper.

What impression does Mohamed create by his use of language?

The student's remark *Give me paper* sounds brusque. However, we cannot be certain that Mohamed intended to be rude or overbearing. We can equally imagine that he probably wanted the sheet urgently to catch up on the work he had missed the previous week. The reason for his choice of language may be that he had not yet learnt question forms such as *Can I have … ?* Instead, he relied on the command or IMPERATIVE form *Give* which conveys an impression of abruptness. However, cultural aspects may also play a part. All cultures have their own ways of marking degrees of politeness. For example, in some cultures, respect for seniors and a strongly defined sense of hierarchy are reflected in the language. By contrast, other cultures, for example, in Australia and the United States, are more 'horizontal' in that members of the community appear to outsiders to share a sense of equality and informality. When people switch between cultures, they often have to adjust to new norms. In the case of Mohamed, if he came from a culture where speakers are more direct than speakers of English, then an adjustment to a greater degree of politeness or formality would be needed.

TASK

What can Mohamed's language teacher do to help him communicate more effectively?

STEP 1   The teacher can respond:

> Mohamed, it's not 'give me paper',
> but 'Can I have the handout, please'?

While this comment gives feedback to the learner, it is doubtful if it is specific enough for Mohamed to understand the implication of his words. The tutor has two options. She can talk to Mohamed individually or discuss this example of language use with the whole group. For example, she can ask the learners what *Give me paper* would be understood to mean. She can raise awareness that this type of language comes across as rude and explore with the students how a request can be expressed appropriately. She can teach beginner learners that adding the word *please* softens the message considerably, as in *Give me paper, please.* She can also help the learners practise the right intonation to express a request.

STEP 2 Since lapses in communication with native English speakers are bound to occur, the teacher provides the learners with strategies on how to repair communication. The learners are asked to work out in small groups what they would say if they felt they had not communicated well. Learners often produce phrases such as: *I say again. Can I say that again, please? I am sorry, my English is no good. I think I said that wrong. Can I try to say that again?*

STEP 3 The teacher suggests to the learners that in the next few weeks they will report on how they communicate outside the classroom, both in terms of successful and unsuccessful communication. This allows the item of maintaining and repairing communication to stay on their learning agenda. She notes this on the group learning plan, identifying Mohamed and any other learners who may need further support.

Register

The term REGISTER is often used to refer to a particular style of speaking and writing. For example, a student may use colloquial language, while dashing off a quick email to a friend. An employee may write a memo to her colleague, using informal language. On the other hand, a job applicant may produce several drafts of a formal letter of application and CV, poring over every word to ensure it is just right. The analogy of choosing the right clothes for the occasion serves as an illustration: we would not normally choose to wear jeans and trainers at a wedding, but would most probably choose a more formal outfit such as a suit for a man and a dress for a woman. Equally, the choice of language needs to reflect the degree of formality of the relationship, and fit the spoken or written form.

Learners who are in the early stages of learning English tend to be pre-occupied with getting their message across in any way they can. It is only in the more advanced stages of language learning, when the learners have learnt a sufficient language repertoire, that they are able to pay attention to register. Here is an example:

CASE STUDY

Lindita is an Albanian speaker who attends a Level I class. She wants to do a travel and tourism course next. For homework she has been given the task of describing her college and the immediate area surrounding it.

What feedback would you give this student on her writing, including her use of register?

> The college of North West London is one of the buildings I like. It is situated in Wembley near the Wembley Park station. There is not much green space, as the area is full of buildings, such as hotels, offices, shops. Anyway it's cool spot and handy for facilities.

The first impression on reading Lindita's description is of a learner who knows English quite well. The reader is struck, however, by the mixture of registers in the text. The first three sentences are relatively formal, apart from the comment *I like.* The last sentence, however, is quite colloquial in its choice of words. Language teachers often see this type of mixture in their students' writing.

As to a judgement on which parts of Lindita's text are appropriate, this depends very much on the brief she was given. If her task was to write a catchy advert for a local newspaper in order for the college to attract new young learners, then the latter sentence would be just right. If, however, she had been asked to produce text for a formal college brochure, then the earlier part of the text would be more appropriate. The teacher needs to clarify with Lindita who the target audience for her text is and revise the text accordingly.

Further reading

Classroom resources

Cunningham, S. and **P. Moor** 2005. *New Cutting Edge.* London: Longman. The students' books in this series, which cover Elementary, Pre-Intermediate, Intermediate, and Upper-Intermediate levels, have special *wordbooster* or *wordspot* sections. Aspects of vocabulary are practised, such as meaning, collocations and phrases, word building, and pronunciation.

Swan, M. and **C. Walter** 2001. *The Good Grammar Book.* Oxford: Oxford University Press.
This grammar book for elementary to lower-intermediate students can be used in class or at home. It contains very simple explanations which are followed by practice tasks. There is an answer key for students to check their work.

Swan, M. 2005. *Practical English Usage.* Oxford: Oxford University Press.
This is a reference book for intermediate and advanced students and their teachers. It contains short and clear explanations of English grammar. Each entry contains an explanation of a problem, examples of correct usage, and some typical mistakes.

Department for Education and Skills. 2003. *Skills for Life Learner Materials Packs for ESOL at Entry 1, 2, and 3; and Levels 1 and 2.* London: DfES Publications.
The learning activities in these packs are mapped to the descriptors and component skills in the ESOL core curriculum and are accompanied by tapes and teachers' notes.

Department for Education and Skills/Home Office. 2005. *Citizenship Materials for ESOL Learners.* London: DfES Publications.
The Citizenship materials pack consists of different versions aimed at people living in England, Scotland, Northern Ireland, and Wales. The packs can be ordered from DfES Publications or downloaded from: http://www.niace. org.uk/projects/esolcitizenship

Background/Theory

Crystal, D. 2004. *Rediscover Grammar.* London: Longman.
This is a very short and simple introduction to English grammar. It provides clear examples to illustrate grammatical terms and their application.

Thornbury, S. 1999. *How to Teach Grammar.* London: Longman.
This book starts with the question: 'What is grammar?' and explains why and how to teach it. It looks at how to practise and test grammar and how to deal with errors. It provides sample lesson plans and practice activities, which are followed by an evaluation of the advantages and disadvantages of the approaches used.

Thornbury, S. 1999. *About Language: Tasks for Teachers of English.* Cambridge: Cambridge University Press.
This book for more experienced teachers deals with many different aspects of language including grammar. It is suitable for self-study, as answers are provided to language analysis tasks.

Aitken, R. 2002. *Teaching Tenses: Ideas for Presenting and Practising English Tenses.* London: Longman.
This is a useful teacher's resource book which gives many practical suggestions for how to present and practise tenses and verb patterns.

Lewis, M. 1997. *Implementing the Lexical Approach: Putting Theory into Practice.* Hove: Language Teaching Publications.
This book explains the lexical approach and the role of lexical chunks in learning English. There are a variety of exercises which show how the lexical approach works in practice.

Thornbury, S. 2002. *How to Teach Vocabulary.* London: Longman.
This book looks at the theory of words and their relationships. It describes how words are learned and gives ideas on useful sources of vocabulary and how these can be put to use in the classroom.

5 THE FOUR SKILLS OF LISTENING, SPEAKING, READING, AND WRITING

This chapter focuses on the four language skills of speaking, listening, reading, and writing. Some aspects are already well-covered in the ESOL classroom, for example, listening for detail and gist, reading to test comprehension, and activities to encourage the learners to communicate. There is also a plentiful supply of resources, for example, speaking and listening activities in the Skills for Life Materials Packs (DfES 2003). This chapter covers aspects which often do not get the same attention: the development of skills that underpin communication and comprehension. For example, the skill of being able to identify individual words when listening to spoken English is an aspect that causes many learners great difficulty.

For reading, we use examples from the National Literacy Test to explore strategies which help the learners handle written texts, both in exam situations and in real life. The section on writing concentrates on activities which teachers can use to expand the learners' ability to write independently. The last section is based on a valuable new concept introduced in the Skills for Life strategy, that of looking at language from the perspective of word, sentence, and text level. This is explored by using examples of communicative interaction, in particular speaking and writing.

Listening

Of the four skills, the teaching of listening is perhaps the hardest to handle in the classroom. One of the difficulties that teachers face is that they are unable to observe listening as they can the productive skills of speaking or writing. They have no direct evidence whether the listeners have understood what they heard. If we compare the receptive skills of listening and reading, we find that, because there is normally no permanent record of spoken language, the listener cannot go over what he or she has heard in the same way that the reader can with printed text. Yet, although spoken language is fleeting and understanding hard to measure, listening is a very important skill for migrants and refugees, both as a skill to learn new language and to survive in their new environment. In this section we will focus on the listening process itself, starting at the beginning of the cycle with how sound is received and processed.

Top-down–bottom-up processing

TASK   Thinking about the process of listening to spoken language

Imagine that a colleague says to you:

I'm having a birthday party. Are you free on the sixteenth of June?

What processes do you use to understand this message?

When you listen to spoken language, your mind engages in two processes. The first is that you hear a stream of sound which you assemble into syllables and words. This process of building small into larger units is called BOTTOM-UP PROCESSING. The second process works the other way round: you use your knowledge of larger units to determine and confirm small units of information, a process which is called TOP-DOWN PROCESSING. You do this by using your knowledge of the language, the world around you, and the context in which you hear the spoken language. In the case of the request above, although the speaker is not saying it explicitly, your prior knowledge will tell you that your colleague is inviting you to a birthday party.

Bottom-up and top-down processing can affect each other. A classic example of this concerns an interpreter who, during a talk on the subject of geography, misheard 'Switzerland' instead of 'Swaziland'. He then used his knowledge of Switzerland (and its mountains) to interpret the talk, to realize to his horror afterwards that he had been using the wrong context. His error in hearing the wrong word, at the bottom-up processing stage, led to a second mistake in top-down processing, when he used his knowledge of Switzerland to interpret the talk.

Like the interpreter, language learners may have many 'Swaziland moments', when they hear sounds, construct these into words, and allocate meaning as best as they can. Since one level of understanding can influence the next and there are many sources of information which feed into comprehension, it is no wonder that learners often feel insecure about their ability to make sense of the language they hear around them.

This poses the question of how language teachers can help the learner make sense of the language they hear, in terms of both top-down and bottom-up processing. Lesson observations show that the top-down element is well-covered through comprehension exercises, especially since that is how listening tends to be assessed in exams. Tricia Hedge (2001) gives an excellent overview of comprehension activities which consist of preparation for listening, the listening activity itself, and the after-phase when extension activities can take place. However, learners often get little training to help them develop bottom-up listening skills and to make sense of the sound stream. This is especially relevant for migrants and refugees who often find themselves in situations where they receive important information, for example, on housing benefit or their child's education. If they have good bottom-up listening skills, that frees the mind to concentrate on the overall meaning of the message. In this section we focus on this aspect of listening, analysing why breakdowns in understanding occur and what teachers can do to help their learners improve their listening skills.

Word boundaries in spoken language

Unlike in written English, the boundaries between words in spoken English can often not be detected. John Field (2003a), in an article on second language listening, makes the important point that pauses in natural speech occur only every twelve syllables or so. This means that listeners often have to work out for themselves where words begin and end. As Field says, it is remarkable that native speakers manage to identify individual words consistently, a process which is called *lexical segmentation.* By contrast, second language learners find this hard to do. Even if they 'know' the words when they see them written down or hear them in isolation, they may not recognize them when they hear them in connected speech. If you have learnt another language, you will know that it can be very difficult to do this and that it is such hard work that the listener soon feels exhausted.

Research evidence also shows that language learners tend to scan for words that they already know rather than listen to the sounds they hear. In their attempt to understand they may even go across word boundaries, divide words into smaller units, or miss words altogether. Here are some examples of the mismatch between what was said and what the learners thought they had heard:

This was said	This was heard
Is she going to sell them?	She going to selling?
It will come in handy.	It will coming handy.
How much are they worth?	How much work?

These and further examples in this section show that many learners find it hard to identify the correct individual words from a stream of sound. Emerging research evidence indicates that the principles of segmentation vary across languages, which may explain why some learners have more difficulties with this aspect than others. As Field points out, many learners do improve their ability over time and training can help speed up the process. Anne Cutler's research (1990) is particularly helpful as she shows that, in English, word stress is an important factor in assigning word boundaries. Let us take some sample sentences to see how this might work:

●   ●   ●

She saw the photograph on the mantelpiece.

   ●   ●   ●

I went to hospital to see my grandmother.

These two sentences both have two main and two lesser stressed syllables, all of which coincide with the start of a new word. This is a usual pattern in English. Cutler calculated that around 90 per cent of content words in a piece of running speech either consist of one syllable only or have stress on the first syllable. She suggests that first language speakers use this knowledge to identify the beginning of a new word. Since it follows that some 10 per cent of content words do not have stress at the beginning of the word, for example, *computer, important,* and *begin,* this strategy is not foolproof. However, it can provide a useful principle when teaching listening skills, especially if learners are accustomed to using a different segmentation strategy in their first language.

Weak forms

TASK

After dictating the sentence *I have lived in his house for three years,* a teacher found that quite a few of the learners dropped one or more of the words to produce: *I lived in house three years.*

What might be the reason why this has happened?

These learners have focused on content words when listening, which in the sentences above are also the words that carry stress. The focus on words that carry meaning, such as *lived, house,* and *years,* is typical of many second language speakers, as we also saw in Chapter 4 in the section on vocabulary. By contrast, learners often do not pay the same attention to words such as *have, his,* and *for.* In the case of the word *have,* it is possible that learners were not familiar with the present perfect tense. On the other hand, it is equally possible that they simply did not notice the abbreviated form /v/. Since *have, his,* and *for* normally do not carry stress in spoken English, they are much harder to notice. Yet WEAK FORMS, as the unstressed variants are called, occur extremely frequently in the English language. They often carry meaning, as in *I lived* versus *I have lived.* That is why it is important that the learners learn to notice these as meaningful words in the sentence. The dictation exercise on page 74 shows how teachers can help the learners work on this feature.

Linking vowels and consonants

When words occur in spoken English, their shape is often influenced by the sounds that surround them. This is one of the major aspects that makes it difficult for language learners to identify individual words in a stream of sound. If we take sentences such as:

Did you hear the sirens? There was an accident on our road.

when these words are said aloud they sound like this:

Didya hear the sirens? There wa za nacciden to nour road.

This example shows that the ends of words are pulled into the beginning of the next word. Michael Vaughan-Rees's (1994) chain of *one apple, two apples, three apples, four apples* provides a useful sequence to help the learners see how words are linked in spoken English:

Written as	Sounds like	Phonetic notation
one apple	wa napple	wʌnæpəl
two apples	two wapples	tuːwæpəlz
three apples	three yapples	θriːjæpəlz
four apples	four rapples	fɔːræpəlz

Here is an outline of how you can work with the learners on linking:

STEP 1 Put the first two columns of the table above on the board and fill in the words in the 'written as' column. Ask the learners group how English people would say 'one apple', etc. If none of the learners produces the correct linking, contrast your own pronunciation with that of the learners to see if they can hear the difference. If they find it impossible to notice the linking effect, write the items in the second column and observe whether they can hear the sound once they see the written version.

The 'one apple' type of linking, which occurs when a word ending in a consonant is followed by a word beginning with a vowel, is by far the most common in spoken English, so it is important for the students to recognize this feature.

STEP 3 During a subsequent lesson you can put some more examples of linking on the board, such as those in the box below, to see if the learners can apply the principle of linking across word boundaries. Please note that the spaces between the words do not imply that there is a pause between the words. The voice is continuous but this visual representation often helps learners understand the principle of linking.

Written as	Sounds like
Take it over there	Ta ki tover there
My name is Allan Underwood	my na mi salle nunderwood
I need an ambulance	I nee da nabulance

STEP 4 In addition to the consonant–vowel 'one apple' type of linking, English also links vowel–vowel combinations. There are three ways in which this is achieved, by inserting the sounds /w/, /j/, or /r/. Here are some examples to show the learners how these links are created.

w	j	r
you‿are	I‿am	four‿applications
w	j	r
too‿old	s/he‿is	for‿ever
w	j	r
Do‿I?	my‿address	here‿and there
w	j	r

Since the pronunciation of /r/ varies according to dialect and national variant, for example, Scotland, the USA, and Southern British English, teachers will need to adjust this aspect to their local circumstances.

Most language learners are not naturally aware that these types of linking occur in English. However, once they know how words are linked together, many find it much easier to understand native speakers. Conversely, once they have mastered these four ways of 'stringing words together', their English also becomes easier to understand.

Linking consonants into clusters

TASK   Consonant clusters

There is one more way in which the sound shapes of words can be changed, this time because two or more consonants at the end and beginning of words find themselves next to each other. Here is a list of words from John Field's (2003a) article on listening. How are these words pronounced?

    ten people
    ten cars
    that boy
    that girl
    good play
    good cause
    this shirt
    those shoes
    right you are
    did you go?

We find that, when these words are said aloud, the consonants at the end and beginning of the words influence each other to create new clusters:

ten people	tem people
ten cars	teng cars
that boy	thap boy
that girl	thak girl
good play	goo play
good cause	goo cause
this shirt	thi shirt
those shoes	tho shoes
right you are	rye chew are
did you go?	di dja go?

How can you make the learners aware that these consonant clusters exist?

STEP 1 To check if the learners can make sense of the clustering effect, either dictate the words on their own or embedded in sentences, for example, *I have invited ten people to the meeting.*

STEP 2 Check with the learners if they have written the right words and, if not, which clusters caused a breakdown of understanding.

STEP 3 If you want the learners to learn to produce these clusters themselves, you can ask them to read the sentences aloud to their partner. It is their partner's task to listen and say if the right cluster is produced.

STEP 4 Now in the whole group, ask each of the learners to read through some of the words on the list and model the right cluster, if need be.

Taking a step back from the detail of this pronunciation exercise, learners often find it helpful to reflect more generally on what spoken English sounds like. It appears that the cumulative effect of the linking of words creates a continuous stream of sound. Learners often like the analogy of spoken English being like a car engine which runs smoothly all the time. They may also be interested to compare the production of their own language with that of English.

Using dictation as a diagnostic tool

Learners find it helpful to check and develop their skills by listening to spoken English and writing down what they hear. This activity works well as a diagnostic tool for the teacher and learners alike. Teachers can use various resources as a prompt for listening. The first is the use of radio broadcasts. While this provides the most authentic material, practical considerations can make these difficult to use. In the first place, if a transcript is not already available, transcribing the spoken text is time-consuming. In addition, the learners will need to hear the text in small chunks and more than once to write down what they hear. This requires accurate rewinding of the tape, which is notoriously difficult. A second option is the use of short texts, such as newspaper articles which are relevant to the learners' lives. Experience shows that these work particularly well in the classroom. Here is an example to show how material can be used with a class of Entry 3 learners. The text used below was taken from a local newspaper as the introduction to a lesson on the learners' local environment. The teacher read out the text in small chunks, as naturally as she could and at a normal speed of speech. She made sure to use weak forms throughout, such as *funds for ... have been allocated.*

Analysing the listening and writing skills of the learners

Overall, the learners managed the dictation very well but in the margins of the article you will find some of the aspects that learners A, B, C, and D had problems with. What do you think might be the cause of their difficulties and how would you help them improve?

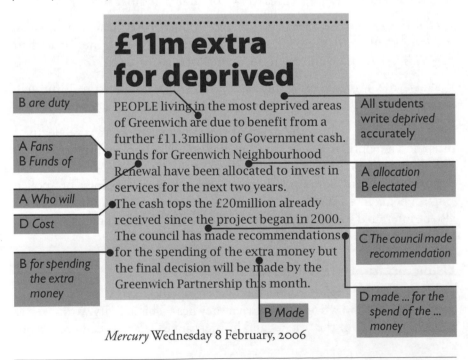

B *are duty*

A *Fans*
B *Funds of*

A *Who will*

D *Cost*

B *for spending the extra money*

£11m extra for deprived

PEOPLE living in the most deprived areas of Greenwich are due to benefit from a further £11.3million of Government cash. Funds for Greenwich Neighbourhood Renewal have been allocated to invest in services for the next two years. The cash tops the £20million already received since the project began in 2000. The council has made recommendations for the spending of the extra money but the final decision will be made by the Greenwich Partnership this month.

B *Made*

All students write *deprived* accurately

A *allocation*
B *electated*

C *The council made recommendation*

D *made ... for the spend of the ... money*

Mercury Wednesday 8 February, 2006

This dictation exercise proved to be a treasure trove of information on the learners' listening skills. It enabled both teacher and learners to work out what the learners already understood and where they needed further help. Although the accuracy of the spelling of words was not the prime objective of this exercise, the learners were keen to find out how well they wrote the text down, so this aspect gets brief attention here. Some words such as *allocated* and *recommendation* caused difficulty but, considering that these words were new to the learners, they made sensible attempts at guessing their spelling. Also good to see was that all learners wrote words like *deprived* correctly, even though they did not know them. This showed that the learners were able to apply common spelling rules to a word with regular spelling. This is an important skill in its own right and useful for looking up new words in the dictionary.

Moving on to the areas where breakdowns of understanding occurred, the first example concerns the word *tops* which was rendered as *cost*. This is a telling example of a learner who, not knowing the word verb *to top*, used the context of the text to opt for a word that she already knew. In other words, rather than rely on her bottom-up listening skills to work out what the word might be, she used top-down processing. This example of mishearing made the learner realize that, in addition to using her knowledge of English vocabulary, she should also pay attention to what the words sounded like.

Like learner D, who wrote *cost*, learners A and B also opted for words that they knew rather than what they heard. They wrote *are duty* for *are due to* and *who will* for *renewal*. By doing so, they failed to locate word boundaries correctly. This is a feature which, as we saw earlier, often presents difficulty. These learners were amused at how they had interpreted the words that had been dictated to them. The examples provided powerful material to make them think about how words are linked in spoken English and how they might recognize word boundaries. The teacher provided support by giving them some sentences in which *duty* and *due to*, and *who will* and *renewal* were used.

The learner who wrote *fans* for *funds* was already aware of her difficulty in hearing (and pronouncing) the sounds /æ/ and /ʌ/. The teacher and learner decided that she needed more listening practice to distinguish between these sounds in the first instance, followed by pronunciation practice once she was secure in her ability to hear the difference. For further discussion on pronunciation, see the next section in this chapter.

Learner B's writing of *funds of* and *for spending the extra money* showed that he focused on words that carried meaning and paid insufficient attention to unstressed words, in this case articles and prepositions. This dictation exercise made him aware that he needed to listen out for weak as well as stressed forms.

This leaves the two examples where the learners missed part of the verb forms. Learners C and D had not registered the weak form of *has made* and needed to hear the sentence read aloud several times before they could. Learner B had also missed out part of the passive construction *will be made*. He was a speaker of Urdu, which does not have the passive voice. Since he felt that he did not understand fully how the passive worked, he wanted to work on the grammar in the first instance. The teacher also made a note that, the next time she used a newspaper article, she would ask the learners to identify passive and active forms. She would then introduce the link between text type and language, using the passive as an example.

This task took about five minutes to dictate and ten minutes to check, and provided many learning points. Many were dealt with on the spot and others were followed up in subsequent lessons. The text worked both as a listening exercise and as a useful introduction to the rest of the lesson in which the learners worked out how they might use the £11m new funding mentioned in the article to improve their local area. The subsequent discussion proved to be interesting as some learners disagreed with the article that their area was deprived. During the last stage of the lesson the learners wrote a proposal on how they would use the money to improve their local environment.

Dictation has not been popular with teachers, at least in part because it has traditionally consisted of dictating lists of words to improve spelling. However, the use of dictation to develop listening skills is essentially a different activity, which many learners regard as a valuable learning opportunity. It helps them practise their listening skills, identify problem areas, and, most motivating, many report that it improves their ability to understand spoken English outside the classroom.

Teacher language as input for listening

Classroom observations show that in many lessons the teacher is the only source of spoken English and that audio material is used to a very limited extent. Since, as we saw in Chapter 2, a proportion of the learners rarely communicate with native English speakers outside the classroom. This means that the teacher may provide their only model of language. In this section we explore how the teacher's spoken English can affect the development of listening skills and suggest ways of broadening access to different voices.

Reflecting on learners' perceptions

Here are comments made by three learners on their listening experiences in and outside class.

> I understand you, nobody else.

> Why I can understand you in class but I have no idea what people are saying outside?

> English people speak too fast but you don't.

What is the reason why the learners make these comments? What should the role of the teacher be when speaking English in class?

These comments give an interesting insight into the learners' perceptions of teacher talk. In many ways they can be seen as positive. Most teachers adjust their English because they know that learners have problems understanding natural speech as it is spoken outside the classroom. This is especially important at beginner level when the learners need modified input to be able to understand what is being said. 'Teacher talk', which is usually pitched at or below the learners' level of understanding, is achieved by using the following techniques:

- simplifying language by using everyday vocabulary and short sentences
- slowing down the speed of speaking
- pronouncing words as individual items
- using the full rather than the weak form of words such as in, for example,
  - You have done very well!

- using exaggerated intonation and pitch to indicate which words are important
- frequent repetition and checking back
- asking open questions.

Many of these techniques are explicitly taught during teacher training courses and rightly so. New teachers often struggle to make themselves understood so they need to know how to communicate with their learners. And yet, learner feedback indicates that there may be an inherent danger in applying these strategies as a matter of course.

Monitoring the use of teacher talk and natural speech

Many teachers develop their own teaching style over time, including the adoption of 'teacher talk'. What can teachers do to review the appropriateness of their language, and the extent to which it prepares the learners to understand English outside the classroom?

1 One strategy is to ask your students. They will be able to tell you if they can understand your spoken English easily and if it differs from the English they hear outside.
2 If you are planning peer observations, you could ask your observer to give you feedback on your language use.
3 The third option is to record yourself while teaching, on either audio or video tape. The recording does not have to be very long: ten minutes can be enough for effective analysis. If you teach different level classes, you should consider taping yourself in these to establish whether you vary your level of English.

If the feedback from one or more of these activities points to a predominance of simplified teacher talk, then you should consider a review of your spoken English. A good starting point is to work out whether you always use the same speed and complexity of language, or whether you adjust your language to the task in hand. This is because it is good practice to let your language use depend on the purpose of the interaction. Teacher talk may be required when you want to make sure that all learners understand what you are saying, for example, when you explain a task or give feedback on language. However, when you are telling a story or chatting to the learners informally, you can expose the learners to more natural spoken English.

Some teachers have said that they feel it reflects badly on them, if their learners do not understand everything their teacher says. But the achievement of total understanding is not necessarily the main objective in the language classroom. It is equally important to extend the ability of the learners to understand natural spoken English. This means providing the learners with language that challenges their capacity to understand. For example, we have already seen in the section on vocabulary that word strings frequently occur together. They, and their pronunciation, appear to be stored as one unit. You can help the learners extend their capacity to handle word strings by using them at normal speed and observing whether the learners have understood what you said, for example, instructions such as: *Whadja wanna do?* or *Gimme the answer*, and the expression: *Do you know what I mean?* /noːʔmiːn/ which is commonly used in London.

The teacher can help the learners extend their listening skills by gradually increasing the speed of speaking, using linking words, and using natural stress patterns. This means, in effect, stripping out more and more of the support techniques that help teachers communicate at beginner level. Teachers should also use authentic materials to help the learners develop their ability to understand spoken English. These can be clips from the news on TV or radio but ads and short scenes from soap operas work equally well. This will provide opportunities of broadening access to different voices and dialects.

Using phonetic symbols

You will have noticed that phonetic symbols have been used in this section on listening skills. They were devised by the International Phonetics Association (IPA) and are the standard system of annotating pronunciation. Teachers often ask if they should teach their learners these phonetic symbols. This depends very much on the learners. Some like to use the IPA alphabet when learning new words, making sure that they notice not just the spelling but also the pronunciation; others prefer to write a rough equivalent following the writing system of their first language. In many ways both are sensible approaches, as the spelling of English words often does not reflect their pronunciation. At the same time, there are learners who find it hard to get to grips with the phonetic script or do not see the point of using it. Experience in the classroom shows that, rather than making the learners use it actively, teachers can use phonetic script to present a word or phrase when they think that it will be useful for the students – perhaps comparing it with others that are pronounced similarly. For example, being able to give a phonetic transcription of words is a useful counterpoint for learners who are heavily influenced by the written forms of words.

STEP 1 A useful experiment to find out whether learners rely on spelling to guide their pronunciation is to ask them how many spoken syllables there are in words like *vegetable* and *chocolate*. If the learners say that there are four syllables in either word, this may indicate that they use their visual rather than their listening skills to guide them on pronunciation.

STEP 2 If you tap out the syllables on the table or your hand while saying the word aloud, you may find that some learners change their mind about its number of syllables. However, others need to see *vegetable* and *chocolate* written in phonetic script with the syllable boundaries marked: /vedʒ/tə/bəl/ and /tʃɔ/klət/. Alternatively, if you judge that your students cannot handle words written in phonetic script, you can consider using English spelling to represent the pronunciation. If you decide to take this option, it is advisable to introduce the concept of schwa /ə/ to the students. This symbol for the *uh* vowel sound is useful because, although it is not represented in the alphabet, it is the most common vowel sound in spoken English. In that case you would present the learners with: *vegtəbəl* and *choclət*. These visual representations make it much easier to see that the words consist of three and two syllables respectively. Many learners report that seeing the word in phonetic script makes it easier to remember the pronunciation afterwards.

Speaking

Language teaching to migrants and refugees differs in one important aspect from just about any other classroom situation: the subject matter and the medium of communication are the same. Let's take, for example, a lesson on asking questions. The teacher starts by demonstrating in English how the grammar and intonation function. The learners then work in pairs to ask and answer questions of each other about their hobbies. The teacher gives feedback to individual learners while they practise and then brings the learners together to review how well the task went. Unless the learners work with speakers of the same language during the pair work exercise, they can be expected to use English throughout the lesson, both to understand the explanation of the grammar and intonation and while they practise their English during the speaking task. This means that in principle all communication in the classroom is an opportunity for the learners to use English.

The frequency with which oral communication occurs in the classroom is also reflected in this book. Tasks in which presentations, pair work, and group work are used to create opportunities for speaking are found throughout, for example, in Chapter 2 the discussion on access to education for boys and girls. In most of the classroom activities described in Chapter 4 speaking plays an important part, such as in the exercise to brainstorm vocabulary, the personality test, and working on everyday language. Later in this chapter you will find examples of how text frameworks can help the learners organize their thoughts before they engage in speaking. The section on feedback in Chapter 6, particularly Paulo's presentation on health and safety (see page 165), analyses the quality of his spoken English and presents ideas on how he can notice and develop these speaking skills.

In addition, many learning opportunities occur in the classroom when learners interact in their own right, for example, when they chat to each other, ask questions for clarification, or need something, as in Chapter 4 when Mohamed says *Give me paper*. The real communication between learners and teachers often provides great opportunities to learn how to handle turn-taking, social chat, and strategies to repair communication. Since what the learners say in class is often an indication of what they would say outside, they are invariably interested in getting feedback on how they come across.

There is, however, one more dimension to speaking: the production of the learners' spoken English. Many achieve a good command of the language in terms of grammar and vocabulary but are let down by their speaking skills, in particular stress, intonation, and pronunciation. This section starts by looking at the need for pronunciation teaching and then explores some of the aspects that are particularly helpful to people who need to communicate in English on a day-to-day basis.

Teaching pronunciation

CASE STUDY 1

You have just started teaching a group of newly arrived learners who have hardly any English. Should you teach them pronunciation?

Teachers often ask this question. Some feel that the learner already has so much to cope with in the early stages of language learning that it is not appropriate to add pronunciation to the list of priorities. Others say that they shy away from teaching pronunciation, because they do not feel that they have the skills to deliver it. It is also true to say that the communicative approach, which has been a major influence in the field of ESOL, has not favoured the teaching of pronunciation. In particular, Krashen's thinking on the use of comprehensible input as the main driver for language learning created an emphasis on the input skills of listening and reading (Krashen 1985; Krashen and Terrell 1983). This has had as its downside that the learners' own language production has received much less attention.

However, a small but growing body of research on the effect of pronunciation teaching by, for example, Tracey Derwing and others (1998, 2003), indicates that explicit teaching does help the development of pronunciation skills, and that training in the use of stress and intonation are especially effective. So, to answer teachers' concerns about whether and when to teach pronunciation, research evidence suggests that learners really do benefit from pronunciation teaching, right from the start and as an integral part of the learning experience. It creates an early awareness of how spoken English works and sensitizes the learner to significant differences between the production of their own language and that of English.

Teaching consonants

Teaching the pronunciation of individual sounds can be difficult. Take, for example, the *th* sound in words like *think* and *through* and which is represented as /θ/ in phonetic script. Teachers often teach this sound by giving instructions such as: 'Put your tongue between your teeth. Make the air come out between your upper teeth and your tongue.' However, more often than not, these instructions do not help the learners create the right sound. Instead, they continue to make the sounds they used before: /s/, /z/, /d/, /f/, etc. There is a practical solution to this problem. If you take some hand mirrors into the classroom, it makes it much easier for the learners to see what they are doing.

Mirrors are especially useful when teaching consonants. They allow the learners to monitor what their mouths are doing, compare the teacher's mouth-shape to their own, and to adjust the position of lips, tongue, etc. Using mirrors does not just help to get the tongue in the right position, it can also help learners see that they need to keep it in place for the duration of the /θ/ sound, which in English is for a comparatively long time. Speakers of Asian languages tend to draw the tongue sharply down and back once they have started to make the /θ/ sound, ending it prematurely.

You may find that some learners are quite self-conscious when you first introduce mirrors in the classroom. However, many find them a helpful observation tool, once they have got used to them.

Teachers have questioned the importance of the pronunciation of *th*, especially since in the dialect spoken in London and the south-east of England, the /f/ sound may be substituted. While this is true and the pronunciation of /f/ may not affect intelligibility, learners should know that this pronunciation would normally not occur in formal situations and that the listener may make judgements about the status and background of the speaker. This consideration is especially important if learners intend to work in an office or professional environment.

Pronunciation activity

Games can provide a useful tool to help learners notice features of English pronunciation which affect the meaning of spoken English. This game consists of MINIMAL PAIRS, which means that words are identical apart from one or two significant differences. To see how it works, look at the word sets below and read the classroom instructions up to step 4, when we shall reflect on its objectives.

STEP 1   All learners will need their own copy of the master sheet with the heading: *Which word do you hear?* Each learner will also need one of the cards A, B, C, or D, which consist of lists of single words. You will need to cut these up beforehand.

STEP 2   Divide the learners into teams of up to four people. Give each learner a master sheet and a card with A, B, C, or D on it. They should not show their cards to the other members of the team.

STEP 3   The activity starts with the person with card A reading out the words on his or her card and the others ticking the word that they hear on the master sheet. Then person B reads card B and so on. If you find that learners read the words too quickly for their colleagues to note what they hear, ask them to slow down. The learners may also ask you for the meaning of words. While it is fine to give explanations, maintain the focus on the pronunciation rather than vocabulary.

STEP 4   Once all cards have been read, the teams should work through the cards again, this time checking if the words on the cards correspond with those ticked by the listeners.

Which word do you hear?

A	B	C	D
1 clock – clog	1 pig – pick	1 dug – duck	1 back – bag
2 rip – rib	2 mop – mob	2 flap – flab	2 belief – believe
3 hat – had	3 mate – made	3 sat – sad	3 hit – hid
4 pick – pig	4 fleece – fleas	4 tuck – tug	4 hiss – his
5 bat – bad	5 hiss – his	5 piece – peas	5 bit – bid
6 price – prize	6 cap – cab	6 rope – robe	6 niece – knees
7 tap – tab	7 back – bag	7 price – prize	7 tuck – tug
8 sack – sag	8 hop – hob	8 pluck – plug	8 nip – nib

A	B	C	D
1 clock	1 pig	1 duck	1 back
2 rib	2 mob	2 flab	2 believe
3 had	3 mate	3 sat	3 hid
4 pig	4 fleas	4 tuck	4 hiss
5 bat	5 his	5 peas	5 bid
6 price	6 cap	6 robe	6 knees
7 tab	7 bag	7 prize	7 tuck
8 sack	8 hop	8 plug	8 nip

A	B	C	D
1 clog	1 pick	1 dug	1 bag
2 rip	2 mob	2 flap	2 belief
3 had	3 made	3 sad	3 hid
4 pig	4 fleece	4 tuck	4 his
5 bat	5 hiss	5 peas	5 bit
6 price	6 cab	6 robe	6 niece
7 tab	7 bag	7 price	7 tuck
8 sag	8 hob	8 pluck	8 nib

TASK

Before we look at the learners' evaluation of their answers, some questions about the purpose of this activity:

Which skills are assessed?

What pronunciation features does the game assess, for example, how do words like *hiss* and *his* differ in their pronunciation?

This game allows the learners to use their listening and pronunciation skills to self-assess their ability to distinguish between paired words such as *hiss* and *his*, and *duck* and *dug*. These words differ in two ways, with one word ending in a voiceless consonant, for example, *duck* which ends in /k/; and the second word *dug* which ends in voiced /g/. The second difference between *duck* and *dug* lies in the length of the vowel. While in *duck* the /v/ sound is short, in the word *dug* the voiced consonant /g/ causes the vowel sound to be lengthened. These are important distinguishing features for many words in English, so they are well worth focusing on.

As to how the learners perceive these sounds, you are likely to find the following pattern. Some have not noticed the difference between voiced and unvoiced consonants such as /s/, /k/, /t/, and /p/ and /z/, /g/, /d/, and /b/. Others are able to hear the difference but cannot produce the voiced sounds at the end of words, for example, /hɪz/ as in *it's not mine, it's his*. By comparison, learners are much less likely to have noticed the difference in the length of the vowel. Yet this is a more important distinctive feature on which native English speakers rely primarily to distinguish between words such as *sat* and *sad*.

We now return to the game being played in class, where the learners are now ready to evaluate their answers.

STEP 5 In many cases the listeners will agree that they heard the word that the card holder said. However, there will also be examples where the listeners ticked a word that was different from the word that is found on the card. This will be for one of two reasons: either the person saying the word did not pronounce the word correctly; or one or more of the listener(s) heard the word incorrectly. Because it is not a foregone conclusion whether the speaker or the listeners are right, teams often really engage in working out what caused the discrepancy. This involves separating out the processes of listening and pronunciation. Some groups are also able to work out the underlying principles of pronunciation, saying 'You said /peas/ when you should have said /piːz/.'

STEP 6 Once the learners have analysed their answers, you can check who had problems with hearing and / or saying the words. This information is worth recording so that you know which learners need further work on one or both aspects.

You can now ask the learners what they think the differences between the paired words are. Some may have noticed the difference in pronunciation between voiced and unvoiced consonants such as /s/ and /z/, /k/ and /g/, and /p/ and /b/. If the learners are not sure about the difference, they can feel the difference by putting their fingers on their throat while they say voiced and unvoiced consonants. You can also demonstrate the length of the vowels visually by stretching an elastic band (for the words with long vowel sounds) while you read through some examples of paired words. Once the learners are confident that they can hear the difference, you can play the game again, this time with you reading one of the words and asking the learners to tick what they hear.

STEP 7 The learners should now be ready to practise saying the words themselves. You may well find that they still find it difficult to voice the consonant at the end of the word but that lengthening the vowel has become easier. While it is desirable to achieve both, the lengthening achieves a major improvement in intelligibility.

Many learners really like this type of activity because they can use their analytical skills to work out the principles that govern the pronunciation of the minimal pairs. They become more aware of the quality of vowel sounds and consonants. This game also sensitizes the learners to the fact that sounds can be influenced by the environment in which they are pronounced, in this case that vowels are lengthened before a voiced consonant.

The principle of this pronunciation game, with its paired words and reading cards, can be adapted to encourage the learners to notice other aspects of the language, too. For example, a game on spelling and pronunciation patterns such as *mat – mate*; *tub – tube*, and *sit – site* is particularly useful at Entry 1 and 2. For suggestions on resources and activities to teach pronunciation, see the Further Reading section, for example, Joanne Kenworthy's (1987) and Rogerson and Gilbert's (1990) books. In addition, many EFL course books incorporate useful pronunciation exercises.

The example below shows what can happen to former learners, if pronunciation is not on the learning agenda.

CASE STUDY 2

Trinh, a hospital nurse of Vietnamese origin, is very competent in the clinical sense but has a reputation for being distant. The families of some of her patients have complained about her lack of communication. Why might this be?

Even when people have been resident in the UK for a long time and have been in work, they can still feel underconfident about their spoken English. Trinh had a good command of English sentence structure as well as general and medical vocabulary. However, she had major problems with her pronunciation, stress, and intonation, which made it hard to understand her. Because of this, she minimized contact with English speakers, which in turn affected her professional behaviour. When she was approached about her ability to function on the ward, she mentioned that she had had very little help with her pronunciation when she attended language classes and that she was willing to attend a special pronunciation class. Her teacher designed a programme which focused on her particular problems: the linking of words, stress patterns, and intonation. By the time she had attended for three months, her spoken English was much easier to follow. Trinh did not just keep her job, she enjoyed her work a lot more because she did not feel so inhibited when communicating with colleagues and patients.

The next pages focus on some key techniques that learners like Trinh have found helpful. The list of resources at the end of this chapter provides further guidance and opportunities for study.

Stress and rhythm

One of the reasons that people have problems being understood is that they handle the stress patterns and rhythm of English differently from what first language speakers expect.

ACTIVITY **1**

Here is a snippet of spoken English:

I'll see you tomorrow at two.

What happens to the individual words when you say these words aloud?

It is very likely that, when you read the sentence aloud, you put strong stress on *see*, *tomorrow*, and *two*. By contrast, other words, such as *you* and *at*, attract so little stress that they are barely audible. This is mainly because the vowels in these words have been reduced to the schwa sound which in phonetic script is annotated as /ə/.

The stress pattern in *I'll see you tomorrow at two*, with its alternation of stressed and unstressed syllables, is typical of spoken English and gives it a unique 'flow'. As the two examples below show, this 'flow' is not accidental.

ACTIVITY **2**

Here are two sentences. How do they compare in terms of rhythm?

What shall we do now?

What do you want to do now?

Although the words and number of syllables are different, the rhythm in these two sentences is remarkably similar.

What shall we	do now?	/ˈwoʔʃəlwiduːˌnaʊ/
What do you want to	do now?	/ˈwoʔdʒəwɒnəduːˌnaʊ/

In these sentences we see a pattern of stressed and unstressed syllables being squashed or stretched to fit into the same intonation pattern. As a result, these two lines have a similar beat. This poses the question of how second language speakers handle these aspects.

TASK   Exploring how language learners handle rhythm in
       spoken English

Either:

1 Listen to some learners while they are speaking English, or even better tape
  them while they are talking. Observe where they put the strong and weak stress
  on words to create sentence stress. How well do they manage the rhythm of
  spoken English?

or:

2 Reflect on this exchange between two learners who are talking about an
  impending job interview. How might they say these sentences?

    Don't think about it.

    What are you going to do when they ask you about job?

Teachers often find that, rather than producing spoken English with its
sequence of stressed and unstressed syllables, the learners put equal or near
equal stress on each of the words and syllables. Thus they are likely to say:

●   ●   ●   ●   ●
 Don't think about it

with strong stress on *about*.

This creates a staccato effect, which can make it hard for them to be
understood. Many language learners appear to be unaware of the rhythm of
English, so the use of poems with a strong rhythmic pattern such as Roald
Dahl's *Revolting Rhymes*, or *Jazz Chants* by Carolyn Graham (1978) can work
well to help them notice. Here is a limerick by Edward Lear which is
reproduced in *Speaking Clearly* by Rogerson and Gilbert (1990).

There WAS an old MAN with a BEARD
Who SAID, 'It is JUST as I FEARED!
Two OWLS and a HEN
Four LARKS and a WREN
Have ALL built their NESTS in my BEARD!'

STEP 1   Ideally play an audio recording of the limerick. However, if a tape is
not available, you can read the text aloud yourself. The first time, ask the
learners to listen for the meaning of the text. Then play the tape again, this
time the learners should concentrate on the beat of the lines. If the learners
find it hard to identify the beat, tap it out on the table.

STEP 2   Give the learners the text of the poem and play the tape again.
Encourage them to mark the syllables which are stressed and to notice what
happens to those which are unstressed.

STEP 3   Now ask the learners to read the text aloud in pairs, making sure that they maintain its rhythm and that they pronounce words which do not attract stress in their weak form, for example, *and a* as /ene/ and *have* as /ev/. (Please note that although 'was' in the first line normally does not attract stress, here it is stressed to maintain the rhythm of the limerick.)

STEP 4   Saying the lines quickly can make it easier for the learners to produce the right rhythm. Divide the class in two and ask the two groups to say alternate lines as quickly as they can. Many learners enjoy this activity, with the two groups competing to say the lines the fastest and with the most accurate stress.

This exercise demonstrates the application of stress and rhythm. It also displays a feature which we have already seen in the section on listening skills. This is the way that word shapes are influenced by the sounds that surround them. If we take the first line:

> There was an old man with a beard

when these words are said aloud they sound more like:

> there wa sa nold man wi tha beard

This example shows that the ends of words are pulled into the beginning of the next word, along the 'one apple' pattern that we saw earlier. Learners who learn to apply this principle of 'stringing words together', often find that they are more easily understood by native English speakers.

STEP 5   As a follow-up activity, choose a short piece of naturally spoken and easily understood spoken English which you have on tape or video and for which you have a written version. Give the learners the written text and play the tape. Ask them to mark the words that they think are stressed. When they have finished, ask them to compare in twos or threes where they put the stress. Once they have agreed where the stress should be, ask them to read the text to each other.

Ideas to help the learners handle sentence stress and linking words
So far we have identified activities to help learners notice sentence stress and linking, such as using poems and limericks with a strong rhythmic pattern and using the 'apple sequence' to help the learners remember how words are linked. In addition, here are some suggestions for incorporating these aspects into lessons.

- If you have done a reading exercise with the learners and they are familiar with the text, you can ask them to read part of it aloud in small groups. For example, you can ask them to concentrate on linking, an aspect that works particularly well when reading aloud. Speeding up the reading slightly can make it easier to achieve the desired linking effect.

- Listen to your students talking to each other during classroom activities and note down some examples of good use of stress, rhythm, and linking as well as areas where the learners need to develop their skills further. Once the activity has finished, debrief the learners on some of the aspects that you identified.
- If you hear that the learners struggle with intonation and stress, provide them with the right model. For further discussion on how to give feedback on speaking, see also Chapter 6.
- One aspect which can affect overall intelligibility is the speed of speaking. There is no absolute agreement among scholars on this and dialects do vary, but the speed of English appears to be about average, compared with other languages. If you have learners in your class who speak English very quickly and who are difficult to understand as a result, you can work with them to see if slowing down makes it easier for them to be understood. This approach has worked well with speakers of languages such as Arabic, French, and Bengali.
- Many learners have never heard themselves speak English. If you record them on audio or video tape, they can listen to themselves afterwards. Many find it a revelation to hear how they sound and the experience is often a catalyst for improvement.

If you record the learners at regular intervals, you create in effect an 'audio portfolio' of performance. This allows learner and teacher to monitor spoken language over time, not only in terms of pronunciation but also use of grammar and vocabulary. Many learners find it very motivating to hear how much they have improved and teachers can record evidence of learning on the individual learning plan (for which see also Chapter 6).

There are various options of activities to record the learners, for example:

- a discussion between two or three learners while they are doing a task
- presentations to the whole class can also be recorded but these tend not to be as successful as more informal interactions, as the learners may not give their best if they are nervous
- a set text which the learners read aloud and which is recorded at regular intervals, for example, every six weeks. Since reading aloud engages different skills from speaking spontaneously, this is not so much an opportunity for assessing speaking but rather an opportunity for the learners to monitor their pronunciation, stress, and intonation skills.

Falling intonation at the end of a list
In the next two sections, two everyday features of sentence intonation are looked at. Sometimes second language speakers report that they have problems ordering items in a shop or at a market stall. You may have observed this happening ahead in the queue while waiting to be served. One cause of communication breakdown is the use of inappropriate intonation.

For example, a butcher selling meat might get the following order: *I'd like a pound of mince, two pounds of chicken legs, a pound of stewing beef, and a leg of lamb.* Language learners may not know it but the butcher would normally know that the leg of lamb is the last item on the list because the speaker would use steeply falling intonation. If falling intonation is used in the middle of the sequence or rising intonation at the end of the list, the butcher is likely to get confused and quite possibly irritated. Because migrants and refugees are likely to have to order goods from the time they arrive, using the right intonation is well worth practising in class.

STEP 1 You need to prepare a list of items to be ordered, for example, fruit and vegetables.

two pounds of potatoes	five onions	some garlic
spring onions	a pack of spinach	three peppers
a pineapple		

STEP 2 Use items on this list to simulate ordering vegetables. Ask the learners to identify whether you are in the middle of ordering or coming to the end of your list.

STEP 3 Tell the learners to cover the list with a piece of paper so that the first two items are visible. Divide the learners in pairs and ask the first learner to read out the items using the correct intonation. The second person then uncovers the third item and reads the new list out aloud; and so on until they have got to the end of the list.

STEP 4 Ask the learners to construct their own lists of items, for example, what they might take when they go and see a friend; or when planning to help a friend fix his car. The learners have to remember all items previously mentioned and add an item of their own, of course using the right intonation.

STEP 5 To see if the learners remember the correct intonation patterns over time, you can also extend the activity to include the giving of telephone numbers. Ask the learners to give each other a (fictitious) number. Make sure that they indicate through their intonation whether there are more numbers to come and when they are coming to the end.

Asking questions

Second language speakers may report that they are ignored when they ask a question. While this may be because listeners are impatient, xenophobic, or racist, it is also possible that they have not realized that they are being asked a question because the right intonation is lacking. Many of the resources which are drawn together at the end of this section provide useful exercises on asking questions, for clarification, etc., but the classroom itself also provides good opportunities to work on this aspect. Learners naturally ask each other and their teacher many questions during lessons. Take, for example, the student in Chapter 4 who wants a worksheet but is unable to produce the right question form and intonation.

Teachers also often use exercises when the learners have to find out information about each other, for example:

> Find someone who
>
> lives in Erdington
> is single
> has a pink cat
> likes strawberry ice cream.

Exercises such as these provide an excellent opportunity not just to observe whether the learners are able to produce grammatically accurate questions, but also whether they use the right intonation. We would normally ask questions like these with falling intonation, for example, ↗*Do you in live in Erdington?* ↘ unless we wanted to express surprise, ↗*Do you really have a pink cat?*↗ John Maidment's websites provide useful models and exercises to practise intonation, including question formation.

This brings the section on pronunciation to a close. We have seen that the application of sentence stress and intonation can improve the intelligibility of the learners' spoken English. As to the desired outcome of pronunciation teaching, the aim of getting the learners to sound like a native speaker is often not realistic or even desirable. What is essential for migrants and refugees is that their spoken English is intelligible. As Setter and Jenkins (2005) say: 'Pronunciation is the major contributor to successful spoken communication, and how anyone learning a language can expect to be understood with poor pronunciation skills is outside of our comprehension.' Learners benefit from regular attention to their pronunciation to achieve intelligibility.

Reading

In this section we look at the interaction between pronunciation and spelling and at the bottom-up and top-down processes that readers use to create meaning. The National Literacy Test, which is used in England, Wales, and Northern Ireland to test reading skills, forms a focal point to review different types of reading activity. It is used to explore how teachers can prepare their learners for the test as well as common reading tasks which they are likely to encounter outside the classroom.

Spelling and pronunciation

One of the main difficulties that new readers of English face—old and young, first and second language speakers—is that many written words in English are out of sync with their spoken form. This means that learners often cannot predict from the pronunciation how a word is spelled and vice versa. The reason for this discrepancy is that, when the first printing presses were introduced in the late fifteenth century, spellings that were common at that time became frozen. By contrast, the pronunciation of English has continued to evolve, causing a gradual separation of spelling and pronunciation. As a result, readers of English encounter very many words that are not spelled as they are pronounced, for example, *knife* and *laugh,* as well as words where spelling and pronunciation match, for example, *hats, club,* and *canteen.* Because of its mixture of regular and irregular spellings, we say that English has an OPAQUE spelling system. By contrast, languages such as Spanish and Polish are described as TRANSPARENT, because their spelling systems represent the pronunciation of words accurately. In these languages the PHONIC system seems perfectly appropriate to teach learners to read because a particular letter represents a particular sound. Because English spelling only partly reflects the pronunciation of words, it seems logical that a multi-skilled approach is needed when teaching reading and writing skills. This enables the learners to learn the skill of matching letters with sounds as well as to use the shape of the whole word when the spelling does not reflect pronunciation. Let us see how this might work, using a text from the Skills for Life reading materials.

TASK   New learners and predictable and unpredictable spellings

This text forms part of unit 2, which is one of the very first units of the Skills for Life materials. It is aimed at Entry 1 learners who have very limited English.

Which of the words in the speech balloons are likely to create problems for the reader because their spelling does not reflect their pronunciation? And what can teachers do to help the learners learn both spelling and pronunciation?

STEP 1 During the preparation for this lesson, teachers will notice that the spelling of most of the words in this text reflects their pronunciation reasonably well. However, there are two everyday words that the learners may not recognize at all because their pronunciation and spelling are so different. They are *Mrs* and *Wednesday*. It is quite possible that the learners would know these words if they heard them but that they are completely thrown when they try to read them.

STEP 2 We now move to the classroom. Ask the learners to read the text balloons on their own and, if they have difficulty, to ask their classmates for help. When they have read through the text, ask them to read the text aloud to each other. While the learners are working on these tasks, observe which words they struggle with and monitor how they pronounce them.

STEP 3 Bring the whole group together and ask two of the learners to read the text in the speech balloons, providing support if they struggle. If they express uncertainty over the reading of *Wednesday* and *Mrs*, put these words on the board and ask how these are pronounced. Alert the learners to the fact that the spelling of these words does not reflect their pronunciation. You can demonstrate this by putting the pronunciation of these words on the board, using English spelling: /misiz/ and /wenzday/. For further discussion on the use of phonetic and English spelling, see page 79.

STEP 4 Use these examples to make the learners aware that there are words in English where the spelling is a guide to pronunciation, but that there are also many cases such as these, where the pronunciation and spelling of words do not match. In the case of the latter, both need to be learnt and stored. As an extension activity, you can ask the learners if they have encountered any other words where the spelling does not match the pronunciation.

The Mrs Baker text shows that, even at beginner level, written text is likely to contain words which leave the learners confused about the spelling of English. Many learners look for regular spelling patterns without realizing that these may not exist. Speakers of languages which have regular spelling systems may find it particularly hard to switch from a predictive spelling system to one where the spelling of many words appears to be haphazard. These learners will find it helpful to know that the spelling of words in English is not always regular and that they may need to memorize whole words rather than look for patterns.

Bottom-up and top-down processing
We saw in the section on listening that top-down and bottom-up processing are useful concepts to understand how the learners make sense of the information that they hear. Learners draw on the same processes when they read written text. During the bottom-up process the reader starts with small units and builds these into larger ones. The learner reader registers the text

visually, identifies individual letters, and assembles these into syllables and words. This process is often referred to as DECODING text. By contrast top-down processing refers to the use learners make of larger units and their prior knowledge, for example, they may already know the phrase *My name is* and be aware that speech balloons are used to indicate that the text represents Mrs Baker's own words.

TASK The interplay between bottom-up and top-down processing

Would the readers of the Mrs Baker text draw equally on bottom-up or top-down processing when reading this text? And if not, why not?

Since the readers of the Mrs Baker text are at an early stage of language learning, they are likely to spend most of their time on the bottom-up process, decoding individual letters and words. Indeed, non-fluent readers often get stuck at this stage. They may be able to read one or two individual words but they cannot process these fast enough to access their meaning. If you find that learners go over the same words again and again, often pointing at the words with their finger, it is very likely that this is what is happening. It is only once the reading of individual words and sentences becomes automatic and the learners have built up sufficient speed that they can read for meaning.

For further information on useful resources to help teachers work with beginner readers, see the section on Further reading where details can be found on, for example, Lisa Karlsen's Literacy Resource Pack (2005) and Marina Spiegel and Helen Sunderland's book on teaching literacy (2006).

Different types of reading

There are many different ways in which we can classify reading, for example, by type of text, the purpose of the task, and the techniques that can be used to access written text. We shall explore some of these aspects, using as examples passages from the Adult Literacy Test. This test is taken by all candidates, both first and second language speakers who are working towards accreditation at Levels 1 and 2. Since exams tend to influence the delivery of programmes of learning, we review its potential impact on the teaching of reading also. More broadly, we reflect on how reading is handled in the language classroom and how it supports language acquisition in general.

TASK Using the National Literacy Test to identify types of reading

You will find below a text reproduced from the bank of test papers which the Qualifications and Curriculum Authority (QCA) makes available on its website (for details, see Further reading).

1 What reading skills do the questions test and how useful are these skills in real life?

2 Are there any types of reading skills that the national literacy tests do not cover and which the learners are likely to need beyond the test situation?

Questions 1 to 5 are based on the following article.

Who's who in denim?

Who first made denim?

The cloth was first produced in France in the town of Nimes in the seventeenth century. When it was brought to England it was called the cloth 'de Nimes'. This means 'from Nimes' in French. English people simply said 'denim'.

Who first wore denim?

Denim was used to make work overalls. When it was taken to America in the eighteenth century, it became very popular with workmen. This was because it was a very strong yet comfortable fabric to wear.

Who made the first denim jeans?

A man called Levi Strauss arrived in America from Germany in 1847 and began to make trousers from denim. They were called waist overalls before they were known as jeans. It is thought that they got the name jeans because they looked like the trousers worn by sailors from Genoa, which were called Genoese trousers.

Who helped denim jeans to become popular?

In the 1930s Hollywood Western films became very popular and people wanted to dress in denim jeans as the cowboys did on the cinema screen. Young people began to wear jeans not just for work but also for leisure wear. Even American soldiers who came to Europe during World War Two brought their denim jeans with them. By the 1950s jeans had become very fashionable. Today, denim is worn by people of all ages all over the world. Not only is it seen in the traditional blue, but in many other colours as well. It is worn by people of all backgrounds and the cloth is made into skirts, shirts, and even handbags.

1 Denim was first popular with workmen in America because

A they wanted to dress like film stars
B it was a strong, comfortable cloth
C it arrived in England from France
D it had become very fashionable

2 Where does the word 'jeans' originate from?

A the town of Nimes in France
B the leisure wear worn by cowboys
C Genoese trousers worn by sailors
D work overalls worn by Americans

3 Jeans were brought to Europe during the war by

A American soldiers
B Genoese sailors
C Levi Strauss
D Hollywood stars

4 What is the main purpose of this article?

A to persuade workmen to wear denim
B to give information about denim
C to tell readers about sailors from Genoa
D to try to sell denim jeans to Americans

5 The last paragraph could be split into two. The new paragraph should start with

A Young people
B Even American
C Today, denim
D Not only

Some background on the National Literacy Test

- The National Literacy Test assesses two major aspects of reading: proofreading and reading for information / meaning.
- The source material consists of short texts up to a full page of A4: letters, tables, memos, leaflets, newspaper articles, and extracts from books.
- The texts cover topics of general interest, such as family and home, leisure activities, work, shopping, and citizenship.
- Dictionaries are not allowed.

From Level 1 Test Paper 16 March 2004 © Qualifications and Curriculum Authority

1 What reading skills do the questions test and how useful are these skills in real life?

Apart from question 5, which is on paragraphing and contributes to the proofreading score, questions 1 to 4 are about reading for information, identifying textual detail, and finding the main purpose of the text. These questions do not require detailed reading but rather the ability to SCAN and SKIM for information. The skill of *skimming* can be defined as getting the gist or general idea of a text. Readers usually skim text to decide if it is of interest to them. They do this by flicking through a book, casting their eye over a text, looking at headings and opening and closing paragraphs. *Scanning* for information is in a sense the opposite of skimming. The reader scans text for specific information, for example, a name in a directory, departure time in a timetable, or a specific detail in a manual.

It may not be immediately obvious but the skills of skimming and scanning are problematic for most second language speakers. Many feel the need to grapple with the whole text, needing to know the meaning of every word, before they can make a judgement on its relevance or interest; and even to answer questions about its detail. This approach is commonly found, even among students on university courses. It is as if the reader does not trust his or her own judgement on the text until it has been considered completely.

The urge to read the whole text in detail, however, is often not the best plan for action. If we take the task above, learners may spend a long time reading, when this may not be necessary to answer the questions. And being able to skim and scan are not just useful exam techniques, they are valuable in personal, study, and work contexts. Because these techniques do not come naturally to many language learners, it is important to alert them to their benefits and to provide ample practice in the classroom.

Tips to help learners develop and expand their reading techniques:

- Texts do not always have to be read in detail. This principle is worth applying in class, too, as learners and teachers tend to mine reading material for every unknown word. While the latter may be useful for learning vocabulary, it is not necessarily the best approach to learning to handle text effectively.
- If a text is accompanied by questions, such as in an exam or to guide an assignment, these should be looked at first. They can be used to work out the type of task, the most suitable method to retrieve the information, and the information that needs to be identified.

In the early stages of learning to scan for information, the teacher could set a clearly defined task, for example, 'Find out how much time you are allowed to do the test. What word are you going to look out for?' Once the learners have got used to carrying out tasks such as these, the teacher can encourage the learners to identify themselves what they are going to scan for. Sam McCarter (2006) provides practical advice on scanning, such as scanning backwards along the lines to make the learners focus on key words rather than reading the text for meaning.

Equally useful in real life is the skill of skimming, for example, to see if an article in the newspaper is of interest to the reader. Learners have various options. They may look at the title of the article, its headings, and subheadings. They may read the first sentence of each paragraph to get an idea of the subject matter. A different approach is to read the opening and closing paragraphs of the text to see what it is about. A fourth option is for the learners to cast their eye over the text, picking out nouns and verbs. Teachers should make their learners aware that they can choose when and how to apply these techniques.

---

2 Are there any types of reading skills that the national literacy tests do not cover and which the learners are likely to need beyond the test situation?

As often happens, practical considerations have driven the design of the national literacy tests. Since the government set itself the target of 1.5 million candidates achieving a literacy or numeracy qualification by 2007, it was decided that, in order to handle the volume of test takers, ease of marking was a priority and hence computerized testing and multiple-choice questions were called for. The testing process is relatively new and improvements have been made over time, for which see details on the Qualifications and Curriculum Authority (QCA) website in Further reading. Nevertheless, while the national literacy tests do assess useful skills, in particular scanning for information, teachers should be aware that marking constraints and the contents of the national standards themselves have resulted in the testing of a narrow range of functions and purposes. If teachers want to prepare their students for further study, employment, and to promote reading for enjoyment, they will need to look beyond the skills required to pass the literacy test. Some of these aspects are explored below.

Topics and text types

The subjects covered in the national tests are confined to topics of general interest. Since topic, vocabulary, and type of text are interrelated, a narrow range of topics will make it likely that learners will encounter a limited range of vocabulary and text types. By text type or genre, we mean the function and purpose for which the text was produced. Texts which share a common purpose are often produced in a similar format and style of writing. These features allow the reader to recognize their purpose. This is not just a limitation of the test but also of many of the materials used in ESOL classes where home and family-related materials often predominate. Learners should experience a variety of text types so that they know how to find their way around them, for example, a leaflet intended for general information, or a letter from the local authority on housing benefits. That is why teachers should consider what text types the learners may need to handle in real life, both to meet immediate needs as they settle down and as they focus on long-term goals. For example, they may want to read for pleasure, or attend a mainstream course where they will need to read technical documents such as a hairdressing manual, instructions for electrical installation, or a method statement in the building industry.

Text length

When the learners take the National Literacy Test, they only need to read very short texts. However, there are serious limitations to replicating this practice in the classroom. Learners who move into further education or employment will need to have built up the stamina and skills to read extended texts, for example, coursebooks or a novel, if they take a GCSE or a Scottish Higher in English. Secondly, short texts are less likely to give the learners practice in finding their way around headings, indices, and other text features. That is why teachers should make sure that, as the learners' English gets more proficient, they are offered longer texts and are encouraged to read in their own time.

Speed of reading

Learners do not just need to be able to understand texts but also to be able to read at speed. This skill is not only required during the literacy test but is also useful for learners who take courses or jobs which require them to manage a high volume of reading material. It can be time-consuming to set the learners extended reading tasks in class but, nevertheless, learners benefit from doing so. Learners should also be encouraged to read in their own time and they should be aware that texts do not have to be complex or challenging. Nation (2001) suggests that to develop fluent reading skills learners should read texts containing a very high proportion of known vocabulary. This may be best addressed by encouraging the learners to read for interest and entertainment and by explaining why this type of reading serves a different, but equally useful, purpose to reading more complex texts.

Factual information and opinion

Because the passages presented in the literacy test are mostly factual, they offer limited opportunity for the learners to see how fact and opinion are handled, an aspect that they themselves often struggle with in their own writing. Learners benefit from reading texts which provide models of how to handle fact and opinion and arguing the case. This is especially relevant if the conventions of their own culture differ in this respect. For example, in UK culture much attention is paid to the separation of fact and opinion and the latter is often only expressed explicitly at the end of the text. Many learners express surprise that this is so because the conventions in their own languages tend to be more fluid. This aspect is explored further on page 112 in this chapter.

Vocabulary load

TASK

The text below was taken from a second Qualifications and Curriculum Authority test paper. It forms the opening paragraph of a newspaper article about an explosion that caused extensive damage to shops and restaurants.

How well would second language speakers cope with the vocabulary in this paragraph?

> Fire officers and police are investigating an explosion that reduced a restaurant and several shops to rubble. One unidentified man was taken to Jubilee Hospital in Park Street after the blast, which involved gas or flammable materials and which is being treated as suspicious.

From Level 1 Test Paper, 24 February 2004 © Qualifications and Curriculum Authority

There are two aspects to notice about this paragraph, the first being that it has complex sentence structure, including the use of a 'which' clause twice in one sentence. The second point is that the vocabulary is more complex than that used in the 'denim' text above, which is likely to cause second language speakers rather more problems than native English speakers. While the latter may not be fluent readers, if they manage to decode the words, they are very likely to know their meaning, apart from perhaps the word *flammable*. By contrast, second language speakers may be able to decode the words but then find that they do not know what they mean. So, having made the effort to read, they may be no further in understanding the text. This is not to say that language learners won't know any of the less common words in this passage, but it is likely that they will not know at least some.

Leech, Rayson, and Wilson's (2001) word frequency list, based on the 100-million word British National Corpus, provides the following information on the vocabulary in the paragraph above: *investigate* (55 occurrences per 1 million words), *explosion* (22), *reduce* (178), *rubble* (fewer than 10), *identify* (133), *blast* (10), *flammable* (fewer than 10), and *suspicious* (14)/*suspicion* (23). The lower the frequency of the words, the less likely learners are, statistically speaking, to have encountered them. In addition, it appears that there is a limit to the ability of second language speakers to deduce the meaning of new words. Research by Laufer (1992) and Nation (2001) suggests that most learners find it difficult to infer the meaning of new words if they know fewer than 95% of the words of a text.

As was mentioned earlier, many learners feel the need to read text in-depth, as if they do not trust their own judgement until they have considered its every detail. Both the analysis of word frequencies and the limited ability of language learners to infer meaning reinforce the notion that second language speakers are likely not to be able to understand at least part of texts such as the one above. One of the factors that language learners and their teachers face is that the topic and vocabulary that the learners will encounter cannot be predicted; nor, it appears, can the difficulty of the text. This means that the teacher will need to provide advice on material to be read in and outside the classroom to extend the learners' reading skills. A second consideration is that teachers often opt for texts with lots of new vocabulary on the basis that it provides the learners with the opportunity to learn new words. Yet as the discussion on vocabulary in Chapter 4 showed, learners may have to encounter new words several times before they know their meaning. Seeing a word once is unlikely to enable the reader to remember it. This calls for careful selection of reading texts and recycling activities in the classroom to give the learners the opportunity to embed new vocabulary. More importantly, learners need to know that reading, both in and outside the lesson, is a prime way to extend and reinforce their range of vocabulary.

Writing

In this section we focus on writing, a skill which demands a particularly wide range of sub-skills, from the ability to handle a pen, or knowledge of spelling, to being able to apply conventions of writing. The profile of the learners is also wide. At one end of the spectrum there are learners who are practised writers in their own language and who quickly get used to English writing conventions; at the other end there are those who have never had the opportunity to learn to read and write in their first language. We begin by exploring what it is like to learn to write. Since for many students putting pen to paper is a major barrier to writing, we then focus on activities to get the learners writing and to gradually expand their skills.

Learning to write in a new script

People who have never had the opportunity to acquire writing skills do not just need to learn about the shape of letters and what they stand for, they also need to acquire the motor skills to produce letters. This means that they must train the muscles in their hand to produce letters in a recognizable shape. If you have worked with learners who are in the process of learning to do this, you will know how hard this can be. To get a feel for what it is like to acquire motor control, try writing your name and address with the hand you normally do not write with. You may find that you cannot create fluent letter shapes and that the muscles in your hand get tired, problems which many new writers face. The task facing language learners is of a much larger magnitude: they have no experience of writing and are taught to write in a language they probably do not speak very well, if at all.

In addition to those who are not literate in their mother-tongue, we also find people who can read and write in their first language but whose script differs from the Roman alphabet which we use to write in English. Although it may appear a daunting task to learn a new script, many learners find the transition much easier than they had expected. This is because generic writing skills, such as motor control and eye–hand co-ordination, are transferable. If you want to experience this, try copying some of the lines from the poem 'The Human Heart', written in Gujerati, below.

માનવીનું હૈયું

માનવીના હૈયાને નંદવામાં વાર શી ?
અધઓલ્યા   ઓલડે,
થોડે   ·   અઓલડે,
પોચાશા હૈયાને પીંજવામાં વાર શી ?

How little it takes to break the human heart!
A word half spoken
A word unspoken
How little it takes to bleed the heart!

from the poem 'The Human Heart' by Umashankar Joshi

If you do not know the Gujerati script, it is likely that you faced two major problems while trying to copy the characters. You kept having to check back what the letters looked like and you did not know where letters started and finished. While writing a new script is undoubtedly challenging, once characters become recognizable and sequences of strokes have been stored in the long-term memory, it rapidly becomes easier to write.

Because a proportion of migrants and refugees need support with learning to read and write in English, teachers have access to many resources, such as Lisa Karlsen's Literacy Resource Pack. These are listed in Further reading. We now move on to focus on a second aspect of writing that preoccupies many learners: the development of their skills once they are able to handle the Roman alphabet.

Getting used to writing

Many students struggle with writing. They often find it hard to write at all, even about topics that they know well, such as their home life, their children, or their job. Just the thought of having a blank sheet in front of them fills them with dread. Yet, like any skill, writing can be learnt, but it does need frequent practice. Since the fear of writing is so often a major obstacle, overcoming it is a crucial step to developing writing skills. However, lesson observations indicate that lessons are often taken up with oral interaction and that writing is assigned to homework, if it is addressed at all. The activities presented in this section have been designed to bring writing into the classroom. We will start with tasks in which the requirement for learner input is limited and well-defined, then broaden out to increasingly independent writing.

Duo dictation

ACTIVITY 1 Duo dictation

This exercise is aimed at beginner learners. It consists of a simple text:

> I live in a flat on the second floor. We have a living room, a kitchen, and a bathroom. There are two bedrooms. One bedroom is for me and my husband, the other bedroom is for my daughter.

This text has been used to create a dictation exercise which the learners do in pairs. Student A reads the words on his sheet to student B, who writes them down in the gaps. Once student A has finished reading, student B takes over and vice versa until they finish the text.

Student A

_____ a flat on _____ floor. _____ living room,

_____ and a bathroom. _____ .

One bedroom is _____ and my husband,

_____ is for my daughter.

Student B

I live in _____ the second _____ . We have

a _____ , a kitchen _____

_____ . There are two bedrooms. _____ for

me _____ , the other bedroom _____ .

TASK

What is the purpose of this exercise and how does it engage the learners in writing?

This dictation exercise allows learners who are new to writing English to tackle a few words at a time. They do not have to start with a blank sheet and can use the gapped text to provide them with an idea of what words are needed to complete it. While this exercise practises writing, it is not a silent activity, as the learners use a lot of oral communication to achieve it. If the learners cannot understand the words that are being said to them, they can ask each other how the word is spelt, a useful technique which will stand them in good stead outside the classroom. And last, it does not matter if the learners do not know all the words, as they have immediate support from their partner.

ACTIVITY 2

Here is another text, this time at a higher level.

> A woman rang the police to report that her car had been stolen. She mentioned that her mobile phone was also in the car. The policeman who took the report dialled the number. He said to the man who took the call, 'I just saw the ad in the paper and want to buy the car.' They arranged to meet and the man was arrested.

> *Adapted from reading material of unknown origin.*

How could you use this text to design a duo dictation exercise for pairs of learners, one of whom has stronger and the other weaker language skills?

Student A

_____ to report that her car had been stolen. _____ her mobile phone was also in the car. _____ the report dialled the number. _____ who took the call, '_____ the ad in the paper _____.' They arranged to meet and the man was arrested.

Student B

A woman rang the police _____. She mentioned that _____. The policeman who took _____. He said to the man _____, 'I just saw _____ and want to buy the car.'

This duo dictation exercise was prepared so that student B, who is at a more advanced level, has to write more and handle more complex language. By contrast, student A has not only less to write but the text to be completed is also less challenging. While it may appear that student A has less to do during the exercise, in fact the two tasks are well matched in terms of time, as this student can be expected to take longer to understand and write down shorter and simpler sequences.

Once the students have completed their texts, they check with each other that they have written the text down correctly.

Whole-group dictation

The next stage in the writing process is to offer the learners whole-group dictation. As far as the choice of text is concerned, a good starting point is to choose a subject that the learners will be interested in. Since teaching learners with mixed abilities is the norm in many language classrooms, particularly suitable are texts which match the language level of the largest group of the learners but which also have some more complex language. This should allow the lower and medium level learners to produce most of the text and the more advanced ones to tackle the more unfamiliar words. Some find the thought of doing any writing intimidating, so not all learners can be expected to take to dictation immediately. However, the teacher can reassure the learners that:

- They will only have to write a few lines and will hear the words several times.
- They should write whatever they can and not worry if they are not able to write much.
- It does not matter if they make mistakes.
- They will check their written work themselves.

CASE STUDY

Illi, an Albanian student, is a very good example of how dictation can help develop writing skills. He was working as a labourer in construction when he joined an evening class. His overall level of English was assessed at Entry 3 but his profile of language skills was very spiky. His spoken English was quite fluent if not always accurate. However, he found it very hard to write. He had problems with spelling common words such as *was*, *should*, *because*, and *arrive*. Although he was initially anxious about doing any writing at all, he soon found the weekly dictation exercises useful, especially the checking afterwards. He would ask for a copy of the dictated text, copy out words that he did not know, and sometimes write whole phrases down again. His teacher observed that he increasingly wrote more quickly and fluently during dictation; and Illi was encouraged to see that he got more and more words right. As we will see from his work later in this chapter, by the end of the year he was able to tackle a free writing exercise with by and large accurate spelling and sentence structure.

Course evaluations show that many learners echo Illi's experience. They find dictation very helpful because:

- They can concentrate on the process of writing without having to think about content.
- They have to write quickly whatever they think they heard, without worrying too much about accuracy of spelling, grammar, etc.
- Many make rapid progress, not just in the spelling of individual words but also in the fluency of their writing.
- They feel much more in control and do not get upset at making mistakes.
- They realize that dictation can provide information not just on their spelling skills but also other aspects of the language, as we saw in the section on listening.

Writing frameworks

The dictations presented so far have provided the learners with well-defined activities during which they only have to concentrate on getting pre-determined words on paper. In this section we look at three different ways in which the learners can use frameworks to develop their writing skills. We start off with a relatively tight structure which provides plenty of support to get the learners writing and then move to increasingly free frameworks to encourage independent writing.

Using spidergrams

TASK

Françoise Grellet's (1996) concept of the spidergram inspired the next stage to get the learners used to writing. You see an example of a spidergram below, which has as its title *Getting to work*.

How does the format of the spidergram allow an element of free writing but in a controlled context?

This writing task works well in a mixed ability class. Why do you think that is?

The task instructions for the learners are as follows:

STEP 1 The learners are told that they should write a story using the words found in the spidergram in Figure 5.1. They should begin their story with the heading 'Getting to work' and use the prompts as a framework to develop their story, choosing any sequence of words they like. They should end with the last phrase at the bottom 'Busy day today!'

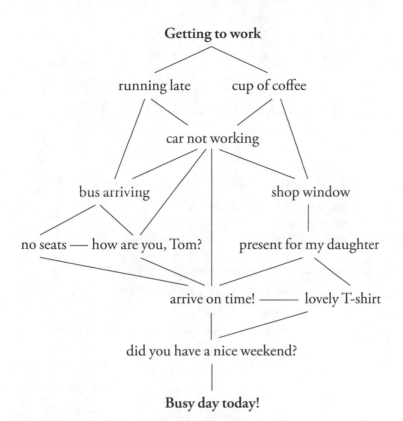

Figure 5.1: Spidergram for 'Getting to work'

Many learners like to work with spidergrams because they combine a defined framework with the freedom to develop their own ideas. Spidergrams suit the needs of a variety of learners because they allow both more and less advanced writers to achieve the task. In this example, less confident writers can take the middle and shortest route, choosing either *running late* or *cup of coffee* and then follow the strand down the middle to get to the end of the story. More proficient writers can roam across the spidergram and incorporate many more prompts to create their story. Some have even been known to include all prompts in their narrative.

TASK   Analysing writing

As to the writing that an exercise like this can generate, here are four samples that learners in an Entry 3 and Level 1 class produced towards the end of the year. We shall start with Illi, the student whose case study we saw earlier. What do you think of the quality and the contents of their writing? And how might you help them improve further?

Illi

I was getting to work little a bit late
this morning. Because, I maked a cup
of tea coffee but milk is ran out
last night. And I get a car but
car was not working. After that, I
called to my friend pick me up.
So I arrived on time.

Agne

I am getting to work. I make a cup of coffee.

I was getting to work late this morning. Because, I
watched football last night. And the car was not working
so I had to get bus. The bus was busy and growed
and so I did not have a sit. While I was on the bus,
(he is my manage)
I called to Tomar tell him that I might shall be there at 10
am. I imagined about my manage's face is angry
the
but without that I arrived on time, because bus driver
driver
was get dir wasn't stop any busstop. A
At lunchtime, I asked Amy about last weekend. She said
" We have a lovely weekend. We have a plan for go on
holiday next month".

Zara

I need to get to work by bus, because if I
work I try Walk the time my run late
so I like to get work before ten minutes so
I can have a cup of toffee. Also my own care
may not work sometimes in many reason, such as!
the betrol may run out and not now where to get
it. That may brought wories to me. Therefore
this may lead to not to arrive on time at work
if the car is not working.

Commentary on the learners' writing

Illi's writing

At the beginning of the course Illi struggled with spelling common words, such as *was, should, because,* and *arrive.* As this sample shows, by the end of the year he had made considerable progress. He was able to write a brief narrative and his spelling and sentence structure are largely accurate.

He finished his work early so the teacher was able to give advice on how he might improve his writing further. She asked Illi to read through his work once more because she had noticed that his use of tenses was not yet secure, for example, *I was getting to work this morning; I maked a cup of tea.* Once he had done that and improved his work further, the teacher asked Illi to exchange his writing with Zara, who was at a similar stage of writing. Their task was to notice what was good in each other's writing and what could be improved. When this process was completed, Illi wrote his story out once more and then handed in his work. With Zara's help, Illi had made substantial progress and had managed to produce a nearly accurate piece of work. The next stage for Illi would be to extend his writing both in length and content.

Zara's writing

Zara, a student from Somalia, had, like Illi, made great progress in the year she had been on the course. She had moved from being anxious when she was set a writing task to being able to produce the writing above. She created coherent sentences such as *I like to get work before 10 minutes so I can have a cup of coffee.* She could improve on this further by adding *[to] work* and reversing *before 10 minutes* to give *10 minutes before / early.* Zara also needed help with her spelling of *betrol* instead of *petrol.* Since Somali has a sound which sits between English /p/ and /b/, its speakers often have problems with these. The teacher planned to deal with this through a listening exercise in the first instance. Once Zara could hear the distinction between /p/ and /b/, she would then move to work on her pronunciation of these sounds. Having learnt to distinguish between these sounds, Zara could be expected to write them without any difficulty.

Agne's writing

Agne wrote a whole sheet of A4 in the 25 minutes allotted to the task, of which you find a paragraph here. The length of the text and use of vocabulary show that she is on the way to becoming a fluent writer. She provides good detail such as the reason why she was late for work and uses link words such as *because, so,* and *while* effectively. However, she needs further work on the difference between *the car was not working* and *the car did not work.* The writing of *the bus driver wasn't stop any busstop* also reinforces the notion that Agne is not yet able to use the verb *to do* to write *the driver did not stop.* Since there were other students in the group who had problems with this, the teacher decided to cover this aspect with the whole group. And finally, the content of the last sentence is not clear, partly because the sentence is very long. The teacher asked Agne to have another look at it to see if she could separate the ideas she wanted to express into shorter sentences.

Structuring written work

When learners need to produce a piece of writing, they often find it hard to know what information goes where in the text. They may need to write a note to their child's teacher, or an opinion piece following discussion in the classroom, or produce a health and safety assignment, as in Chapter 6, but they simply do not know where to start. In this section we offer a general plan which the learner can apply to many situations.

STEP 1 Tell the learners that they are going to work on the general structure of written text, for example, an assignment, essay, or, in a work context, a report on new office equipment to be ordered. Give them the sheet below and ask them to work out in small groups what information might go in each of the three blank boxes.

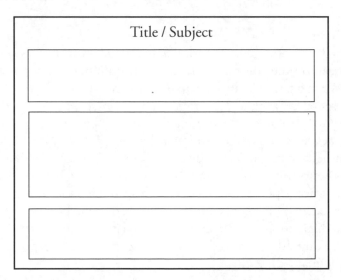

If at all possible, give the learners the opportunity to work out by themselves what information goes in what box because, even at lower levels of language, they often have an idea of how text is structured. However, if you are certain that the learners will not be able to manage this task, cut out the three boxes in the table below and ask the learners to put them in the right order.

STEP 2 Check in the whole group that the learners are thinking on the right lines about the structure of writing. Compare the result of their deliberations with the table below.

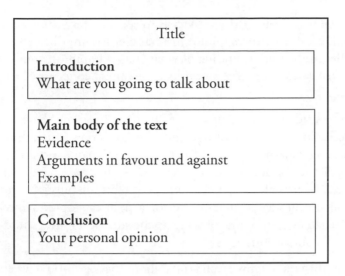

STEP 3 Ask the learners to think also how they would structure writing in their own languages. They can create as many or few boxes as they like.

STEP 4 In the whole group ask the learners to compare the characteristics of English writing with the conventions found in their own cultures. Be prepared for major differences, for example, the vertical, linear sequence of English writing against the circular approach that is found in Chinese writing. In the latter model the narrative unfolds without the overt testing of a statement or theory and no personal viewpoint is taken.

Figure 5.2: Chinese model of writing

STEP 5 Provide the learners with written texts which match their level of language and which they will be able to read fairly easily, for example, a simple memo to complain about the late delivery of goods, a newspaper article, or an essay. Ask them to highlight the introduction, the body of the text, and the conclusion. If more advanced learners complete the task before the others, they can make a note of useful language to introduce the topic, to put forward arguments in terms of advantages and disadvantages, and to produce a conclusion. When all have completed the task, compare findings in the whole group. While you and the learners may find examples where different text organization is required, in general the sequence of introduction–body of text–conclusion is a standard feature of English writing.

STEP 6   The next stage of the activity is to see how texts deal with fact and opinion. Different cultures do not just handle these in different ways, they often differ in the understanding of what fact and opinion are. Be prepared for the learners to need time to explore how these concepts are handled in English.

STEP 7   The students should now be ready to put what they have learnt so far into practice in their own writing. Choose a subject on which they are likely to have strong views and / or of which they have personal experience. Topics with which the learners have engaged well in the past have included the threatened closure of a local school, the quality of public transport, the traffic congestion charge in London, or a political topic of international relevance such as, at the time of writing, the situation in the Middle East or measures to combat Aids.

You can start the activity with an article about the topic you have chosen, for example, on the congestion charge. Ask the learners to explore the arguments for and against this during group discussion. They should use the format presented in step 2 to note what information might go in the three boxes. Ask them also to identify what the facts are that they want to present and what their own opinion is.

STEP 8   Once the learners feel that they have sufficient content in the boxes on their sheet, they can start to work on their first draft. Be on hand to give advice, if they ask for it, but otherwise let them write by themselves.

STEP 9   The last stage in the writing process consists of revision. Most commonly this consists of checking for spelling and grammatical errors but often the structure of the text also needs attention. For example, have the learners developed their argument in sufficient detail? Sometimes they repeat the same statement more than once. You may also find that students write very long sentences in which meaning peters out. If this is the case, alert them to this fact and ask them to break these long sentences into shorter chunks. For an example of this, see Agne's work earlier in this section.

Providing models for writing a CV
Text models to help the learners produce their own CV form the third, and last, writing framework in this section. These enable the learners to see how text is constructed before they attempt to produce it themselves.

STEP 1   For this activity you will need to gather a sample of CVs and covering letters, ask the authors for permission to use them, and make sure that you remove personal details.

Distribute copies of the CVs and ask the learners in small groups:

- to rate the CVs from the one they like best to the one they like the least
- to provide a rationale as to why they rated the CVs as they did

- to notice whether the CVs were the same or different from those that they might expect to see in their own country.

STEP 2 The learners present their findings to the whole group. Here is an extract from a CV that the learners liked least:

EDUCATION:	GCSE
QUALIFICATION:	SECRETARIAL COLLEGE – ADVANCED TYPING, COMPUTER WORD EXCEL AND ACCESS
NOV 04–TO DATE:	PART TIME ADMINISTRATOR – BUSINESS ACTIVITY CENTRE. DUTIES – CLERICAL DUTIES, PETTY CASH, REIMBURSEMENT, PHOTOCOPYING
JAN 01–OCT 04	ASSISTANT SECRETARY – HAREWOOD CENTRE DUTIES TYPING, FILING, ANSWERING THE TELEPHONE

And a second example, the CV that the learners liked best:

NAME	JASON X
CONTACT DETAILS	XXXXXXX
SKILLS PROFILE	
Communication (written)	• Drawing up guidelines for managers to assess sales proposals
Communication (verbal)	• Excellent interpersonal skills developed through working with customers, staff, and management team
IT skills	• Advanced knowledge of Windows, MS Office, Excel, and typing speed of 50 wpm
WORK EXPERIENCE	
March 05–present	ABC Company, London Temporary administrator in purchasing department
Jan 03–Dec 04	Open Door Project, Mexico Volunteer in outreach team, supporting children up to 12 years old.
EDUCATION & QUALIFICATIONS	
2000–03	University of Durham BA Hons in English Language and Literature
1995–2000	Broadway High School A levels: Spanish, English, Economics GCSEs: English, Maths, Art, History, Geography, Science, French, Spanish, PE

INTERESTS/ACHIEVEMENTS

Sport	• Keen cyclist, swimming on a regular basis
Travel	• In addition to my stay in Mexico, which I planned and funded myself, I have traveled to Australia and Thailand.
Other	• Certificate in Health and Safety Standard First Aid

REFEREES   XXXXXXXXXXXXXX

STEP 3 Features the learners rated as important included:

- a short CV of ideally no longer than two pages
- a clear layout with the same style of headings throughout
- text produced in lower case, as capital letters are hard to read
- start with the most recent events and qualifications and work your way back in time
- a CV that underpins the skills set out in the letter of application.

The CV above, which the learners found the most appropriate, provided a useful model for constructing their own.

When choosing samples of CVs for this activity, teachers should try to find up-to-date material which meets the job interests of the learners. For example, the public and private sectors tend to use different formats. Secondly, the presentation of information may change over time, e.g. the practice of presenting the most recent job first in Jason's CV.

Planning, writing, and revision

The last stage in the sequence of learning to write is planning. This may seem paradoxical because planning comes first in the process of writing, followed by the production of a first draft, which is then revised and a final version produced. However, experience in the classroom shows that the planning stage is the hardest. The learners are able to handle it much better once the process of writing has become automatic through activities such as dictation and writing frameworks, and learning how to draft and revise.

Students tend to develop their own ways of planning over time but models for planning are a useful starting point. Many learners find the concepts of mind mapping and spidergrams so useful that they adopt these to plan writing their own assignments. For example, Tula, who was studying for her Accounting Technician's exam, used the mind mapping model in Figure 5.3 to produce the first draft plan for her project review below:

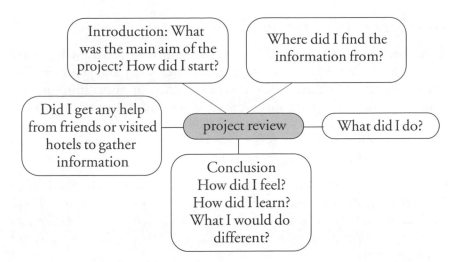

Figure 5.3: Spidergram for 'project review'

When asked why she used this format, Tula said:

> I did not always do this. Before I used to just start writing and then I would repeat same thing in different places. It was mad, I would get confused about what I wanted to write. Now I put everything I want to say on paper like this and then I can see which goes to where.

Here is the first paragraph of her introduction to project evaluation:

> I have been working on my project, which is part of my syllabus. The project is about managing people and system in the accounting environment. This is the first time in my life making huge project so emagine how difficult it would be for me. First of all, I read the whole case study for about five-six times to understand the structure of business organization. This hotels organization used Activity Based Management system, which is the main control device and create profitability. Before I didn't even know what is the ABM is? So I did some research on the ABM system.

While there is clearly more work to be done on the text, Tula has made a good start, presenting her ideas in a logical order. Having built up her basic writing skills through dictation, then writing increasingly long chunks of text independently, she is now at the stage where she can produce a first draft. After revision she can be expected to hand in a piece of work that meets the required standard.

Word, sentence, and text level

In the past, much teaching of ESOL has tended to focus on the small building blocks of the language, in particular vocabulary and grammar. The national literacy standards, which were launched in 2001, introduced a helpful new tool to observe the wider development of learner language in terms of word, sentence, and text level. This has provided an opportunity to look more holistically at how the learners put sentences together and whether they are able to create coherent text.

These concepts are so useful that in my view they deserve to be applied not just to reading and writing, as they are in the literacy standards, but also to the skills of speaking and listening. We shall start by looking at some samples of writing and deal with oral communication later. First, here is a piece of writing by Mina:

> Dear teacher,
> My name is Mina I am come fohm Afghaniston I am Live in hear about 10 years I like England. because my county is fighting I can't live more. I like tosted, English and the four work in the post offic I hope so on dag my wish come toro
>   Mina

Mina's writing shows that she is not a pure beginner. She is able to write short sentences and, although not all words are expressed perfectly, it is possible to get a sense of what she is trying to say. On the other hand, her sentences are very short and the text she has produced lacks fluency and coherence. The text shows that Mina needs a lot of help with individual words and tenses, such as the spelling of *toro* for *true* and *I am come*. Yet, even at her level, work can be done at sentence and text level. For example, she should work on her sentence boundaries and learn how to use punctuation more consistently. She could reorganize her text chronologically, starting with her life in Afghanistan, then move to her experience of living in England, and conclude with her aspirations for the future.

Mina's writing shows a common pattern of language learning. Teachers working with learners at beginner level can expect to spend most of their time at word and phrase level. However, as the learners progress, the balance should shift towards work on sentence and text level, including strategies to link ideas within and across sentences.

Link words and discourse markers

LINK WORDS and DISCOURSE MARKERS are important tools which the learners can use to create coherent text. These are words that link ideas and events within sentences and across paragraphs. First, we look at *link words*, which are used to link events, objects, and ideas within sentences. For example, a link word such as *because* is used to explain why something has happened; and *either … or* to give alternative options.

In the left-hand column below you will see some typical examples of language produced by learners at different levels of proficiency. Apart from the first example, these learners use accurate language to express their ideas but what these sentences lack are link words. These are supplied in the right hand column and instantly lift the language to a different level.

We see my brother sister.	We see/saw my brother *and* sister.
We left Pakistan. We came to London.	*After/when* we left Pakistan, we came to London.
We had no money. I lost my job.	We had no money *because / when* I lost my job.

Many learners write the type of staccato English which we see in the left-hand column. However, they often quickly catch on to using link words. Here are some suggestions as to how the teacher can help the learner notice and use these link words.

STEP 1   If the learner is just beginning to work on this aspect of language, the teacher underlines the space where a link word would be useful and supplies the word.

STEP 2   Once the teacher has supplied link words a few times, she underlines the places where link words are missing and lists them on the page or on the board. The task for the learner is to put the link words in the right place where the text is underlined.

STEP 3   The teacher underlines the space where a link word is required, writes 'link word' alongside it, and this time the learner supplies it him or herself.

TASK

So far we have looked at ways of connecting events and ideas within sentences. A second aspect to look at is the creation of links across sentences and paragraphs. Here are some lines which were written by Ashfaq from Afghanistan about his family outing. How could he improve his writing?

> We went to London at weekend. We went Hyde Park. We had lunch. We took bus to see London Eye. We went home very tired.

Ashtaq's level of language is typical of Entry 2, when learners have learnt to formulate short phrases and sentences. His language is really quite accurate but the use of short, unconnected sentences creates a staccato effect, which leaves the reader the task of creating links between them. Ashtaq can improve his writing by adding discourse markers, for example:

> We went to London at (the) weekend. *First* we went to Hyde Park. *Then* we had lunch. *After that* we took (the) bus to see (the) London Eye. *Finally* we went home very tired.

First, then, after that, and *finally* are examples of *discourse markers* which are used here to frame a sequence of events across sentences. Discourse markers are used extensively in English and fulfil a wide range of functions. Some examples:

Let's start, OK, or *Well* are used to introduce a new topic.
Anyway signals a change in the topic under discussion.

You know confirms common understanding.
On the one hand … on the other hand contrasts two arguments across sentences.

Since language learners do not often use discourse markers, here are some ideas help them notice them and practise their use.

STEP 1 When the teacher marks the work produced by Ashtaq and other learners in the class, she sees that they have used few discourse markers. She designs an activity in which she plans to use commonly used markers to describe how she spent her weekend. To help the learners, she prepares a list with some of the discourse markers that she is likely to use while talking.

later on	☐
at the beginning	☐
last	☐
then	☐
finally	☐
first	☐

STEP 2 The teacher uses informal language to describe her weekend to the learners and tapes herself while talking. She asks the learners to listen out for the discourse markers on the list and to note down any others that they hear.

STEP 3 The learners compare their findings, first in pairs and then in the whole group. If they get stuck, the learners can go to the tape recorder to listen to the tape.

STEP 4 The teacher asks the students to look at their own written work again in pairs and to decide where they would insert the discourse markers that they have just heard.

There are a number of teaching materials which focus on the use of discourse markers, for which see the list of resources at the end of this section. While discourse markers are particularly common in speech, apart from Carter and McCarthy's work (1997 and 2006) there are relatively few teaching materials that deal with this aspect. There are two reasons why it is well worthwhile making sure that learners are aware of the use of discourse markers and know a good selection. Learners often ask for explanations of phrases which they hear outside the classroom and they are right to do so: spoken English is littered with phrases such as: *actually, by the way,* or *as I was saying just now.* These phrases are not just important to understand, they also provide a very useful function, because language learners can use them to buy thinking time while formulating the next chunk of words. Because discourse markers are such a useful tool to keep communication going, teachers should consider introducing them at all stages of language learning. Simple phrases, such as: *Please, Right, I see, OK, I mean* can help learners maintain communication, which is especially useful for beginners who are likely to get stuck more frequently.

The second reason for paying attention to discourse markers is that, compared to many other languages, English tends to make heavy use of them. They are used to express cause and effect, and sequences of events and actions, where other languages are often less explicit and leave it to the reader to deduce them. You may have noticed the difference yourself, for example, when reading translated instructions to new equipment that you bought. These can be very confusing to the English reader but not necessarily because of a poor translation. It is equally possible that the original instructions did not contain signposting discourse markers in the first place. Because the learners may not be aware of the difference between their own language and that of English, it is well worth exploring with them how they might organize spoken and written text in their first language and how this might differ from English.

Using a textual framework for speaking

As we saw earlier, the organization of language at word, sentence, and text level is not just relevant to written text, it can equally be applied to spoken language. This is because, in spoken English, information is often sequenced using standard features and markers. Let us see how this might work in practice.

TASK Using textual organization for spoken communication

Learners often express anxiety that their English is not good enough to handle everyday communication. They find that they do not know how to open a conversation or discussion, how to get their point across, and what they should say when. Here we take the making of a complaint about the delivery of faulty goods as the focus for a learning activity.

How could the learners use the concept of text organization to structure their communication effectively?

STEP I Many learners find it helpful to plan interaction before it takes place. This allows them to work out what they want to say and in what order. If we take the general framework which the learners used to organize their writing in the previous section, we find that it can also be applied to structure text for speaking.

Tell the learners that they are going to play the role of a customer who has had goods delivered which turn out to be faulty. Ask them to brainstorm what they might say and in what order. Give them the textual framework below to help them organize their thoughts. Provide the learners with support while they are working in small groups.

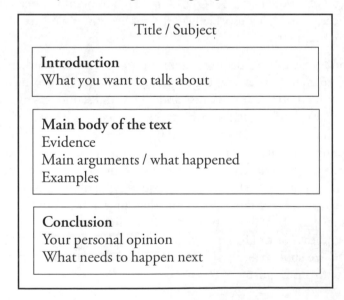

Title / Subject

Introduction
What you want to talk about

Main body of the text
Evidence
Main arguments / what happened
Examples

Conclusion
Your personal opinion
What needs to happen next

STEP 2 Bring the learners together in the whole group and pool the results of their preparation. If necessary, help them place the topics and language into the right boxes. For an example of the type of script the learners produce, see the box below.

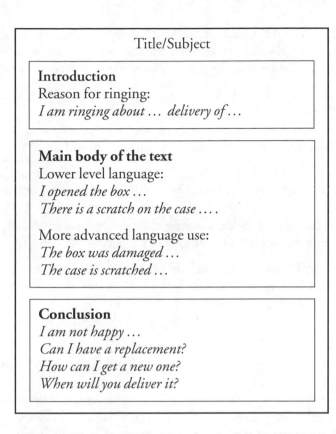

STEP 3   The learners should now have sufficient information to manage the interaction when they role-play the exchange with a fellow student who will take the part of the person receiving the complaint.

This format is simple, easy to remember, and can be adapted to many situations. It allows the learners to organize their thoughts and arguments at text level, sequence their ideas, and pay attention to how they can best open and close the conversation. Once they have practised using this format a few times, the learners may well find that they can use it automatically. You can check this by giving them a similar task without providing ample time to prepare.

Further reading

Practical resources

Carter, R. and **M. McCarthy.** 1997. *Exploring Spoken English.* Cambridge: Cambridge University Press.
This book and accompanying tape provide authentic samples of spoken English as well as transcripts which can be used to demonstrate the use of discourse markers.

Cunningham, S. and **P. Moor**. 2005. *New Cutting Edge*. London: Longman. Increasingly coursebooks contain systematic practice of pronunciation skills. Two examples are *New English File* (see below) and *New Cutting Edge*.

Davis, P. and **M. Rinvolucri**. 2000. *Dictation*. Cambridge: Cambridge University Press.
This book has many ideas for using dictation in the classroom, for example, the game *Running dictation*, which many learners enjoy doing.

Department for Education and Skills. 2003. *Skills for Life Learner Materials Packs for ESOL at Entry 1, 2, and 3; and Levels 1 and 2*. London: DfES Publications.
These resource books provide learning materials which were designed for each of the language levels of Entry 1, 2, and 3; and Levels 1 and 2.

Graham, C. 1978. *Jazz Chants*. Oxford: Oxford University Press.
This book and subsequent titles such as *Jazz Chants Old and New* provide chants to practise intonation and stress. There are also tapes available. Even though the chants are spoken in American, *Jazz Chants* is a useful and fun book to use with your students.

Hancock, M. 2003. *English Pronunciation in Use: Intermediate*. Cambridge: Cambridge University Press.
This is a comprehensive reference and practice book suitable for self-study or classroom work. Sixty units cover all aspects of pronunciation, including individual sounds, word stress, connected speech, and intonation. Each unit is supported by audio material in a range of accents, available on audio CD or cassette.

Karlsen, L. 2005. *The ESOL Literacy Resource Pack*. Second edition. www.esolliteracy.co.uk
This pack is designed to meet the needs of ESOL students who speak little or no English and who are not literate in their mother-tongue. It contains materials, pictures, record sheets, and guidelines to enable systematic acquisition of basic literacy skills.

Northedge, A. 2005. *The Good Study Guide*. Buckingham: Open University Press.
While this book is not specifically designed for people whose first language is not English, it has lots of sensible advice on how to study, develop ideas, research online, and write essays. The Open University also publishes specific guides for the study of the arts and the sciences. http://www.ouw.co.uk/

Oxenden, C., C. Latham-Koenig, and **P. Seligson.** 2004. *New English File Pre-Intermediate*. Oxford: Oxford University Press.

Rogerson P. and **J. Gilbert**. 1990. *Speaking Clearly.* Cambridge: Cambridge University Press.
This pronunciation book is aimed at intermediate and advanced learners. In addition to providing speaking and listening tasks, the book has a useful pronunciation test which allows the learner to identify areas for development. The student's book is accompanied by a teacher's book and tapes are available.

http://www.handwritingworksheets.com
This website makes it easy to create worksheets for learners who need practice in handwriting. You simply key in the text and a worksheet is automatically produced in a variety of formats.

Websites dedicated to pronunciation
http://www.speechinaction.com
This website teaches listening and pronunciation skills through recordings of spontaneous speech. British, Irish, American, and international accents are used. The programmes are best suited to Level 1 and 2 learners but, with the help of the teacher, parts can be made suitable for lower levels, too. There are opportunities for the learners to record themselves and self-assess.

John Maidment's websites contain exercises to identify various aspects of spoken English, for example:
http://www.btinternet.com/~eptotd/vm/plato/platmen.htm to identify the main stress in the sentence.
http://www.btinternet.com/~eptotd/vm/toni/tonimenu.htm to identify intonation.
http://www.phon.ucl.ac.uk/home/johnm/oi/oiin.htm to identify intonation patterns in sentences.
http://www.phon.ucl.ac.uk/home/johnm/eptotd/tiphome.htm This contains a wide range of tips on how English works.

Background/Theory

Carter, R. and **M. McCarthy**. 2006. *Cambridge Grammar of English: A Comprehensive Guide to Spoken and Written English Grammar and Usage.* Cambridge: Cambridge University Press.
The A–Z section at the beginning of this book and Chapters 1 to 3 cover discourse markers extensively. The CD-ROM has spoken versions of samples of text which demonstrate language points as well as intonation.

Field, J. 2003. 'Promoting perception: lexical segmentation in L2 listening.' *English Language Teaching Journal* 57/3: 325–43.
This article provides a clear overview of the processes involved in second language listening as well as exercises which help the learners improve their listening skills.

Hedge, T. 2001. *Teaching and Learning in the Language Classroom.* Oxford: Oxford University Press.
This book contains a thorough overview of the four skills and how they can be taught in the ESOL classroom. Aspects such as selecting materials, setting tasks to introduce listening activities, and managing interaction are well covered.

Kenworthy, J. 1987. *Teaching English Pronunciation.* London: Longman.
This handbook for language teachers provides a clear overview of aspects of pronunciation such as combinations of sounds, sentence stress, setting goals, and providing feedback.

Millar, R. and **C. Klein.** 2002. *Making Sense of Spelling – A Guide to Teaching and Learning How to Spell.* London: SENJIT/Institute of Education.
This short guide, while designed with first language speakers in mind, provides practical ideas and activities on how to develop spelling strategies.

Spiegel, M. and **H. Sunderland.** 2006. *Teaching Basic Literacy to ESOL Learners.* London: LLU+.
This book provides an overview of basic literacy teaching and learning. It covers aspects such as reading and writing skills, learning styles, materials, and planning and managing provision.

http://www.qca.org.uk/6449.html
The Qualifications and Curriculum Authority website provides sample national literacy tests as well as details of the test specification.

6 MANAGING LEARNING

Teachers face a multitude of tasks both in and outside the classroom. They need to assess their learners, plan learning, and be able to manage large classes which may consist of learners with a wide variety of skills and learning needs. This chapter deals with some of the major aspects that the language teacher will encounter on a day-to-day basis.

Language assessment

Many organizations require that teachers and learners spend time on assessment. This is, at least in part, because the British government has come to see assessment as an important tool to measure national performance in education and training. The focus on assessment is particularly strong during the recruitment of new learners, as organizations and their teachers want to make sure that the learners are placed on the right course. In addition, the results of the initial assessment provide a useful basis for target setting with the individual learner.

By introduction to the topic of assessment, the sections below set out the context in which assessment commonly takes place and other major aspects which teachers will want to bear in mind when planning and administering assessment.

The purpose and context of the assessment

Language teachers find that they are expected to carry out an increasing amount of assessment but there is often an underlying anxiety that 'We are measuring something but we are not sure what'. That is why, when designing assessment tasks, it is crucial to ask 'What information do I need to get from the assessment?' Here are three examples of situations in which you may want to plan assessment:

- You are interviewing a group of new learners who need to be placed on a suitable course.
- You are interviewing learners who want to join a speaking and listening class.

- You have been teaching a group of learners for six weeks and want to check the progress that they have made.

These three contexts are likely to need different tasks to give you the information you and the learners need to make a judgement on their English. In the first example, which concerns initial assessment, the test would need to cover a broad range of language aspects to indicate which course and level would best suit the learner's needs. In the second example, it is important to capture the learner's speaking and listening skills. Sentence structure, pronunciation and intonation would be a likely focus as well as the ability to identify individual words in a stream of sound (for which see Chapter 5). If the learners are at Entry 3 or higher, then it is useful to see whether they are able to handle more formal language. In the third example, teachers will want to know to what extent course objectives have been met so far and whether further work is necessary.

All assessment activity will need careful planning but the administration of the assessment does not necessarily need to be presented as a formal 'test' occasion. Assessment can equally form part of the lesson.

Language assessment in the teaching cycle

There are three key stages during which assessment normally takes place.

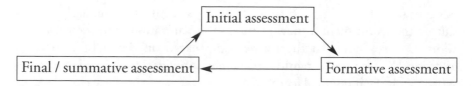

The purpose for which you want to carry out assessment is likely to have an impact on the type of task that you present to the learners. During initial assessment you are more likely to want to get a broad picture of what the learners can already do and what they need to learn. During formative assessment you will want to find out how well the learner is doing and to give feedback on progress. Then we have final or summative assessment which is carried out at the end of the course to see whether the learners have met their goals and achieved the required standard. This is increasingly important as teachers are expected to show funding bodies both evidence of progress during the course and the level at which the learners are able to handle English.

The learners' other skills

Many learners have other skills and knowledge which teachers need to be aware of when planning learning programmes. Here is a list of aspects which can inform placement and planning of learning:

The learners' first language and any other languages they are able to use.
It is useful to know whether the learners are able to use more than one language. If the learners have learnt languages beyond childhood, then the skill of language learning is likely to be transferable to learning English as an adult.

Teachers may meet learners for whom English was the language of instruction at school, for example, people who were educated in Nigeria, Ghana, or India. If this is the case, teachers need to make a judgement whether English language classes are the right option or whether other provision suits the needs of the learner better, for example, a basic skills or GCSE class.

Educational achievements and study skills

Learners who went to school in their country of origin will have acquired learning and study skills which can often be transferred to learning English. It is worth finding out how many years the learner attended education, since the longer they attended better their learning skills are likely to be.

As we saw in the section on writing, learners who have never learnt to read and write in their own language are likely to need extended time to learn to write in English. On the other hand, learners who have learnt to write in their own language, even if their script differs from the Roman alphabet, can be expected to learn to read and write in English quite quickly.

Since expectations of education are shaped by the culture in which learners grow up, it is good to be able to anticipate what teaching methods, such as communicative activities and multiple-choice questions, may be unfamiliar to learners. If you are a new teacher, it is worth asking more experienced colleagues before you meet your new class what the learners' likely experiences of education may have been. Once you are teaching, you can also find out from the learners directly.

Occupational skills and work experience

Many learners will have worked in their country of origin and skills acquired there may be transferable. It is worth assessing if the language classroom is the best environment for learners. For example, an experienced carpenter who wishes to continue to work in his field may be better referred to carpentry provision with language support attached. For the provision of language support, see Chapter 7.

Keyboard skills

Considering the importance of typing and word processing, both in the learning environment and in employment, it is important to find out if the learners already have these skills. If they do not, they can be referred to separate provision where they can learn to type or spend part of their time in language lessons to acquire keyboard skills.

The learners' reasons for wanting to learn English and their aspirations for work and study

This aspect is crucial since information from the learners on the context in which they want to use English can guide you on the type of topics that interest them. For example, a learner who has children and wants to be able to communicate with their teachers, will find it useful to know more about the educational system. A learner who wants to study nursing will benefit from reading texts on this topic.

Establishing the effectiveness of assessment tasks

If you design an assessment task which is going to be used more than once, or if you want to use an existing test, it is important to pilot it to see if it works before it is introduced. You can do this by finding some learners who are at the level that the assessment is intended to test and asking them to do the tasks. Their responses will give you an insight into how learners are likely to react to the assessment. For example, sometimes the learners interpret a task in a different way from what you had intended. You may also find that the task does not give you the information on language performance that you had expected. In addition, it is difficult to write clear task instructions which are at the same level of language difficulty as the task itself. Piloting the task will give you information on how effective the task instructions are and the learners participating in the pilot often give useful feedback.

In the case of initial assessment, it is important to check at the end of the course if the tests you used gave you the right information to place the learners accurately. This can be done by checking not only on the results achieved by the people who stayed for the duration of the course but also those who were moved to another class, and, if you can, those who dropped out. This process allows you to adjust existing tasks to get a more accurately predictive assessment and to introduce new items if you find that the assessment lacked information on aspects of performance.

Marking the assessment and processing outcomes

If you are asked to mark students' work, it is useful to find out if a marking scheme is used in your organization and whether there is training available in how to mark. It is often found during inspection that there is wide variation in the marking and grading of assessments. This can mean that learners with similar language skills are placed in different level classes. In addition to standardizing marking within the organization, many teachers find it useful to compare the results of their own assessments with the test scores achieved by the learners when they take externally accredited or moderated exams. This is especially important when new qualifications are introduced.

Initial screening and assessment

So far we have looked at general aspects of assessment. Now we look at initial assessment in more detail. In the UK the initial assessment process consists potentially of two phases. The first phase, called screening or skills check, is used to find out whether an individual is likely to have a language need and to sort the learners roughly in broad levels. The process usually involves the learners taking a brief test which is completed in about ten minutes, for example, filling in details on a form or identifying the right grammatical form in sentences. This type of test is sometimes called a barrier test because, if the learners get a certain number of answers right, they are deemed to be at a particular level. Screening was much used for a time, not least because providers were required to carry it out by funding bodies. While some providers still use screening tests because they make it possible to process large numbers of enrolments, many have come to the conclusion that they have limited value. This is because they provide little information on what the learners can and cannot do in language terms. Instead these providers prefer to skip the screening stage and to concentrate on initial assessment because that provides in-depth information on the learner's language skills which also makes placement on the right course more secure.

TASK   Evaluating an initial assessment task

Here are samples taken from two tasks which are typical of those used in some institutions.

Who are these tasks aimed at and what information can they be expected to provide about the learners' language skills?

Are there any aspects of the assessment task that you think could be improved?

1   Please link the words that mean the same. The first one has been done for you.

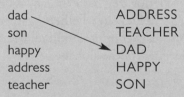

dad	ADDRESS
son	TEACHER
happy	DAD
address	HAPPY
teacher	SON

2   Please link the letters that mean the same. The first one has been done for you.

a	H
f	A
g	R
h	F

These two samples are aimed at learners who are in the very early stages of learning to read. They assess the ability to recognize and match letters and words written in lower and upper case. This type of learner may have no English language skills at all. However, it is equally possible that their spoken language skills are much more advanced because they speak English in daily life. A full assessment of the four skills of speaking, listening, reading, and writing will enable the teacher to put their literacy skills in context.

The structure of these assessment tasks is puzzling. Both engage the learner in essentially the same activity: recognizing and matching letters and words written in lower and upper case. Normally tasks start with the simplest activity and then build up to more complex items. Here the reverse has happened, with the first matching task being more complex than the second. The assessment under discussion is based on actual practice in the field. When completed assessments were looked at, it became clear that indeed the order of the tasks was problematic. None of the learners who could not manage task 1 had attempted task 2.

A third aspect to notice is that the task instructions are misleading because the words and letters 'are the same' rather than 'mean the same'. Also worrying is that the instructions are more complex than the task itself. It could be argued that, if the learner can understand the instructions, then they should have no problems with matching letters and words. On the positive side, the task does include a helpful example of how to match the letters and words.

The analysis of these tasks shows that it is not easy to produce reliable assessments. At the same time, piloting them would have highlighted the weaknesses in the tasks and made it possible to improve their effectiveness.

To improve these tasks, a first step would be to reverse the order of the two activities, to simplify the task instructions, for example, to 'draw a line between the letters that are the same' and to make sure that the learner has access to a person who can explain the task orally. Considering that basic literacy is being tested, it would also be good to extend the task to find out whether the learners can copy words, as below. This would give the teacher information on whether the learner can both recognize and write the letters of the alphabet.

Below are some words. Please write these words on the line on the right. We have done the first one for you.

book   _book_

child   _____

my name   _____

school   _____

Making use of the initial assessment

Teachers and learners invest time and effort when they engage in initial assessment. Learners may spend well over an hour being assessed on their speaking, listening, reading, and writing skills. Teachers work with the learners to assess their oral skills, mark reading and writing tasks, and complete paperwork to indicate levels of language skills and assign the learners to classes.

INITIAL ASSESSMENT TASK

Here are two samples taken from pieces of writing which were done as part of an initial assessment. What do these samples tell you about the writers' language skills?

Please write below about yourself
My name Haweya. I from Somalia. I come in London 3 years. My femly 1 dohther 2 son. My house semal, 2 bedroom, 1 kitchen.

Please write below about yourself
My name is Hatice, but I prefer to be called Hattie, which it's easier to pernance. I am 25 years old who come from Turkey. I like sociulise with my friends and family this by to going to out and go out for meal. I want study law. I would like to use my qualification for the people who need profacional leygal services. Advising and listining and also solving the problems.

Most providers use writing, such as that produced above, to decide what class will suit the learner best. It is much less common practice, however, to analyse the language produced during initial assessment and to use it as the basis for setting language learning goals. This is a pity since the learners' work can provide valuable information on their ability to handle English.

If we take the case of Haweya first, her writing shows that she can write simple sentences which are well demarcated with capitals and full stops. She has some control of sentence grammar. On the basis of this sample she would be referred to a beginner's class at Entry 1. She has the following learning needs:

- to improve her spelling of words to describe herself, her accommodation, and her family
- to use the verb 'to be' as in *my name is* and *my house is small*
- her writing of *semal* indicates a pronunciation need, as Somali students tend to insert the sound /ə/ between consonants, for example, /səkul/ for 'school'.
- to increase the volume of her writing to produce a full paragraph.

The second sample, written by Hatice, shows that she is able to get her message across. Many features of her writing, such as her sentence structure and use of vocabulary, indicate that she is at Entry 3. Hatice's learning goals are:

- to improve her spelling. It appears that she writes some words as they are pronounced, for example, *sociulise* and *listining*
- to work on aspects such as *I want to study law* and the use of articles such as in *solving problems*
- to learn to use the gerund accurately such as *I like socialis<u>ing</u> … and go<u>ing</u> out for a meal.*

The analysis of the learners' writing can provide a very useful starting point to drawing up learning plans, as we shall see below. It is also good practice to give the learners feedback on how well they did in their assessment, as these findings provide a good basis for discussion on target setting. Giving feedback to the students is also covered elsewhere in this chapter under 'Progress reviews' and 'Giving formative feedback'.

Individual learning plans and target setting

Individual learning plans, or ILPs as they are commonly called, were introduced in England in 2001 as a measure to help teachers focus on the needs of individual learners, and were subsequently adopted in Wales and Northern Ireland. The concept of the individual learning plan was originally established in the fields of adult literacy and numeracy teaching, on the premise that adults who are actively engaged in deciding what they are going to learn are more likely to remain on the course. It was the government's intention that teachers should negotiate learning goals with their learners. These would provide the basis for a learning programme as well as ongoing assessment and progress reviews. As examples later in this chapter show, a major benefit of this approach has been that the learner's short- and long-term aspirations are now better taken into account when planning learning. Nevertheless, other aspects of the application of ILPs have proved to be problematic. Teachers have found that it is particularly difficult to negotiate learning plans with learners who have low level language skills. Completing the ILPs has proved to be time-consuming and in the eyes of many teachers the format of the ILP makes it difficult to capture learning goals effectively. A third difficulty is found in the target setting itself. Teachers are expected to set SMART targets. This means that targets should be:

Specific
Measurable
Achievable
Realistic
Time-related

TASK   Identifying smart targets

Here are targets set for Miriam, who has just joined her class. Which ones can be said to be specific and measurable and which not?

Miriam's targets for Term 1

- improve the spelling of common words
- be able to use language for going to the doctor
- talk about past and present events using tenses accurately
- improve writing
- use link words such as *and*, *because*, *so*, and *although* in spoken and written English
- listen and respond to requests for personal information
- speak clearly to be heard and understood in simple exchanges

---

Two of these targets are specific and measurable: 'talk about past and present events using tenses accurately' and 'use link words such as *and, because, so,* and *although* in spoken and written English'. The others are problematic because they are hard to measure progress against, for example 'improve writing' and 'be able to use language for going to the doctor'. In the latter case, language for going to the doctor can be applied to any language level and can encompass a wide variety of functions, such as booking an appointment, explaining symptoms, and understanding the doctor's diagnosis. Statements from the national literacy standards are also often adopted as targets, of which the last two on Miriam's list are examples. However, teachers have found that it is difficult, if not impossible, to measure progress against these because the national literacy standards themselves are not specific and measurable.

In addition, I explore in my NRDC paper (2004) a fourth aspect as to why teachers and language learners have found completing the ILP so difficult. This is the ability of the learners to reflect on their own language use and hence to contribute meaningfully to target setting. This aspect is addressed below.

TASK   Reflecting on language and other skills

Here are Larisa and Monique, two advanced language learners, who participated in a research project to establish among other things how they reflected on their language learning and job search skills. What do the comments made by these learners tell us about their ability to evaluate their own language?

  L Well, I've been here for nearly four years so I think it's, it's … I can't say that it's high but people can understand me and I can understand them as well, so you see that it's quite OK.
  M Yes, I think, … I can make myself understood … People understand me.

These comments made by Larisa and Monique show that they struggled to analyse their language skills in any detail. Not only were the comments made by Larisa and Monique typical of their group, this is what their teacher said about her students:

  E Well, I think their predictions tend to be very general. You know, if you ask a student how they want to improve and how they need to improve they generally tend to say something like: 'Speaking, or more grammar or eh, or more listening' so it's a very broad sort of answer.

Larisa and Monique's reflections on their ability to use English formed part of a wide-ranging interview during which the learners talked about the new things they had learnt during the course. Larisa, a maths teacher from Belarus, was one of the students who responded to this question. She had come to the UK four years previously and had learnt English from scratch since then. She was a particularly articulate student but otherwise in many ways typical of her group. Compare her thoughts on her ability to speak English to those on her newly acquired job-seeking skills:

  L Obviously, I'm more confident than I was before because, if you know what you're doing, it gives you confidence. So before I didn't know how to write CV, I did not know how to describe my skills, I didn't know where to find the job, so I didn't know any websites, I didn't know any resources, magazines, newspapers so I was really confused. I didn't know where to start, so it really helps; this course really help me, to give me, help me where to start. So I can write nice CV, I can describe myself. Well I didn't realize that I've got all these skills and I know where to look for my job. Now I think every day, I just look at all these resources, one day I'm just looking at the newspapers, another day I look in the magazines and other day I'm looking at websites and they just, I can write a covering letter, so it's really helpful.

Larisa's descriptions suggest a qualitative difference in the way she reviews her language learning and job skills. She is able to recall and enumerate job-seeking tasks in specific detail, listing skills such as CV writing as well as the tools she has learnt to use for job hunting. By contrast, she is unable to define her language skills in the same way. This poses the question of why a learner like Larisa, who is able to express herself so clearly on the development of her job seeking skills, has problems with reflecting on her language learning. And she is not alone in this: her inability to do so appears to be typical of language learners.

In the first place, language learning cannot be described as a stable process, with the learners understanding and then being able to apply a feature of the language systematically. Readers who have learnt another language may well have found themselves that learning a new language is a voyage of discovery with awareness of the new language emerging sometimes gradually and retrospectively. Secondly, learners are so busy processing language, taking in information, and trying to create meaning that there is hardly any 'space' for the monitoring of performance. In addition, the learners may lack linguistic knowledge to describe their language needs. These reasons all appear to contribute to the fact that it is hard, if not impossible, for language learners to reflect on their language performance. It is even more difficult for them to predict language needs in that they cannot be aware of aspects that they have not yet uncovered.

This finding indicates that teachers and learners cannot take for granted the learners' ability to reflect on their learning needs, even when they have an advanced level of language skills and have by and large been successful language learners. Undoubtedly more research is needed, as only a small number of learners participated in this study. However, since the Skills for Life strategy aims to strengthen the involvement of the learner in the planning and review of their individual learning, a limited ability to reflect on and predict language needs goes beyond an academic interest: if the learners are unable to predict their language development, this will impact on the process of negotiating the individual learning plan and the review process. This finding has two major implications. In the first place, it appears not so much that the ILP process itself is faulty but rather that its application could be improved. Secondly, considering the limited capacity of the learners to reflect on their language needs, this reinforces the importance of the teacher in the assessment process. However, this does presuppose both a language-analytical approach and an understanding of the functions and contexts in which the learner wants to communicate.

Looking at how assessment and target setting can be achieved in practice, it is essential that drawing up an ILP is both a meaningful experience for the learner and administratively manageable for the teacher.

The following steps provide a guide for teachers to plan and negotiate learning:

- Use the results of initial assessment and any in-class assessment activity to work out what the learners can already do and not yet do in language terms.
- Elicit from the learners the purpose and context in which they want to learn English. This can cover a wide range but most commonly given reasons are: to communicate for everyday purposes, work, study, and self-employment.
- Create language goals which will enable the learners to function in the contexts that they have prioritized.
- Discuss the language goals with the learner and, if necessary, explain how they relate to the functions that he or she has identified.
- Write the language goals on the ILP form and explain that you and the learner will review these goals during the next tutorial.

Here are three examples of individual learning plans. They record both the objectives identified by the learners and their accompanying language targets, as expressed by the teacher.

The learners' functional objectives	Language learning goals to achieve these targets
Mahini is at Entry 1. She wants to be able to talk to her neighbour, whose children play with hers.	• Understand common word strings for greeting and small talk, for example, *Hello, how are you? I am fine. Is it OK if the kids play at our house today?* • Intonation and grammar for question-and-answer exchanges • Pronounce words such as *fine* and *kids* with accurate vowel length and final consonants

The learners' functional objectives	Language learning goals to achieve these targets
Ali is at Entry 2. He wants to be able to complete an application form so that he can apply for work at the local supermarket.	• Write in legible handwriting • Use the past tense to express previous work experience • Produce with help the application in the appropriate register and understand why this is important • Use language for job application accurately, for example, word strings such as *I would like to apply, I can offer, I look forward to hearing from you* • Read through written work before handing it in, checking capital letters, full stops, and spelling
Soraya is at Entry 3. She wants to move to an access to nursing course next year.	• Be able to understand commonly used medical vocabulary, such as *patient, medicine*, and *equipment* • Understand common language used to give instructions, for example, sequencing actions: *first you do x, then y.* • Read basic texts on nursing • Practise skimming to see if the text is relevant, scanning for specific detail; and reading for meaning. • Use material from nursing course to manage written assignments

This format combines both learner objectives and language-specific targets. You will also have noticed that Mahini and Soraya's targets include the development of speaking and listening skills. Since most learners see it as a priority to learn English for oral communication, it is important to give speaking and listening appropriate attention in the learning plan. For ways of analysing and teaching spoken language, see Chapter 5.

Teachers may also consider setting targets to help the learners develop their ability to learn and use the language independently. In Ali's case this has been identified in his learning plan: to read through written work before handing it in. A second example is that initially Mahini did not have the language skills and confidence to speak to her neighbour. However, once she had learnt some basic expressions, Mahini and her teacher agreed that she would try to talk to her neighbour.

This poses the question of how a teacher, especially teaching a large group of learners, can handle all these different targets. Some teachers have also expressed anxiety that, having collected all this information on the individual learner, they cannot possibly meet all the needs identified. This calls for a twofold approach. In the first place, analysis of the individual learning plans often shows common themes, which can be used to direct whole group teaching. Secondly, it is important to discuss with the learners how the teacher plans to meet the variety of targets. For example, she may put some of the major language aspects identified on the board and discuss how and in which order the class might tackle them. Teachers should also explain that inevitably not all lessons will be of relevance to all learners but that she will strive for a fair balance. If learners feel that the learning does not relate to their needs, they should feel free to come and talk to the teacher about it.

Setting challenging targets

Teachers increasingly experience tension between the notion that they should set challenging targets while at the same time meet targets for qualifications on which the funding of their courses depends. If teachers set challenging targets and the learner fails to achieve them, the organization loses out financially and may not be able to offer the same number of places in subsequent years. This awareness of a potential financial penalty may cause teachers to set targets which the learners can achieve comfortably and which do not stretch them.

Setting challenging targets is a subject on which John Hattie's work (1999) provides interesting information. Hattie analysed the outcomes of a large number of studies on factors influencing teaching and learning. He did not just take into account teaching methods and resources, for example, the quality of instruction, the use of computers, and setting homework. He also looked at their impact for different groups of students. He found that one of the aspects that had the most positive effect on learning was the setting of specific and challenging goals. Sound target setting and providing feedback on learning were found to be mutually supportive and provided the best drivers for success.

Expectations of progress

While setting targets, learners and teachers may want to consider what the projected timescale to learn English might be. For example, learners may have decided that they will spend a year learning English in the expectation that they will then have sufficient language skills to find a job or move to a vocational training course. Without guidance, they are unlikely to know whether their goal is realistic. They may also become demoralized during the course when they realize that they are not going to achieve their target and give up as a result. That is why the initial interview with the learner provides a good opportunity to look at current language skills, long-term targets (for instance to get a job), and the likely level of language skills that will be needed to achieve it.

This poses the question of how long it might take to achieve the required language competence to achieve long-term goals. Literature on this aspect is scarce, not least because learners show great variety in the progress that they make. At the same time, not being able to give an indication of the likely time needed to acquire new language skills makes it difficult for teachers to advise the learners on this important aspect of their learning experience. The Qualifications and Curriculum Authority (QCA) estimates that it takes at least 100 hours of learning to complete each of the three skills of Speaking and Listening, Reading, and Writing. This means that a learner who needs to improve by one level across the three skills would need to spend at least 300 hours of learning. It is important to be aware that these numbers of hours can only be seen as averages because individual factors, such as aptitude for language learning, literacy in the first language, and learning outside the classroom create wide variation in the achievement.

At the same time, learners should know that language learning is a time-consuming business, as two investigations show. At Canberra Institute of Technology, Australia, data have been collected since the mid-1980s. These indicate that it takes on average 1,765 hours of learning for learners to progress from pure beginner level (including a proportion of the learners who have no literacy skills in the first language) to the point where they can undertake study of another subject or take on a job with routine communication requirements. The Center for Applied Linguistics in the United States found that 'it would take 500–1,000 hours of instruction for an adult who is literate in the native language but has not had prior English instruction to reach the level of being able to satisfy basic needs, survive on the job, and have limited interaction in English' (National Center for ESL Literacy Education 2003).

Progress reviews

A recent development which is much liked by teaching staff and learners is the introduction of the progress review. This is not to say that progress reviews did not happen in the past, but previously they would normally have consisted of asking the whole group what they thought of their course. The new approach is to offer the learner an individual tutorial at regular intervals to review learning against the targets that were agreed previously. The tutorial also provides an opportunity to set new targets as well as to review other factors which have a bearing on the learning process. For example, a learner who has previously not indicated a long-term goal may mention that she has become interested in a career in nursing. Teachers can use this information to identify materials which meet the interest of the learner, for example, by asking a colleague who teaches nursing for advice. They may refer the learner to events, such as an open day at the college where information on nursing is available. Or they may arrange for the learner to attend a taster course. Since the learners find individual tutorials so beneficial, increasingly teachers are given additional time to carry these out. For example, some organizations allow fifteen minutes before or after the lesson to talk to the learners about their progress. Even more effective is the practice seen at Greenwich Community College where a second tutor is allocated to each course for a certain number of hours. This enables the class tutor to hold individual tutorials while the other tutor teaches the class.

To see how a progress review can work, here is a copy of Ali's progress review which is based on his learning plan which we saw on page 137.

Ali is at Entry 2. He wants to be able to complete an application form so that he can apply for work at the local supermarket.

Current targets

1 Write in legible handwriting

- Handwriting is still hard to read but A is increasingly using the computer

2 Use of the past tense to express previous work experience

3 Use language for job application accurately, for example, word strings such as *I would like to apply, I can offer, I look forward to hearing from you*

- See completed job application attached. This shows definite improvement in targets 2–4

4 Produce with help the application in the appropriate register and understand why this is important

5 Read through written work before handing it in, checking capital letters, full stops, and spelling

- Evidence of checking written work for most tasks.

New targets

6 A got the job at the supermarket: needs practice in speaking and listening skills to deal with customers

7 Word order in English

This report shows that Ali has made good progress and that new targets have been set. For example, Ali became aware of the principle of word order in English while he was working on his use of the past tense. This was incorporated in the updated version of his learning plan.

Learners really appreciate the opportunity to talk to their teacher about their individual progress. In practice, however, the time to carry out progress reviews may be limited, not least because funding for this type of activity is vulnerable to cuts. If this happens, strategies for effective group tutorials can help to preserve the benefits of reflection on learning. If you find that no additional time is available to talk to the learners about their individual progress, a mixture of group and individual discussion can work well. For example, you can ask your learners to reflect on their learning goals in small groups of learners who have similar targets: What have they achieved, and where do they think they need more work? Once they have given their feedback, you can present them with your findings on achievement, which you prepared earlier on an overhead or PowerPoint slide. This allows you and the group to compare findings and use these to agree new targets, both group and individual. You could then set the learners some independent work and talk to them one by one to confirm that they are happy with their targets and to see whether there is anything else that should be incorporated into their learning plan.

In addition to reviews with the teacher, some organizations rely on progress reviews of the type below.

TASK   Using the learners' own perceptions of their learning

Here are two examples of forms which are typically used to review progress against targets.

- How well do these forms meet the needs of the learners?
- How well would learners at Entry 1 be able to understand the language used?
- How could teachers use the information provided by the learners?
- How reliable is the documentation as a record of progress?

Form 1		ESOL Individual Learning Plan and Record of Progress							
Learner name _____ Level *Entry 1*	Curriculum reference	I need more work			I can do this			Comments	
Target		start Sept	mid Oct	end Dec	start Sept	mid Oct	end Dec	
Ask questions to get specific information	Sc/E1.3							
Listen and respond to requests for personal information	Lr/E1.2							
Read and get information from texts	Rt/E1.1							

Form 2			
Learner name _____ Course *Entry 1*	**Record of achievement** **Individual learning plan**		
	Still learning	I can do but need help	I can do on my own
Say where I live Learn words for my cleaning job Write my address without mistakes			

These two forms are quite different in their approach. Form 1 does not meet the needs of the learners very well. General descriptors have been taken from the national literacy standards, which learners who are working towards Entry 1 cannot be expected to understand. Equally, the curriculum references would not have any meaning to them. It is not clear how the boxes should be completed and unlikely that the learners would know the abbreviations used for the months. By contrast, Form 2 is much more user-friendly. The targets have been personalized and are expressed in language that the learners can be expected to understand. The form is also easier to complete.

Forms of this type are commonly used to collect information from the learners on their own perceptions of progress. If produced in a format and language that the learners can understand, they do have their use: they give the learner an opportunity to reflect on their own learning. Teachers can compare their own conclusions on achievement against the perceptions of the learners. However, there is a question over the validity of these feedback forms as a record of progress. This is because there is no way of knowing if the learners have accurately identified whether they are able to handle the language associated with their targets or not. For this, the reflection and professional judgement of the teacher is required.

Using learner profiles

TASK

Many organizations expect their teachers to produce a learner profile for their classes. Here is a typical example.

Learner profile for Entry 2–3 class   Monday 2–4 p.m.

Student name	Country and language(s)	Time in UK	Background	Language needs	General comments / differentiation
Mohamed L	Pakistan Urdu	10 years	welder, now unemployed, married, 5 children	E2	Shy and under-confident in class, needs help with writing
Mariam U	Lebanon Arabic	4 years	married, 3 children, son in crèche	E2 E2 E3	Needs help with all skills
Ali M	Somali	6 years	student on IT course, single		Help with spelling and vocabulary
Halina T	Polish	2 years	single, working in hotel	E2	Give easier reading exercises

What are the strengths and weaknesses of this format? In particular, what important information is missing?

These learner profiles provide background information, such as country of origin, first language, and the length of time that the learners have spent in the UK. While this information is useful, information on the learners' language skills and learning needs is lacking. If this information was included, it would provide a useful overview not just for the teacher but also for any other staff that teach this group, for example, when cover is needed because of illness.

Here is a different model which the teacher updates twice a term. It contains information on the learners' language skills and shows that the learners' progress is monitored over time.

Overview of writing class term 2

The main objective of this class is to improve writing skills, but other skills are also covered, for example, reading and discussion as a prompt to writing. Many learners want to prepare for progression to vocational training next year. The programme of work is negotiated with students on a weekly basis. Overall, really motivated students make good progress considering that many only get four hours of English a week.

Term 2: This term the class is starting work on more advanced writing skills, especially the structure of short reports and memos, identifying fact and opinion, and the use of link words and more formal language.

The students

Sri Lata From India. Has been in UK for 5 years and while shy, has good spoken English: Level 1. Wants to go into hotel management.

Term 1: Oct 10th : Has major problems with spelling of common words, for example, *would, because*. Grammar: Needs more work on articles and past participles. Dec 15th: Rapidly developing confidence and tackling less common words. Speed of writing has improved, too.

Term 2: Feb 7th: Starting on more advanced aspects of writing, such as paragraphing. S is using some link words already, for example, *because, though* but the task for this term is to expand to using *since, on the one hand – other hand*, etc. April 20th: Is really improving and more confident in handling writing such as letters and memos but also giving personal opinion. Still struggling with articles, which we will focus on in term 3.

Mateus From Angola but lived in Zaire for a long time. Wants to do sound engineering. Language level: E3 overall but weak writing skills

Term 1: Oct 29th: Mid-term start. Not used to writing and has low starting point compared to the other students. Needs help with all four language skills as well as grammar so giving individual support where possible.

Term 2: Jan 16th: Regular attender and improving from week to week, not only in the length of writing but also range: from bitty to increasingly full sentences; see work attached. March 10th: M got on access to engineering course. He is working on his project assignment with me providing guidance on structure and language. April 28th: M completed access course and so proud of his assignment!

Fumi From Zimbabwe but also spent time in Sweden where he has family. Wants to set up in business in UK. Good language skills, esp fluent in speaking.

Term 1: Oct 10th: Target for this term to improve accuracy in written English, especially spelling, tenses, and use of discourse markers. Dec 15th: Use of tenses and accuracy of spelling much improved (see work attached). Needs to produce longer texts. Recently attending less regularly because has new-born baby.

Term 2: Feb 10th: dropped out because of family commitments.

While this method of recording progress looks less neat than the pro forma with its boxes that we saw on page 142, it has many advantages. It can be kept as a diary on which the learners' progress can be recorded over time. This should not take an inordinate amount of time as notes can be made during lessons, and as learning points and new goals arise. This format can be used to track group learning as well as individual progress. It can be used to provide evidence of achievement but perhaps more significantly, this process encourages the teacher to think about the learners' strengths and weaknesses and how they are progressing in their learning on an on-going basis.

Planning and delivering lessons

Lesson planning

In this section lesson planning takes central stage. For new teachers the lesson plan is an essential lifeline, without which they are likely to feel adrift. But more experienced teachers also rely heavily on the planning stage because it is a crucial first step to good teaching and learning. As to what goes into the lesson plan, that depends in essence on two aspects: the learners' needs that have been identified and the information that the teacher needs to record to deliver a good lesson. The latter is likely to change over time because, as teachers become more experienced, the need for very detailed planning is likely to decrease.

Lesson planning can be an exciting process since it allows teachers to think through what activities will most benefit the learners and what would fire their enthusiasm. Here are some core indicators which are often found in sound lesson plans:

- challenging tasks which are achievable over time
- tasks which create real interest and communication
- a good variety of well-paced activities and materials
- a blend of activities which involve the four skills
- learning which gradually becomes more complex and which extends the learners' skills.

TASK   Evaluating lesson plans

You will find below extracts from two lesson plans. Please evaluate these against the criteria set out above. If you find that you want to add criteria of your own, do add these to the list.

Lesson plan 1

					Date and time of class	
Group working towards level *Entry 2*					*Mon 25 November* *9.30–12.30*	
Topic: Using the present and past tense[1]						
Time	**Topic/Teacher input**	**Language focus**	**Learner activity**	**Feedback/ Assessment**	**Learning styles**	**Differentiation**
10 mins	Collect homework Revision of what we did last week	Vocabulary and pronunciation to describe where you live: for example, *flat, kitchen, Deptford, Woolwich, school*		Recycle and confirm learning from last week		Make sure to recycle pronunciation with Maria: *flat*, Suleiman: *through*, Damian: *work ↔ walk*
25 mins	Read story about John and Sheila's old house and where they live now	-ed for regular verbs: *loved, helped,* and *started* irregular verbs: *brought, bought, had, been*	Read text Answer questions and compare answers	Monitor	visual	Read text aloud to Farzana and Ishmael; then get them to read the text by themselves
20 mins	What did you do in your country that you do not do any more?	3 types of pronunciation of -ed: for example, *loved, helped,* and *started*	Discussion and description in pairs and then in the whole group	Observe language use Give feedback on present/past tense after discussion	oral/aural	
10 mins	Writing: complete text frame on life in country of origin and life now	Use word strings accurately and spell common words	Write	Take work in and mark for next lesson	visual	Give Farzana, Ishmael, and Jusuf the complete text so they can check their work and copy from if it they get stuck

Evaluation

Recall of last week's vocabulary initially not great but much better when we did revision at the end of the lesson.

After reading aloud twice to Farzana and Ishmael, they were able to read by themselves!

Ran over time because topic on speaking created lively discussion on lack of contact, greeting, etc. with people in London. Writing now to be done for homework.

Most improved on pronunciation of *-ed* but Ishmael still struggling. Reinforce next week.

[1] For readers who are not familiar with the National Literacy Standards, learners who are working towards Entry 2 are expected to be able to handle the simple present.

Lesson plan 2

Entry 1 class Tues 1–3
Objectives: Students will be able to:
- use word order
- make simple statements of fact (Sc E1 4.a, 4.b)
- give personal information (Sc E1 4.b)

Time	Content	Method	Assessment method	Resources	Differentiation
10 mins	Check homework	Elicit right answers	Check answers		
50 mins	Word order	Look at written examples of sentence order Put cut-out words in the right sentence order	Go around the group and check answers	Worksheet with short sentences Sentences cut up into individual words	Individual support
25 mins	Give personal information	Ask each other questions and give answers	Check pair work	Cards with words like *name*, *live*, *married*	Strong learners work with weaker
10 mins	Word order	Feedback on using word order			

Evaluation
Lesson went well but learners struggled with asking each other questions to elicit personal information

When we compare the two lesson plans against the criteria above, the first example on teaching the Entry 2 class comes out well. The lesson is coherent, with the use of the past and present tense providing a common theme throughout. The activities allow the learners to practise these aspects across the four skills of speaking, listening, reading, and writing. The first activity, which consists of reading a story, allows the learners to recognize features of both regular and irregular forms of the past tense. The learners then transfer their skills to use the past and present actively in the discussion on what they did in their country of origin that they do not any more. The writing task occurs last because, for the vast majority of learners, writing is the most difficult skill to handle. The activities are short and focused, which creates good pace. Another area where this lesson plan scores well is that the tasks are challenging. As the evaluation indicates, the learners improved their ability to use the past tense but in particular the pronunciation of *-ed* needs further work. Also attractive about the sequence of planned activities is that they are relevant to the learners' lives. This applies in particular to the discussion where the learners are asked to contrast how people behave in their country of origin against what they perceive the norm to be in their new environment. The lesson evaluation indicates that this topic fired up the learners and that they made it their own by discussing how people deal with each other in public.

By contrast, the second lesson plan meets the criteria to a much lesser extent. The activities are not well-defined and it is much less clear what the teacher and learners are expected to do. It appears from the learning objectives that the learners were to work on word order for statements only. This created problems when they had to ask each other questions, such as *'What is your name?'* and *'Where do you live?'* because, without the prompt question the learners could not give information in the form of statements. The comments in the evaluation box confirm that the sequence of activities did not prepare the learners to carry out the final activity. Overall, the lesson lacks pace and, while the use of cut-up sentences to practise word order is good, the time given to this activity is over-long. The last column is headed 'differentiation', which is the term often used to describe meeting the learning needs of individual learners. However, there is insufficient information on which learners need individual support and what this will consist of. Since meeting the needs of individual learners is increasingly seen as a priority, this aspect is analysed in more detail later in this chapter.

Learning styles

The first lesson plan contains a column which records 'learning styles', a feature which is quite often used in lesson plans to reflect the fact that different people learn in different ways. There are many products on the market to identify learning styles, of which Frank Coffield and his colleagues reviewed 13 in their two reports published in 2004. Learning styles consist of tools to investigate for example thinking styles, motivation, and learning preferences. The use of the term in the lesson plan above reflects part of one model, that of learning preferences. Learning styles here refers to the learners' visual, auditory, kinaesthetic, and tactile senses, i.e. the use of vision, hearing, movement, and touch. However, as Coffield *et al.* comment, 'this is a model of instructional preferences, not learning'. Their concern applies to this lesson plan, too. Rather than referring to learning styles, here the term is linked to speaking, listening, reading, and writing activities, which by their nature are oral or visual anyway. More broadly, Coffield *et al.* raise the lack of evidence for the effectiveness of learning style models and their impact on learning. In the case of this lesson plan, it is hard to see what the impact is of the recording of learning styles.

Evaluating lessons

The lesson plan produced by the first teacher shows that not only did she produce a well-planned lesson, she also provides useful notes on how well it went. This confirms the impression that she is an able teacher who plans for and reflects well on learning.

You will find below an evaluation by the same teacher of the next lesson, when the class reviewed the writing that they had done previously.

> **Evaluation**
> Review of writing went well, learners able to improve on their own work, for example, *I go school last year*
>
> Word order still an issue, needs more work.
>
> More work on pronunciation of /juː/, for example, in *refugee, excuse me*
>
> New vocabulary to be recycled: *happy, sad, hopeful, settle down*
>
> Discussion went on too long, next time keep better pace.
>
> Patrick very shy still but seems right for the class.

This type of evaluation helps busy teachers keep track of how well the lesson went, for example, any topics that need further work or revision; whether all students managed to do the task well, and who found it difficult. It is also an important tool for reflection on the teacher's own performance, for example, whether the task was successful and how it could be improved next time.

Scheme of work

Many organizations require that their teachers prepare a scheme of work at the beginning of each term. On the next page is a sample of a scheme of work which includes the Entry 2 lesson plan that we saw earlier.

This scheme of work gives a concise overview of planned activities. It is undoubtedly useful for teachers to plan ahead, not least because, should they be absent, the scheme of work allows substitute teachers to provide continuity of learning. However, the status and intent of the scheme of work deserves attention. The premise that underpins this book is that the planning of learning is guided by the identification of the learners' needs. If this premise is accepted, this means that the scheme of work (including lesson plans) can only be a 'declaration of intent', because aspects of learner needs may surface at any time. These may influence the delivery of the rest of the lesson and even the course. Teachers and managers should be aware that projecting a term's work is fine, but that changes to the document can be expected.

Group working towards level	Entry 2		Date and time of class	Mon 9.30–12.30	
Week	**Topic/theme objectives/ skills and grammar**	**Learning outcomes**	**Assessment/ notes**	**Other**
7	The present and the past	-*ed* for regular verbs 3 types of pronunciation of -*ed* irregular verbs: for example, *brought, bought, had, been*	Accurate use of tenses throughout pronunciation for oral and spelling of written work	
8	Talking and writing about events	Using link words to describe sequence, reasons, etc. for events in the past and present: *and, but because, or*	Written work using tenses and link words	
9	Ask for factual information	Use of *do* and *did* in questions	Observe students asking each other questions	

Teaching and learning

The examples above show that a sound lesson plan sets the scene for a good lesson. A well-prepared teacher is also more likely to be able to respond flexibly to the needs of the learner. For example, it may become apparent during the lesson that the learners cannot manage a task because some of the underpinning language is not yet secure. In the case of the Entry 2 lesson on the present and past tense, the learners may struggle with describing customary behaviour. Because the lesson plan is well laid out, the teacher can take a quick overview and decide to keep the topic but to confine the discussion to what the learners think of their experiences in their new country. This allows the learners to consolidate the use of the present tense first.

Interlanguage and the order in which language is learnt
When teachers analyse the language used by their learners, it is quite easy to be overwhelmed by the sheer variety in terms of structure, pronunciation,

vocabulary, etc. This is especially the case with classes which consist of speakers from many different countries. This is where research findings which categorize some of the major types of language can be helpful. The first useful concept is that of *interlanguage*. This term was first introduced by Larry Selinker in 1972 to describe the emerging language produced by adults who are learning a new language. Interlanguage is not static but changes as the learner develops from stage to stage. It is made up of three features, as Figure 6.1 indicates.

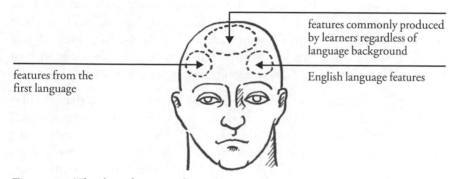

Figure 6.1: The three features of interlanguage

The first component that forms part of interlanguage is the language that the learner can already use well. The appropriate use of English language features provides useful information of both achievement and progress, and its identification is an important objective throughout the assessment cycle. Teachers of migrants and refugees are right to pay attention to the achievement of appropriate language in class, for example, vocabulary choice, use of grammar, and pronunciation. This is because the learners need to know that they are doing well and because it is encouraging to get positive feedback.

At the same time, many learners tend to be preoccupied with what they cannot yet do. They are particularly aware of the second component of interlanguage: the impact of the first language on the way they use English. This aspect was indeed identified as a significant factor in the 1960s. It was assumed that learners would learn new language structures with ease if the same or similar structures were found in their first language and that they would have difficulty if the two language structures were different. A good example of the latter is the use of articles in English, which cause Slavonic language speakers, for example, Poles and Russians, considerable difficulty because this feature does not exist in their languages.

However, researchers such as Patsy Lightbown and Nina Spada (2006) suggest that the picture is more complex. What is particularly puzzling is that learners sometimes make errors that bear no relation to the first language. There is a body of linguistic evidence to support the notion that learners go through a similar sequence of language development regardless of their first language. While there can be variation between language groups, the learning of features such as negation, question formation, and the formation of the past tense go through 'systematic and developmental sequences in second language acquisition'. As Lightbown and Spada say, these stages are not closed, as if the learners pass through one room at a time, leaving one before they enter another. The movement between stages is fluid and learner language often spans multiple stages of development. This has important implications for language teaching. On the one hand, teachers can plan learning opportunities which are likely to be useful to speakers of a variety of other languages. On the other hand, the development of individual learning is likely to span multiple aspects at any stage.

To complicate matters even further, it may appear at times that learners regress. For example, a learner may have learnt to use a common phrase such as *I bought*. When he realizes that there is a rule to add *-ed* to indicate the past tense, he may shift to *I buyed a ticket for the bus*. This is not necessarily a negative development. It shows that the learner is getting to grips with a new aspect of the language, even if this results in the temporary application of a rule beyond its normal context. Over time, learners can be expected to learn that the past tense *-ed* form is only applied to certain verbs. So the use of *buyed* may look like regression but may in fact be a sign of progress. This variation in language use confirms that teachers cannot expect linear progress along the path to proficiency.

Lightbown and Spada identify another aspect that can surprise new teachers. It can take learners a long time to apply language rules which on the face of it look really easy. A good example of this is the third person singular *-s* as in: *the woman buys a paper every day* or *the window cleaner comes once a month*. The use of *-s* is so simple, yet many second language speakers find it hard to apply the rule, even at advanced level. This means that teachers need to be prepared for a much longer learning trajectory than they might have imagined.

This leaves teachers with the challenging job of keeping an overview of the various stages that any of the learners may be going through and using their professional judgement and knowledge of language to assess how they are progressing. In this respect the learner's interlanguage can provide valuable insight both for the teacher and the learner. For example, learners may find it difficult to produce the correct word order in English, an aspect which was looked at in Chapter 4. Its cause may be that the learners apply the word order of their own language to English. If teachers ask the learners what the word order in an equivalent sentence or phrase would be in their first language, this serves two purposes. The information the learners provide can help the teacher identify the reason why they struggle with this aspect and at the same time help the learners notice how English word order works.

Meeting individual learning needs

As we saw in Chapter 2, people who have settled in English-speaking countries and attend language classes bring with them a wide range of language skills, backgrounds, and aptitudes. While there have been trends in migration, such as the large numbers of Iraqis and Somalis who fled their country of origin and the arrival of people from Eastern Europe in search of employment, potentially teachers can find learners from any country in the world in their classroom. The same is true of people's education and employment history. It is possible to find people with very different skills attending classes, for example, a university graduate, a person who cannot read and write at all in his or her first language, and someone who attended secondary school and has good study skills. In addition, not all learners progress at the same pace, so even if teachers start with a group of learners of a similar level, they are likely to find that their skills and needs diverge as the term progresses.

Clearly, it is an important part of the job of the teacher to provide learning opportunities which reflect learners' needs whenever possible. Here is an example of such an activity taking place.

TASK Identifying individual needs

Linda has just started teaching a new Entry 1 class. When she discussed with the learners what they wanted to learn, it became clear that they wanted to be able to write a note in case they or their children were unable to attend school. As a first activity Linda asked the learners to write a message to their class teachers, Krystyna and Bernie, to explain the reason for their absence and to leave their note with Lesley, the college secretary.

Here are three examples of the students' writing. How well do they cope with the task and what does their work tell you about their individual needs?

Usha

hallow, good morning Lesley,
please give massage to may Teacher Krytyna
I am not feeling well today I have appointment
with Doctor
My I.D.No DIA05035197

Thank you.
bey

Nasra

My name is nasra I Cant Came to my Class
Tuday I have appointment hostietel

My iD namber ·mAH04016895 and my Teacher
name Bernie Driscoll

Safia

Hullo My name Safia. I can't came Today
my classed peckoos: am not filwol.

Linda marks the learners' writing and creates an overview of their strengths and weaknesses:

Can the student write a simple message?	Usha	Nasra	Safia
provide essential information	✔	✔	✗
write at sentence level	✔	✔	✗
use articles	✔	✗	✗
use capital letters	✔	✔	✔
use full stops and apostrophes	Not consistent	✗	✗
spell words accurately	Not consistent	Not consistent	✗

These three learners form part of a class of twelve. It turns out that, while Usha's and Nasra's work is typical of the group, Safia and one other learner are clearly weaker.

Having analysed the learners' work, Linda works out how the needs of the learners will be met in the lesson plan below.

Topic	Learner activity	Individual learner needs
Feedback on writing letter notifying absence	Learners review their own writing	Safia and Eustace to complete text frame to help review their writing and to prepare for leaving a phone message
Leave phone message	Learners ring the college secretary's number and leave a message on her answerphone	

This is how Linda worked with the learners. Usha, Nasra, and their peers checked their written work, which Linda had marked by underlining the text that could be improved on. She asked the learners to work together and construct an improved version of their writing. While the learners were working on this, Linda gave the two weaker learners a partly completed text frame which she had based on their work.

Date _____
Dear _____
I am sorry, I can't _____ to class today. I am not _____well.
My teacher's name _____ Krystyna / Bernie.
Thank _____
Name _____

Linda spent time with both groups of learners but made especially sure that the weaker learners could manage the tasks. Once Safia and Eustace had completed the text frame she helped them compare it with the written work which they had produced themselves.

When both groups had completed their tasks, Linda brought the learners together in the whole group. She extended the activity by asking the learners to prepare a message which was to be left on the answerphone. While the more advanced learners prepared notes for this task, Safia and her classmate used the written text frame that they had just completed to rehearse their telephone message.

This is a good example of a teacher keeping in focus the needs of the whole group as well as individual learners. Tasks were set so that individual learners could manage the work but equally all learners participated in whole group tasks, where possible. Linda had also anticipated different speeds of working and made sure that all learners were engaged throughout. No one was bored because they finished before the others. Nor did the less advanced learners panic because they could not manage the task.

Since this lesson took place at the beginning of the course, Linda used the lesson plan and group profile to note down her thoughts on the learners' strengths:

> **Safia** Hesitant when writing. Has substantial literacy needs at word and sentence level. Manages capital letters but not consistently. Needs to practise spelling common words and grammar, for example, *am not fil wol.*

> **Usha** Writes fluently and to a standard expected at Entry 1. Mostly well-formed sentences and accurate spelling. Will need extension activities when more basic features are addressed in class.

Recording this information provides a good starting point to track the learners' progress. This information is also very useful, should another teacher need to take her class. See also page 144 for other examples of learner profiles.

CASE STUDY Individual learning needs

Here is another example of a learning activity and a description of the lesson that followed:

Topic	Resources	Activity	Differentiation
Reading sentences on daily activity	Sentences and pictures which have been cut up	Match the sentences and pictures	The weaker students to work with the stronger Students work according to their ability

This teacher sets her class of ten beginners the task of matching pictures of daily activities with written descriptions, such as *She reads a book* and *She goes to work*. She asks the learners to work in small groups and arranges it so that in one group the strongest learner works with two students who have very little English. The strong learner is clearly keen to do the exercise and works through it essentially by herself, moving the pieces of paper around and saying the sentences. The other two learners look on and try to say some of the words after her. Although the language use of the strongest learner is by no means perfect, the others repeat after her without support from the teacher.

This is clearly not a satisfactory set-up but how can it be remedied? In the first place, the tutor could have defined more clearly on the lesson plan how she planned to deal with the learners' individual needs. Once in the classroom, she should have observed what the learners were doing and ensured that the slower learners get sufficient opportunity to do the exercise. The teacher could also have provided the faster learner with additional work while she spent time with the other learners.

While most language teachers cope well with this type of differentiated learning, it is at the same time opportune to question to what extent teachers are able to deal with a multitude of language needs. Here is Shelley, who teaches English language in the community, talking about her classes:

> I teach outreach classes and the students are at every level and so there is no alternative but to differentiate, however difficult it may be. I try to have a theme so that they can work on common things, so that they can do common vocabulary and maybe common listening but they have to work at differentiated tasks because of their different levels.

Shelley is clearly working hard to make her lessons work but at the same time it sounds as if she is under strain. Sometimes organizations place learners with a wide range of needs in one class. This is most likely to happen when a small number of classes is held in one venue but equally, poor initial assessment and placement may be at fault. Inspection reports frequently comment that teachers do not meet the individual needs of the learners. However, the underlying factor is often that the range of needs is simply too wide for even an experienced tutor to handle them well. This is especially the case when teachers have to teach large classes at beginner level.

If you feel that the range of language levels and needs is too wide to manage, then it is a good idea to ask your manager for advice. There are times when learners with a wider range of needs than normal are accepted to keep classes viable. In that case a good compromise may be to limit the size of the class to a number where the teacher is able to deal with individual needs. For example, a course provider may have a policy to recruit a maximum of sixteen learners for each class but the manager may agree that at beginner level up to twelve learners are accepted. This can be in the interest of the provider, too, since classes where the needs of the learner are not met are much more likely to suffer from high levels of drop-out.

Activities that work well in mixed ability classes

While learners benefit from activities which have been carefully thought out by their teachers, there are many other tasks which are suitable for a variety of learners. Here is an example of such an activity:

TASK   Spot the difference pictures

How might you use these pictures and at what levels?

These pictures were produced as a prompt to get beginners writing everyday words such as *table, chair, teapot,* and *mug,* as well as constructions such as *there is* and *there isn't.* Their use in the classroom, however, showed that learners at higher levels also enjoyed working with them. First here are three examples of writing at Entry 1 and 2:

> *One poto woman is reading newspaper. There is two chair.*
> *Nothing on table.*
> *Door open.*

> *The under picture doesn't have girl.*
> *Two cups are leave on table in the under picture.*
> *It have a flowerpot on the right of door.*

> *First picture:*
> *There's one girl is sitting the chair. He's reading a book.*

> *Second picture:*
> *The girl isn't there. Somethink's (I don't understand, what is that?) on the*
> *table. A flower is front of the door.*

When these photographs were used as a prompt by more advanced learners in an Entry 3 class, in addition to describing the pictures they extended their writing by exploring what they liked about the house and garden. One learner imagined what the young woman in the picture was reading and why.

Using, creating, and adapting materials

One of the major considerations which teachers face when planning lessons is the selection of appropriate materials. Until 2002 there were few published resources which suited the needs of migrants and refugees living in the UK. There certainly were no coursebooks such as those available to EFL teachers. Instead teachers were expected to design their own materials or to adapt existing resources to the needs of the learners. Teachers used mainly authentic materials such as leaflets advertising goods or a bus timetable to set language learning in real life contexts. They might also use materials taken from EFL books, most likely because they wanted to teach a particular language point. While the vast majority of teachers still create materials taken from a variety of sources, the choice of published materials is much greater than before. The Further reading section at the end of this chapter contains details of publicly available materials, many of which can be downloaded or ordered free of charge. Publishers increasingly map materials to the national standards as well as producing customized material for language learners. This is a very welcome development since not all EFL materials are culturally appropriate or reflect the lives and priorities of migrants and refugees. For example, traditional EFL materials tend to focus on leisure topics, such as travel, hobbies, and holidays and are aimed at learners who are in their late teens or early twenties. By contrast, migrants and refugees tend to be older, are likely to have family responsibilities, and need English to settle down in their new country rather than go on holiday there.

Many course providers stock a selection of resources and, if you are a new teacher, it is useful to familiarize yourself with these before you start teaching. If you are offered an induction, that provides a good opportunity to ask for guidance on what materials are available and how they are typically used.

In addition to printed coursebooks and materials, commonly used teaching resources include:

- authentic materials, for example, articles and adverts from local and national newspapers, leaflets on goods and services, job application forms
- pictures and posters to prompt discussion and writing. These are especially useful with lower level students.
- specialist materials packs to help learners who are learning to read and write; for which see Chapter 4
- DVDs, CD-ROMs, and audio / video tapes
- materials made available on the web, such as on the talent and British Council websites. In addition, many publishers offer free resources and teaching activities as well as materials for use on interactive whiteboards.

Here are some questions which can be used to assess the suitability of teaching materials for particular groups of learners:

- What are the key learning points?
- What level of language is the material pitched at?
- Which aspects will be new to the learners and may need pre-teaching?
- How will the activity develop the learners' ability to communicate in everyday life and in the contexts they identified in their learning plans?
- Will other resources be needed to use this exercise effectively?
- Which learners may need extra support to handle this activity?
- Which learners can be expected to finish this activity quickly?

CASE STUDY   Selecting materials from citizenship materials pack

New citizenship materials were commissioned by the Home Office and the Department for Education and Skills to help learners of English learn about Britain. For details of how to access these, see the Further reading section at the end of this chapter.

Darren teaches a class consisting of Entry 2 and 3 learners. He wants to familiarize himself with the citizenship materials and one of the tasks he reviews is the Diverse History exercise below.

Using the questions above, he evaluates the activity to see if it would be suitable for his learners. What do you think Darren's findings might be?

A diverse history   4.2

Roots in the future: Dates of immigration to Britain

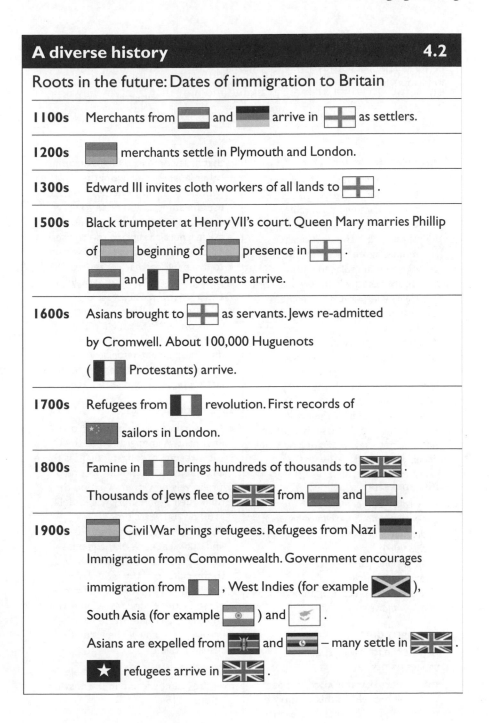

1100s Merchants from ▭ and ▭ arrive in ⊞ as settlers.

1200s ▭ merchants settle in Plymouth and London.

1300s Edward III invites cloth workers of all lands to ⊞.

1500s Black trumpeter at Henry VII's court. Queen Mary marries Phillip of ▭ beginning of ▭ presence in ⊞. ▭ and ▮ Protestants arrive.

1600s Asians brought to ⊞ as servants. Jews re-admitted by Cromwell. About 100,000 Huguenots (▮ Protestants) arrive.

1700s Refugees from ▮ revolution. First records of ▭ sailors in London.

1800s Famine in ▭ brings hundreds of thousands to ⊠. Thousands of Jews flee to ⊠ from ▭ and ▭.

1900s ▭ Civil War brings refugees. Refugees from Nazi ▭. Immigration from Commonwealth. Government encourages immigration from ▮, West Indies (for example ⊠), South Asia (for example ▭) and ▭. Asians are expelled from ▭ and ▭ – many settle in ⊠. ★ refugees arrive in ⊠.

Material produced by NIACE

Entry 1	Entry 2	Entry 3
Write and spell countries and nationalities. (Ww/E1.1)	Identify meanings of high frequency words in a text. (Rw/E2.2)	Read about and discuss the history of immigration to Britain. (Rt/E3.1)

Suggested procedure (Entry 2)

- Pre-teach '*merchants*', '*clothworkers*', '*protestant*', '*famine*', '*expelled*', '*settle*'.
- Give out the immigration table opposite, and ask learners to try to identify the countries/nationalities mentioned in the text from the flags they have been replaced with.
- Check answers, making sure learners are clear whether it is the name of the country or the nationality that is required.
- Ask learners to discuss what evidence of any of these nationalities they can see in their own neighbourhood. (For instance, an Irish-themed pub or a Vietnamese restaurant.)
- Ask learners to draw their own flag, and then to discuss what other nationalities they think are presently coming to the UK.

Differentiation

- *For weaker learners turn each flag gap-fill question into a choice between nation/nationality (for example Spain or Spanish?)*
- *Allow dictionary use with text (mono or bilinguals).*
- *Give additional practice of pronunciation of dates and years.*

Language points

Integrate the following specific language points:

- tell learners that the word 'refugee' was itself brought to this country by the French Huguenots. Ask learners to suggest other words that have come into English from other languages, or from the nationalities mentioned in the text;
- use the immigration table to draw attention to note form; you could ask learners to replace the ellipsed, missing words and expand the text to make full, 'formal' sentences.
- highlight or revise 'dates' vocabulary and pronunciation;
- do extended collocation/metaphor work on 'settle' – a high frequency verb. For example, *settle a debt/dispute/argument, settle down, settle on something, settle in a place, settle into a job/role/property*, and so on.

Extension activities

- Ask learners to discuss their own nationality/s immigration to the UK – is it recent, or longstanding? Is there an established community here, or a relatively new one? What do they think their community will look like in 50 or 100 years time?
- Ask learners to do research to find out what each of the groups mentioned here have contributed to the culture of the UK.
- Ask learners to look back at the personalities encountered in 4.1, and to try to relate these to the immigration table. (They could research this.)

Answers to the immigration table exercises can be found in the answers section, p. 319.

The key learning point of the Diverse History exercise is to teach the names of countries and their adjectival forms, for example, *Spain–Spanish* and *France–French*. The text also contains quite a number of words which are likely to be new to the learners. Learners who are unfamiliar with the flags and the countries they represent are also likely to learn what they stand for.

The complexity of the vocabulary and the pictorial representation of the flags create quite a high-level text. The guidance notes advise that new words such as *merchants, cloth workers, famine,* and *expelled* should be pre-taught. However, Darren anticipates that, in addition to these words, other vocabulary may also be new to the learners, for example, *presence, servants,* and *re-admitted.*

The purpose of this exercise appears to be not so much to extend the learners' ability to communicate in their daily lives but rather to provide them with information on the history of immigration to the UK, an aspect which can be expected to be of interest to learners. On the other hand, the chances that the learners will encounter the new vocabulary in their daily lives and hence practise and retain their meaning over time are likely to be small. (See also Chapter 4 on the learning of new vocabulary.)

Darren decided also that it would be important to photocopy this worksheet in colour because the colours of the flags would be needed to determine what nationality they represented. In addition, a list of country names and flags would be required to help the learners complete the exercise.

This exercise requires quite a high level of reading and could be taxing for people who were unfamiliar with the history of Great Britain. Therefore Darren decided that it was more likely to be suitable for learners who are at E3 than E2. At the same time, the first activity mentioned under the heading 'extension activities', is very well-suited to a mixed-ability class. It suggests that the learners should discuss the arrival of their own community in Britain, a topic which is likely to engage the interest of the learners very well.

Having taken into account these factors, Darren decides to use the arrival of the learners' own communities as a discussion topic with the whole group. A week later, he uses the reading exercise as an extension activity for the stronger learners, while he works with the other learners on revising other language.

Having alternative materials to hand

CASE STUDY

During a previous lesson you have identified a learning need for a third of the learners. You decide that you will plan for a whole group activity because the other learners would benefit from it as revision of what they have learnt before.

When the lesson starts, you find that some of the learners who were the primary target for the lesson are missing. What do you do?

This is a tricky but not uncommon situation, so well worth planning for in advance. If you specially prepared an activity for learners who then do not show up for their class, it makes sense to postpone it to a later stage. However, this means that you should have some other materials to hand to replace the activity that you had planned. A useful strategy to pre-empt a late switch in activities is to mention to the learners that you intend to plan a particular exercise for them and to check that they are definitely going to be there.

However, there is a second reason why it is a good idea to have back-up materials. There is always the possibility that you move more quickly through your lesson plan than you had anticipated. While it is possible to stretch the activities you had planned to fill the time, this creates the danger that the lesson starts to drag. That is why it is a good idea to have some additional materials with you just in case. Especially useful are those which can be handled by learners who are at different levels, for example, a speaking or writing activity such as the photographs on page 158 or a spidergram which can be found in Chapter 5.

Giving formative feedback

Teachers and learners spend much of their time in class talking to each other. Common types of interaction are: teachers giving instructions and explanations, telling stories and anecdotes. The learners themselves talk and listen while carrying out tasks, checking that their answers are correct or discussing, for example, an article that they have just read. In principle, any instance of communication, whether between learners while they work together or between teacher and learner, provides opportunities for the teacher to observe how the learners use English. The transcript below of a presentation given by Paulo, a student on an Entry 3 course, gives an opportunity to analyse his use of English.

TASK   Reflecting on the transcript of a presentation

Paulo's presentation forms the final stage of a project on health and safety on which he and his colleagues have been working. Paulo has produced a portfolio on his findings and used this to prepare a PowerPoint presentation .

What are the strengths and weaknesses of this presentation, for example, in the way he sequences the text and the language he uses?

How would you help Paulo to improve his talk?

RESTAURANT

In the restaurant, Inside the
floor must be dry, because
can become damaged people.
The staff must be clean, There
hands about germs. When
you use a grill pan you must
wearing a special glove for
hand be safely, like in bakery.

P	Today I need to show everybody my health and safety course file ... a comparison of the different safety hazards: restaurant and hospital. Now, first in the restaurant, in the restaurant, inside the restaurant must be dry because can be damaged people to the floor. The staff must be clean, their hand about germs. You know germs?
Other learners	Yes.
P	You know germs.
	When you use the grill pan you must wearing a special glove for hand be safely like in bakery if you are working in a bakery. Because inside bakery is too hot you must [inaudible] is weak often.
	The next one hospital. In the hospital the visitor must be quiet for the patient. Then, you can use your mobile, you can't use your mobile, a needle twice, before you give someone a needle must wearing a glove, after that take off your glove and clean your hands. Go to the next one.
	Then the last one, my, my conclusion. My conclusion is: people must be take precaution himself before the disease to become. Don't give 100 per cent for the restaurant is food, maybe is bad, make sure before you eat. Check. In the hospital, in the hospital make sure you are protected.

This transcript shows that Paulo's choice of vocabulary is good, especially his use of nouns such as *germs* and *safety hazards*. His talk also has sound structure, consisting of an opening statement of what the talk is about, followed by a description of the two environments in which he reviews health and safety: the restaurant and the hospital. His conclusion rounds off the presentation appropriately. At the same time, there are numerous occasions when his poor use of language interferes with what he wants to say. Many sentences lack coherence, for example in the opening paragraph *inside the restaurant must be dry because can be damaged people to the floor. The staff must be clean, their hand about germs.*

The analysis of Paulo's presentation shows that he needs feedback on his use of English and advice on how he can improve. For example, where the message is not clear, the teacher can ask him to explain what he meant, for example, in the case of *Don't give 100 per cent for the restaurant is food.* Once the meaning has been clarified, the teacher can then support the learner with the creation of the phrase or sentence which gets the meaning across. Since in Pablo's case part of the spoken text is produced on the PowerPoint slide and reflects his spoken English, this also gives the teacher a great opportunity to look at the text in detail. She can use this to help the learner notice patterns of language use on which he needs to improve, for example, *you must wearing.* Paulo also needs to rethink the coherence of statements such as *you can use your mobile, you can't use your mobile, a needle twice.*

Paul Mennim (2003) provides a useful study on how to engage the learners in the evaluation of their presentation skills. He reports how he asked his students to rehearse their presentations two weeks before they were due to give them formally. These were recorded and part of them transcribed by the learners themselves. The learners were then asked to comment on their language use and to make suggestions for improvement. They also received feedback from their teacher. The final presentation was then also recorded and analysed by the teacher. Mennim found that the quality of the English had improved in the second presentation and that the content was more comprehensible. It would be useful to apply this model with a learner such as Pablo to see to what extent the process of rehearsal and feedback enables him to improve his language and presentation skills.

Mennim is not the only researcher to find that giving feedback to learners helps improve the quality of language they produce. Studies by 'connectionists' such as Nick Ellis provide insight into the processes that underpin language learning. Their work is based on the assumption that humans 'learn language in much the same way as we learn everything else' (Ellis 2006). When we learn languages, we create meaning out of new information, social interaction, and experiences. Through the context in which communication occurs and the frequency with which language is used, we develop an understanding of how the language works, creating connections between meaning, form, and situation; hence the use of the term 'connectionism'. Ellis, however, identifies one aspect which sets adult language learning apart from other types of learning: the learners are already 'tuned' to the first language and this influences the way they handle the learning of the new language. Without outside help, the learners are likely to get stuck at a basic level of language, a process which is often referred to as FOSSILIZATION. In Ellis's view, language learners can only improve if they get both explicit feedback on their use of the new language and on the tension between the patterns of language use in the first and second language. This echoes Schmidt's finding (2001), which was referred to in Chapter 1, that language learners need advice and feedback to help them 'notice' patterns of use in their new language. Hattie (1999), whose research is referred to in the section on target setting, also identifies feedback as the single most important intervention to enhance learning. His comment that 'the incidence of feedback in the typical classroom is very low' is also borne out by my experience of observing ESOL lessons. These show that many opportunities for feedback are missed.

Cyril Weir (2005) in his book on language testing identifies an external factor which has influenced teachers' attitudes to formative feedback. He suggests that there is a growing tendency to associate assessment with final testing as part of a drive to make providers accountable to external bodies. This has been to the detriment of using assessment and feedback to help the learners develop and improve their ability to use the language. However, as the literature reviewed here shows, a focus on formative assessment and feedback can bring substantial benefits to the learners, improved performance, and, as a consequence, better results during final assessment. A study by Ammar and Spada (2006) forms part of a growing body of research that shows that learners who receive explicit feedback on their language make better progress than their peers who do not. Their second finding was that teachers' prompts to invite the learners to self-correct worked particularly well with beginners.

When teachers are asked why they do not comment on the learners' language use, two responses are often given. In the first place, teachers may not have noticed that the learners have problems with an aspect of the language. Second, teachers reported that they were reluctant to give feedback, for fear that it might embarrass or even intimidate the learner. The latter concern can be easily resolved by asking the learners how they feel about getting feedback, and when and how much they would like to receive it. Teachers are likely to find that their learners really welcome the idea that their teacher will comment on their spoken as well as written language. The next activity looks at the impact of giving feedback on spoken language in more detail.

EXTRACT 2 Classroom talk

Here is the transcript of classroom interaction taken from my NRDC study on advanced language learners (2004). The subject is the concept of equal opportunities which Elena, the teacher, and her students explore. Elena directs the focus to India, where Malini was born.

When and how does the teacher give feedback in this extract? Can you see advantages and disadvantages to her approach?

E   In India, it does exist, doesn't it, the concept, the idea?

M   Yes.

E   People know about it.

M   Yes, it exists but like government are putting forward many steps for giving equal opportunities to women also, like they are, ... they have given thirty three per cent seats in er parliament [pronounced as /pA:liAmxnt/]

E   ...parliament, yes [models the pronunciation: /pA:lxmxnt/]]

M   parliament [repeats using the correct pronunciation]

E   To who?

M   For whom, to whom

E   Oh, to women!

M   ... to women.

E   So they've had, like a, positive erm

M   Yes

E   Affirmative action, yes

M   But still in rural areas ...

E   Yes

M   ... it's not true.

E   Yes did you catch that er word, what kind of areas?

M   Rural ...

E   Rural yes, another lovely pronunciation word, yes rural means in the ... countryside

M   Countryside, yes.

This extract shows that much useful activity is taking place. The overarching objective is to explore the concept of equal opportunities, the application of which Malini describes in her native country. While the learner is talking, the teacher introduces language-specific aspects. For example, she responds to Malini's pronunciation of 'parliament' by modelling the correct pronunciation, which the learner in turn repeats. Elena also picks up on the pronunciation and meaning of the word 'rural'. She is clearly an engaging and supportive teacher who works hard at communicating with the learners. Yet as this extract shows, her inherently good teaching techniques, such as helping the learners with pronunciation and finding the right words, also have disadvantages. The drawback of Elena's approach is that the instant interventions repeatedly interrupt the flow of the student's input. There is a concern that this hampers the development of fluency and extended talk, a skill which language learners need when communicating with first language speakers.

This poses the question of how teachers can find a balance between giving feedback and allowing the learners to talk without interruption. A useful approach would be to give the learner space to express her thoughts, unless she gets stuck and needs help, and not to interrupt until she is finished. While the learner is talking, the teacher could make notes of examples of good language use and areas for improvement. If the teacher writes her comments on an overhead transparency or PowerPoint slide, she can use these straightaway to structure her feedback. This approach also enables the other learners in the group to participate. For example, the teacher might ask 'What would you have said? How can this be improved on?' and 'Remember we did this last week?'

This technique not only allows the teacher to focus on the detail of language use and pronunciation, it also allows for reflection on more global aspects, such as the structure of the narrative. For example, teachers may find that a learner starts an explanation with the least important argument first and that he or she builds up to end with the most important argument last, as is common in some cultures.

Working with external qualifications

Until 2005 proportionately few of ESOL learners in the UK sat exams to achieve a qualification awarded by an external examinations body. Some organizations provided learners with an in-house certificate to indicate language achievement but, since there were no national standards in the UK, judgements made were of necessity impressionistic. This situation has changed dramatically recently because all four countries now have a much greater focus on the measurement of language achievement against common standards.

The introduction of any externally accredited exam can be expected to have an effect on classroom teaching, a phenomenon which is called *washback*. This can impact both positively and negatively on the content of lessons and on the perception of teachers and learners. The closer the test reflects the situations and types of language which the learners use in their day-to-day life, the more we can expect the effect of the test to be neutral or positive. Many learners also respond well to the challenge of an exam and will make an extra effort to prepare for it. By contrast, the further the test is removed from the learners' communication needs, the more likely it is that the washback effect of the exam is negative. The latter is most tellingly described by teachers as 'having to teach to the test', which means that they provide activities to prepare the learners for the test and which otherwise they would not have chosen.

While exams are a fact of life, at least for the foreseeable future, teachers need to consider how they can accommodate them in their teaching. In the first place, it is important to be sensitive to how the learners feel about the idea of taking an exam. Many learners are very positive; others see exams as normal as they would have expected to take them in their country of origin. The third category, those who are anxious about the exam, is the most worrying as it can be hard to decide how best to prepare them for it. These three categories of learners may need different approaches while at the same time teachers need to bear in mind that the learners will need to be familiar with the exam format. The teacher's own attitude towards the exam is also worth reflection, especially if they feel negatively about it, as they may project their feelings on to the learners. So how can teachers best deal with the preparation for the test?

In the first place, you need to find out as early as possible what the test entails and evaluate your normal practice against the types of activities and level of language that the test will demand. See if you can incorporate any elements that you do not normally address into your teaching. For example, if the learners need to be able to handle multiple choice questions, provide them with some practice. If there are strict time limits to doing tasks, you should consider setting targets for completion in class. It is useful to keep a record of the activities that you use to prepare the learners over time and to look back on them in the light of the exam results. If you feel unhappy about aspects of the exam or the negative effect it has on the appropriateness of teaching and learning, do discuss this with your manager or take your concerns to the awarding body direct. Most are keen on finding out what teachers think of their exams and willing to consider changes to meet the needs of the learners better.

Further reading

Classroom resources

Cliff, P. and **T. Bradbury.** 2005. *Skills for Life Exam Preparation Pack.* Oxford: Oxford University Press.
This pack helps learners prepare for the Skills for Life exams at all levels. It contains practice tests, a teacher support book, and CD for listening practice. The OUP website also has downloadable sample writing tasks, written by real ESOL learners, and a mark scheme and examiners' commentary.
http://www.oup.com/elt/local/gb/skillsexamppreppack?cc=gb

McGovern, E. and **G. Smith.** 2006. *New English File ESOL Teachers' Resource Book.* Oxford: Oxford University Press.
This resource book is specifically designed for learners of ESOL. It contains practical and photocopiable materials.

www.dfes.gov.uk/readwriteplus
This website contains a publications list which provides details of assessment materials, learning resources, and reports and case studies on Skills for Life-funded projects. Most are free and can be downloaded and/or ordered in hard copy.

http://www.oup.com/elt/teachersclub
Many publishers offer teaching materials online which are well worth a look such as the Oxford University Press's Teachers' Club.

www.niace.org.uk/projects/esolcitizenship/
This website provides access to citizenship materials which help develop the learners' knowledge of life in the UK. Different versions of the packs have been produced to reflect practice in England, Scotland, and Northern Ireland.

http://www.talent.ac.uk
The talent website is hosted by Tower Hamlets College in London. It contains a wide selection of teaching materials and worksheets produced by teachers for teachers. Information on training courses and job opportunities is provided as well as links to other websites, e.g. on how to create your own interactive resources.

http://www.teachingenglish.org.uk/
This website is run by the British Council and contains a host of material on language teaching. There is a section with many practical activities as well as articles and reflections on teaching.

Theory/Background

Swan, M. and **B. Smith** (eds). 2001. *Learner English*. Cambridge: Cambridge University Press.
This book provides useful descriptions of languages such as French, Spanish, Portuguese, Arabic, Farsi, Turkish Swahili, Chinese, and Vietnamese. Pronunciation, spelling, grammar, and vocabulary are explored as well as typical problems with English.

Hughes, A. 2002. *Testing for Language Teachers*. Cambridge: Cambridge University Press.
This book provides a practical and clear overview of the concepts of assessment and testing. It covers aspects such as reliability and validity, testing the four skills, and grammar and vocabulary, as well as commonly used assessment techniques.

Lightbown, P. and **N. Spada**. 1999. *How Languages are Learned*. Oxford: Oxford University Press.
This book provides a clear and informative overview of how languages are learnt. Not only do the authors bring together research on first and second

language acquisition, they also explore how principles can be applied in the classroom.

Weir, C. 2005. *Language Testing and Validation.* Basingstoke: Palgrave MacMillan.
Chapter 6 provides a useful overview of aspects to consider when designing assessments, such as task setting, learner motivation, and the skills of speaking, listening, reading, and writing.

Alderson, J. C., C. Clapham, and **D. Wall.** 2006. *Language Test Construction and Evaluation.* Cambridge: Cambridge University Press.
This book provides a clear overview of the various stages of planning and implementing testing and assessment. Of particular interest are the chapters on monitoring examiner reliability and developing and improving tests.

Coffield, F., D. Moseley, E. Hall, and **K. Ecclestone.** 2004. *Learning Styles and Pedagogy in post-16 Learning.* London: Learning and Skills Development Centre.

Coffield, F., D. Moseley, E. Hall, and **K. Ecclestone.** 2004. *Should We Be Using Learning Styles? What Research Has to Say to Practice.* London: Learning and Skills Development Centre.
These studies, which overlap to a degree, provide a comprehensive overview of commonly used tools to assess learning styles. Their authors indicate that there is currently insufficient independent research evidence to substantiate claims of effectiveness, especially in the context of further and adult education.

Mennim, P. 2003. 'Rehearsed oral L2 output and reactive focus on form.' *English Language Teaching Journal* 57/2: 130–38.
This article provides a useful example of how to engage the learners actively in the evaluation of their own oral presentation skills. It appears in a periodical which aims to bridge the gap between theory and practice in the classroom.

Schellekens, P. 2004. 'Advanced learners' in Roberts, C., *et al.*: *ESOL Case Studies of Provision, Learners' Needs and Resources.* London: National Research and Development Centre 114–28.
This case study looks at the ability of the learners to reflect on their language learning. It also looks at how language and non-language teachers address learner needs in the classroom.

http://www.openquals.org.uk/openquals
This page on the Qualifications Curriculum Authority website provides an up-to-date listing of the ESOL qualifications and the awarding bodies that offer these in England, Wales, and Northern Ireland.

http://www.sqa.org.uk/esol
This website provides information about SQA qualifications and resources. Information on assessment materials is also available on the secure part of the website.

The inspectorates
http://www.ofsted.gov.uk/publications.
The Office for Standards in Education (Ofsted) website contains all information related to inspections in England.

http://www.hmie.gov.uk
This is the website for the Scottish Inspectorate of Education (HMIE).

http://www.estyn.gov.uk
Estyn is the office of Her Majesty's Chief Inspector of Education and Training in Wales.

7 LANGUAGE SUPPORT

This chapter is devoted to an increasingly important area of language teaching: the delivery of language support to learners who are on mainstream vocational courses. Since there is uncertainty in the field over what 'language support' means, the term will be defined and different types of delivery investigated. We explore how support can be set up and evaluated and look at some key indicators to ensure successful delivery.

Defining types of provision

Historically, ESOL provision in the UK has consisted of discrete English classes which have been predominantly targeted at migrants and refugees with minimal language skills. More recently, however, the focus on provision has widened to include those who want to access mainstream training courses. This has created exciting opportunities as well as challenges for the profession. Language support is being introduced as the major tool to provide the learners with language skills that are directly related to vocational content and the workplace. Since the delivery of language support is relatively new, organizations and teachers are in the process of experimenting with methods, staffing, and resources. Some aspects of these are explored in the exercise below to set the scene for this chapter.

TASK Types of provision

Below are four types of provision which contain an element of support. Which do you think can and which cannot be described as language support?

1 An NVQ 2 plumbing course which has a support teacher attached to help with language aspects such as understanding vocabulary and writing up assignments.

2 A catering course where the learners have access to an open learning centre and support workers are available as a general resource to help learners with their assignments.

3 An IT course where the tutor has both an IT and an ESOL qualification and is able to teach both.

4 An ESOL course which contains two modules on maths and IT.

Of the examples above, the two courses in plumbing and IT can be said to offer language support. The learners are on a course leading to a mainstream vocational qualification. To achieve their goal, the learners receive language support which relates directly to the vocational content. For example, learners on a plumbing course will be expected to communicate with their boss. To achieve this occupational goal, they may need opportunities to learn to communicate effectively face-to-face and over the phone. Or they may need advice on how to complete a log of what they covered on placement, presenting information clearly on what tasks were undertaken and how they were carried out. This type of provision has also recently been called 'embedding'. However, this term is potentially confusing, as embedding implies that the support is or should be fully integrated into the course itself. In this book the term *language support* will be used to refer to various types of support which can be attached to vocational courses, and of which embedded learning is a variant.

As to the second example in the task, the classification of the catering course is problematic. While help is provided with assignments, there is no support to help the learners cope with in-class activities. Secondly, many support workers are not qualified teachers, but are trained to provide general assistance with learning. They are expected to help learners with a variety of aspects such as literacy for first language speakers, numeracy, ESOL, dyslexia, and study skills. Because of the nature of their training, they cannot be expected to have the subject-specific skills that are required for the delivery of targeted language support.

In the fourth example, the ESOL course which offers maths and IT modules, the roles of language and vocational skills have been reversed: the main learning goal is to learn English, for which the subjects of IT and maths are used as the context. Many language departments now offer this model of learning. While very useful, this provision cannot be described as offering language support. In this book we shall refer to this type of provision as *contextualized language learning* or *contextualized learning*.

In summary, the following terminology will be used in this chapter to refer to the three major ways in which language and vocational learning can be brought together:

● *general support*, most commonly delivered through sessions which are open to any learner who wants to come along

- *contextualized language learning* where a vocational element is introduced in ESOL classes
- *language support,* by which we mean language learning which relates directly to the learners' main vocational course.

At the same time, these three methods should not be seen as existing in isolation, because a blend of options may well best suit the needs of the learners. As we shall also see, needs beyond direct course content can also prompt opportunities for learning, for example, skills requirements in the workplace.

The nature of our target group also deserves consideration. Many adult language learners already have substantial skills and experience, including strong study skills and a positive attitude to learning. They may be well-qualified and bring prior experience of the workplace. These skills are particularly useful when they enter mainstream vocational courses. However, because of the general history of support in education and training, organizations may have come to see its delivery as part of a deficit model, i.e. teaching struggling students. This is not an accurate interpretation of language support, which should be seen as building on the learners' existing skills and helping them develop the language skills they need to achieve their vocational goal.

Reflecting on language and course content

TASK Looking at course content and language requirements from the learners' perspective

When planning language support, it is important to anticipate at what stages the learners may be in most need of support. You will find below a snippet of the national occupational standards for Warehousing and Distribution to explore what type of tasks, content, and / or language learners may need help with.

- What language skills and vocational competences will be required to carry out the different tasks described in the unit below?

- Can you predict what the learners will find easy and what is likely to cause difficulties?

- Might there be differences between the language skills needed during the training course and in the workplace?

Unit	Skills for logistics	Element	
Dealing with payment transactions		Collect and account for payments for goods delivered	
		Code LOG 4.2	Issue May 2003

Description of this element

You must be able to collect and account for payments for goods delivered. You must confirm the delivery of goods, the amount and the method of payment to be received. Goods are items that make up a load. A load is any goods moved by road. You will need to collect payments when goods are delivered and issue the appropriate receipts. You will need to ensure cash amounts are carried securely in accordance with operational and organisational procedures. You will reconcile the payments received with the documentation and hand over or deposit the completed documentation and payments collected in accordance with operational and organisational procedures. Report any discrepancies with payments to the relevant persons.

When we analyse the work functions that the learners will be expected to carry out, we see that they need to deliver goods, issue receipts, make sure that paperwork is in order, deposit payment, and report any discrepancies. These functions are simple and routine and should be easy to master. By contrast, the language requirements are potentially much more complex and variable. While they are being trained, the learners may have to read written instructions such as those contained in the description above and understand their tutor's explanations. While at work, the learners will need to communicate with colleagues, customers, and their managers, for example, when there is a problem with delivery or payment. They will also need to be able to complete and check paperwork.

The description above indicates that the language and communicative load is very much higher and more complex than the skills required to deliver goods, as shown in the cartoon in Figure 7.1.

Figure 7.1: Delivering the communicative load

This calls for the planning of a variety of language development activities, both to support the learners while they are on the course and in the workplace, for example, by working on the learners' intelligibility of their spoken language and practising scenarios of likely interactions with customers, for example, answering questions such as: *I've come to pick up my computer. When can I collect the goods? Why is my order not ready yet?*

The difference in language and vocational requirements we see in this Warehousing and Distribution unit is by no means unique. As to vocational courses, many have well-structured curricula. Their content evolves gradually from a basic level to increasingly complex concepts and tasks. If we take as an example an IT course for beginners, we see that simple concepts are introduced first, starting with switching the computer on, followed by managing passwords, creating text files, copying and pasting text, etc. Thus the learners acquire new skills in a gradual and methodological fashion.

By contrast, the language demands of courses develop differently, as shown in Figure 7.2. Overall, the language load starts at a high level and then stays relatively stable. This is because major aspects, such as the tutor's explanations and instructions, the written language in handouts and textbooks, and communication with customers, change little. If there is an increase in complexity, this is mainly brought about by the introduction of new vocabulary. So, if we look at the course from the perspective of the learner, we see that, because they have to get used to new and often complex language, they face a lot of pressure right at the beginning of the course. At the same time, any poor understanding of language can directly affect the understanding of course content. It is well known that many second language speakers feel overwhelmed and drop out in the very early stages of the course. The pressures just outlined are the most likely reason why so many do.

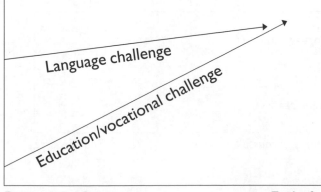

Figure 7.2: A comparison of language and vocational learning loads

TASK Models of delivering language support and contextualized learning

You will find below three models of supporting learners who are planning to go on vocational courses. In the light of the discussion on the learning loads that the learners face, which model do you think would be most appropriate for second language speakers?

Model 1

This is the most commonly found model of delivering language support. It consists of a fixed number of hours throughout the course, typically two hours a week.

Language support
Mainstream vocational course

Beginning of course   *End of course*

Model 2

In Model 2, the learners have access to more hours' language support at the beginning of the course to help them cope with the new language they encounter. As they settle down and increase their ability to manage independently, language support is gradually scaled down. However, it is not completely withdrawn because the learners may need help with new tasks, such as producing a final written assignment or a formal presentation of findings.

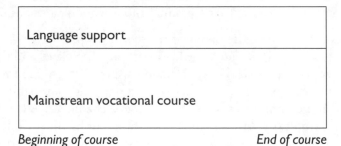

Beginning of course   *End of course*

Model 3

In addition to attending a vocational course with language support attached, as described under model 2, learners have the opportunity to attend a contextualized module while still on a general language course. To prepare the learners for progression to the mainstream course, the language team have worked with the vocational tutor to plan a three-staged approach. First, the language teacher pre-teaches some of the key language, after which the vocational tutor has her input. These activities allow the learners to become familiar with the style of delivery in the vocational department, typical activities, and vocabulary and jargon. Last, the language teacher follows up the vocational sessions. She may cover learning techniques, such as listening and note-taking skills, or how to do an assignment as well as recycling important vocational vocabulary. Some providers have even offered contextualized courses based on a unit which is particularly language rich, such as one of the hairdressing units which we shall explore further in this chapter.

Beginning of course   End of course

We began this section by asking which models of delivery would best suit the needs of second language speakers. In the first place, it is important to say that all three models would benefit the learners, provided that the language support relates directly to the mainstream course they attend. However, not all models match the needs of the learners equally well. Model 1 is the least attractive because the fixed two-hour slot is unlikely to offer the degree of support that learners need at the beginning of the course. Models 2 and 3 meet the needs of the learners better because the learners get extra support in the early stages of the course, when they need it most. And model 3 works best of all because, in addition to language support, it also prepares the learners for the transition from ESOL to mainstream provision. The main disadvantage of models 2 and 3, however, is organizational: many providers would find it difficult to provide flexible staffing, especially if all vocational courses start at the beginning of the academic year. This may be overcome by offering staggered starts of courses throughout the year. While colleges of further and adult education mostly recruit learners only once a year, vocational training providers in the UK are often more flexible and provide good models of staggered recruitment which allow for more responsive delivery of language support.

Language audit

Tutors will want to familiarize themselves with course content and the language requirements of mainstream courses before they start offering language support. This is especially important if they are new to the mainstream subject area or if support is being introduced for the first time. This activity is often called doing a *language audit* and should not be confused with a second, separate use of the term which describes the process of information gathering on the language backgrounds of the learners. The activities outlined in this section can also be expected to be useful for language tutors who want to introduce contextualized language learning.

TASK Identifying sources of information

What sources of information might you use to analyse mainstream courses and plan language support or contextualized learning? How would you use these sources?

Your first port of call to get access to sources of information is the vocational department, especially the vocational tutor with whom you will be working. In addition, there are also general sources of information, which are mentioned in the text below and details of which can be found at the end of this chapter.

National occupational standards

Courses that are accredited externally through an awarding body are nearly always derived from a national set of occupational standards. These standards are easily accessible through the UK Standards website. This provides information by unit and element, which is a subdivision of a unit, as well as assessment guidance and requirements for underpinning knowledge and skills. A unit on hairdressing is used below to demonstrate how language support tutors can draw on these occupational standards to establish communication requirements.

TASK   Using national standards to plan for language and communication training
Hairdressing level 1 – salon reception duties

In this exercise, we use two samples of the national occupational standards for hairdressing, which were taken from the unit on salon reception duties.

How can you use the performance criteria and knowledge requirements below to plan for the delivery of language and communication training? What activities might you design to help the learners check if they have the right language skills?

National Occupational Standards
Level I Hairdressing
Unit G2   Assist With Salon Reception Duties

Performance Criteria

In order to perform this unit successfully, you must:

2. Attend to clients and enquiries by:
  a) treating all people making enquiries in a positive and polite manner
  b) correctly identifying the purpose of the enquiry
  c) confirming appointments and promptly informing the relevant member of staff
  d) promptly referring any enquiries you cannot deal with to the relevant person for action
  e) recording messages correctly and passing them to the relevant person at the right time
  f) giving all information clearly and accurately
  g) giving confidential information only to authorised people.

Knowledge and Understanding

To perform this unit successfully, you will need to know and understand:

Communication
7. the importance of taking messages and passing them on to the right person at the right time
8. the importance of effective communication to the salon's business
9. how and when to ask questions
10. how to say things that suit the purpose of your discussion
11. how to speak clearly in a way that suits the situation
12. how to show you are listening closely to what people are saying to you
13. how to adapt what you say to different situations (i.e. the amount you say, your manner and tone of voice)
14. how to show positive body language

These performance criteria and knowledge requirements indicate that the learners will need to have good language and communication skills to cope with reception duties. You may want to go to the UK Standards website yourself to see if you agree that, out of the units that make up the N/SVQ, both this unit and a second unit on style and colour consultation require the strongest communication skills.

Language support tutors can use these two units to work on the learners' language skills. They could, for example, video some typical exchanges between a customer and receptionist who are both native English speakers. These can be used by the learners as models of communication and as a prompt for role-plays, which in turn can be videoed and used to help the learners evaluate their performance. Areas that are likely to need work include the accuracy and fluency of language, and the use of intonation and pronunciation when reception staff and hairdressers converse with their clients by asking questions, such as: *Who is doing your hair today? What are you having done today?* and that question so typical of the communication culture in hairdressing salons: *Are you going anywhere nice on your holidays?*

This also poses the question of what level of language skills the learners might need to have on entry to the N/SVQ hairdressing course. Experience of working with second language speakers at Tower Hamlets College shows that learners who are at Entry 3 can be expected to achieve their hairdressing qualification, provided that they have access to sufficient language support. At Tower Hamlets College this consisted of an additional five hours a week. The team felt that a major part of the effectiveness of the support lay in the course design, with ESOL and vocational tutors collaborating closely. They drew up a shared syllabus from which each tutor then derived their own scheme of work. An informal measure of success lay in the fact that trainees whose first language was English noticed how well the language learners were doing on their course and became interested in the type of activities that the language support team offered.

Syllabus, coursebooks, handouts, and other course materials

Language teachers will need to find out what documentation the vocational team uses to deliver the course. Some vocational tutors design their own materials, but many use those produced by awarding bodies. Increasingly, these are of high quality and are written in plain English, with some awarding bodies even offering complete courses which follow a detailed syllabus. These curricula and materials give support teachers a good idea of course structure, training activities, and where support is likely to be needed. Details of awarding bodies and links to their websites can be found on the UK Standards website.

Course delivery

Occupational standards and the course syllabus will give you an idea of the content of the course. What it cannot tell you is how it will be delivered. It is worth asking your vocational colleagues to talk you through the timetable and to explain what activities typically take place. However, best of all is to negotiate access to mainstream lessons before you start delivering support, so that you have an opportunity to observe what happens in the training room.

You may find that the approach to teaching differs from that used in the language classroom. For example, some craft-based courses start the day with an hour's theory which is not necessarily related to the practical work that the learners will be doing later in the workshop. This is particularly common if the course allows for the continuous intake of trainees which means that, as soon as one leaves, another is recruited. The teaching styles of individual tutors can also vary considerably. For example, some mainstream tutors are skilled communicators, and are good at simplifying language and checking back that the learners have understood. Others use lots of complex language and irony, which can be hard to understand if English is not your first language. The pace of learning on vocational courses also deserves reflection, especially compared to discrete language courses which tend to be more nurturing and allow more time for the learners to get to grips with new material.

Spending time in the training room can serve three purposes: it allows you to see patterns of delivery and individual teaching styles; it can help you spot areas on which you can work with the vocational tutor to improve the quality of teaching; and it allows you to identify suitable opportunities when you and the vocational tutor can deliver joint training.

While negotiating access to mainstream tutors and lessons, please bear in mind the perspective of the mainstream tutor. Some may feel that their territory is being invaded, others are worried about their own use of English, most commonly their writing skills and understanding of grammar. If you are working with a mainstream tutor who is new to language support, it may be a good idea to invite him or her to attend one of your lessons first. That way they will get to know you in an unthreatening situation and gain a better understanding of language teaching and learning. What also can work well is to offer the vocational tutor an observation of a lesson taught by a colleague who also teaches on a vocational course and who is skilled at working with second language speakers. This promotes cross-fertilization of good practice.

Language in the workplace

The national occupational standards describe the functions that the learners will need to carry out in the workplace and from that you can work out what language skills will be needed to underpin these. However, a visit to a company that provides work placements can give you direct experience of the type of language the learners will need to be able to handle, for example, reporting a fault in the company log book or communicating with colleagues and customers, in particular being able to handle small talk. Your colleagues in the vocational department should be able to advise you as to which companies will be most suitable for you to visit.

Wider needs related to employment may also present themselves. For example, the vocational and language team at Tower Hamlets College realized that, once learners on childcare courses in Tower Hamlets had got their qualification and a job, they would need to be able to travel to a variety of council venues at short notice. Since some learners were not familiar with public transport, the college used a variety of venues to get the learners used to travelling to different destinations confidently.

Assignments, assessment tasks, and (mock) exam papers

Providers often rely heavily on a bank of assignments and exam papers, again provided by awarding bodies, to prepare the learners for assessment and / or exams. These will give you a good idea of the type of tasks that will be used to assess the learners, for example, multiple-choice questions or open questions which require free writing. You will be able to find out whether oral and/or taped evidence is allowed as evidence of occupational competence, if there are any time restrictions on completing the tasks, and what categories of learners are allowed extra time. Sample papers and exams will also give an indication of what language skills will be needed to complete tasks, for example, being able to read instructions and to produce written answers. It is also important to be alert to the fact that the language required to pass the exam may not be the same as that to complete the course and that often the language requirements for the assessment are higher.

Using course evidence produced by fellow trainees

So far we have looked at occupational standards, documentation, course delivery, and the type of tasks that the learners will need to be able to do. These sources undoubtedly provide useful information, yet they can only give indirect insight into what the learners actually need to do to achieve their qualification. To get direct evidence, there is an excellent source of information available: the course work produced by trainees who have been on the course previously.

TASK Assessing the language requirements of the course

The text below was produced by Adam, a learner on a BTEC Business Level 2 course. Adam is of West African background, was born in the UK, and speaks English at home. The passage below forms part of an assignment on business development. How effectively does he express himself?

> **Describe ways in which your selected business could respond to key competitive force.**
>
> I would recommend a few ways in which Tesco could respond to competitive forces.
>
> *Adverts*
>
> Tesco could do very well if they could advertise more of their product. For their customers to be aware of it.
>
> *Cheaper Goods*
>
> They need to sell more of their product at cheaper prices. They should also provide discount and bonanzas.
>
> *Opening more stores*
>
> Tesco should expand their stores as many as possible, so that they could meet customers expectations.
>
> Tesco has to make sure they keep an eye on their rivals for changes in prices, new goods, etc.

While Adam's use of headings is effective and he makes some good points, the text is obviously not perfect. His course tutor graded Adam's work as sufficient to pass the course, which he did at the end of the year. Examples such as this give the most telling information on the level of language that second language speakers need to aim for. It may come as a surprise to some language teachers that the quality of writing does not need to be perfect, but it is also positive to know that learners can achieve their vocational course aim while they are still learning English. In addition, previous learners' work not only provides a practical benchmark for teachers, it can also inform the learners. For example, if the concept of competitiveness which Adam addresses above is new to learners or they are not sure how to structure an analysis of this type, seeing models of writing, by both first and second language speakers, can make it much easier for them to produce a piece of work to the required standard. In the case of Adam's work, however, it would be advisable for teachers to present the learners with a corrected text or to make sure that the learners know that the work is not perfect.

In the same way that language teachers can use written work produced by previous learners, they can also make use of audio- or video-taped evidence to assess spoken skills requirements. The results of the analysis can then be used to benchmark, for example, Pablo's presentation on Health and Safety, which we analysed in Chapter 6, and help him improve his language skills.

TASK

By way of contrast, we now look at a piece of work that was produced by Ali, a young learner who was on a motor vehicle maintenance course at the time that he wrote the text below. Ali, like Adam, was born in the UK but he spoke Urdu as his first and English as his other language. What can we say about the quality of this writing and its use as evidence of his understanding of Health and Safety?

> 2. Explain why it is important to use the correct tools
>   for the job you are carrying out
>   *Be Cause you will need right thungs for
>   what are opening for saftey to move sure
>   Inng's are tight Hed*

Taken from Full on English *produced for Birmingham and Solihull LSC 2005*

We can look at this writing from two perspectives, the first as a piece of text which language teachers can use to help Ali improve his writing. However, the second perspective is at least as important. The vocational tutor had asked Ali and his fellow learners to answer a list of questions to show that they had understood the health and safety implications of using tools. What we find here, unfortunately, is that the weakness of the writing affects the validity of Ali's statement. He may have understood the concept of health and safety, but the reader cannot be sure. This example of writing shows that, if written work is intended as proof of subject knowledge, the learners will need to have a sufficient level of English to convince the assessor and examiner that they have the required vocational skills and knowledge. This is an important consideration for teachers who support language learners on mainstream courses.

Analysing the language of mainstream courses

So far we have looked at the types of information that teachers can use to get an understanding of the language demands of vocational courses. Next to be investigated is what types of language skills the learners are likely to need. The list below identifies some of the major areas that the learners may need support with.

- Frequently used language in the workplace, for example, verbs like *set* and *set out*; *run* and *run out of*; *pop in, pop this on*, etc.
- Idioms, for example, *He's tied up at the moment* or *I was thrown in at the deep end in my new job*, which do not make sense when taken literally.

- The use of vocabulary and jargon. However, please consider that often it is not specialist vocabulary that second language speakers struggle with. This is because the learners are in the vocational environment where they soon pick up specialist language.
- Grammar, in particular language for instruction and description of process as expressed through the use of the passive voice: *The engine should be turned clockwise before inserting it.*
- Understanding language for instruction and explanation, for example, second language speakers can get confused by instructions such as *Before you do X, do Y.* They may take the first part of the instruction as the first action they should perform.
- Being able to handle the right register of formal, informal, and colloquial language. These all occur in the workplace and depend on the communication partner, for example, a trainee talking to peers in the canteen would use colloquial language; an employee advising a customer would use formal language; colleagues in a meeting with their boss would probably use informal language; and an employee in a job-appraisal meeting with her boss, most likely formal language.
- Language for social interaction. Second language speakers can be seen as aloof by their peers and tutors because they lack the necessary language to handle small talk, slang, and irony.
- The use of the four language skills and study skills, for example, the need to be able to listen to a presentation and take notes at the same time. Vocational tutors have commented in the past that learners who cannot take notes miss out on an important tool for learning and revision.
- Producing extended spoken and written text, for example, how to prepare for and give a presentation, or how to write a project assignment.

Looking ahead to the planning of learning activities, many of the teaching ideas which were explored in the chapters on grammar and the four language skills can be equally well applied in the vocational context. Techniques to develop speaking and listening skills can help the learners improve their ability to communicate in the training room and the workplace. And the use of text models and frameworks is particularly useful when the learners need to tackle tasks with which they are not yet familiar. For example, learners may not know how to take notes during presentations. They find it really helpful to have access to examples of how to do this. You can anticipate this need by working with the mainstream tutor to create notes for one or two of the first presentations that the learners will encounter on the course. These will make it easier for the learners to follow the talk. They also provide models which the learners can then use to produce their own notes. If you can, it is a good idea to cover this aspect of learning during an extended course induction or contextualized module before the start of the vocational course.

Working out language levels on entry to and exit from the course

By now you will have built up a picture of the contents of the course, its delivery, and the language needed to demonstrate vocational competence. You will have used the work produced by learners who attended the course previously to assess the type and level of speaking and writing skills that will be required on the course. You are now in a position to establish what the likely language levels should be on entry to and exit from the course. In the case of mainstream courses, calculations of this type must take place in the knowledge that the achievement of the vocational qualification is the main objective, with language as the underpinning skill needed to complete the course. A second consideration is that language levels and skills requirements can vary considerably from course to course. If we take, for example, Business Administration, we find that, while the functions of answering the telephone, filing papers, and booking appointments are simple and routine, the language required to carry out these tasks can be complex and unpredictable. Employers' expectations should also be taken into account and realistic levels of language built into the course so that the learners stand a good chance of being recruited once they qualify. In the case of an N/SVQ Level 1 Business Administration, a target of language at level 2 would be realistic; whereas for Hairdressing, Level 1 is likely to be sufficient for Speaking and Listening and Entry 3 for Reading and Writing.

The next step is to work out what the minimum levels of language should be on entry to the course. Since this depends on many factors, this is not an easy task. However, here are some basic principles which can be applied to get an indication of the level of language skills. The aim of this task should be to set a minimum language level which assures a successful learning experience and achievement of the vocational qualification, while at the same time not excluding learners unnecessarily.

The first principle is to assess the degree of improvement that the learners can be expected to achieve by attending the course. This can be done by calculating the total number of hours which the learners will spend on the vocational training and language support components. For example, a year's course to deliver Hairdressing N/SVQ Level 1 may consist of one day of vocational training plus four hours' language support a week. This means that the learners will have roughly 400 hours of classroom contact during which they will be expected to communicate in English. This figure can be set against the minimum of 100 guided learning hours estimated by the Qualifications and Curriculum Authority (QCA) for an average learner to progress for each of the skills of Speaking, Listening, Reading, and Writing. At the same time, it is important to consider that not all vocational training will provide the context for language learning and that not all skills may be used to an equal degree. The information taken together indicates that learners should be able to achieve a degree of improvement of one level while on the course. This means that learners on the Hairdressing course should be at Entry 3 at the start of the course. If we apply the same principle to the Business Administration course for which the learners should be at Level 2 on exit, then they should be at language Level 1 on entry. It is important to point out that this calculation is made on the basis of the improvement in language skills, not the achievement of the language qualification itself, because the preparation for taking the Skills for Life exams demands an additional allocation of time.

And last, if you are planning to run language support for the first time, you may want to set the minimum language level for entry to the course at a level where you are confident that the learners can complete the course in the time allowed. Once you have completed the first delivery of the course, you can then evaluate the entry requirements and decide if it is possible to adjust the minimum level of language.

Assessment and guidance

Once language levels have been set for entry to the course, you can plan for initial assessment and any guidance that the learners will need to decide whether the course is right for them. The general principles of assessment and guidance, which were set out in the previous chapter, apply equally to the context of mainstream delivery. However, the setting of language learning in the vocational context creates some additional considerations, which will be addressed in this section. The first is that, in order to get relevant information on what the learners can already do and need to learn, the language assessment should be set in the vocational context. Secondly, since most mainstream courses will have been in existence before language support is attached, assessment of vocational and other skills will already be in place. If this is so, it may be possible to use existing tasks to incorporate the language assessment component within it. Here are some thoughts on what assessment tasks should elicit about the learner:

- prior occupational skills, educational achievements, and work experience, as these can have a significant impact on capacity to achieve
- language skills and needs
- study skills, which will depend on the course, but most commonly required are the ability to assimilate information, take notes, read materials, and write assignments
- keyboard skills, which may be a necessary skill in the workplace but may also be of immediate importance if the learner has to produce written work on the course in the form of assignments, reports, and projects.

Initial and formative assessment tasks are best constructed jointly by the mainstream and language support tutor and are most effective if they explore the ability of the learner to handle language, vocational, and study skills in one integrated task. For example, if face-to-face communication with customers is an important aspect of the course, a task designed around this topic will give important information on what the learners can already or not yet do.

Once you and the vocational tutor have carried out the initial assessment and worked out the learner's strengths and weaknesses, you can brief the learner on your findings during the guidance interview. If you find that the profile of skills does not meet the minimum requirements for entry to the course, be ready to refer the learner to a course which helps them develop their skills further and encourages them to apply again once they have achieved the agreed target. This is also a good opportunity, if you have not already done so, to check that the learners know what the course is about and are aware of alternative options. For example, there are many courses in the Health and Social Care field, and learners may not be clear that they can opt for a variety of areas, for example, working with children, in care homes, or with people with learning disabilities. The guidance interview also provides a good opportunity to explain what the language support will consist of and whether attendance will be compulsory. It allows you to prepare the learner for the fact that he or she is likely to find the first few weeks of the course challenging for the reasons set out earlier in this chapter. You will also be able to explain what you and the vocational tutor have planned to help them cope with the early stages of the course. Many learners are reassured to know what to expect and have reported that, having had this information, they felt much better able to stay the course as a result. And once they are on the course, language teachers can refer back to this discussion when following up on how the learners are doing.

Delivering support

Three methods of delivery are most commonly found:

- There may be an element of double-staffing or team-teaching, when you and your vocational colleague work in the classroom together.
- You may be allocated time to work outside the training context on language-related aspects.
- There may be open-learning facilities where the learners can go for help, use self-access packages, such as spelling, or write their course assignments.

Although rare, there may also be a need to support a learner on a one-to-one basis with a particular aspect.

Whatever the method of support, liaison with the vocational tutor is crucial to establish what the learners will need to learn and when. On a more elementary and personal level, if the vocational and language support teachers are going to work well together, they need to get on as people and feel comfortable in each other's presence. It is important to be flexible and to give the partnership every chance to work. However, sometimes it turns out that the vocational and language tutor just do not get on, in which case it is important to let your manager know.

Being a language support tutor is undoubtedly challenging but also rewarding. You may well find that, while working alongside your vocational colleague or colleagues, you learn from them and they from you. In particular, once the vocational tutor sees how you apply language teaching techniques, they are often well able to use these in their own teaching. As a result, they may start to break down information into smaller units rather than give an uninterrupted talk. They may simplify language and check back if the learners have understood at regular intervals. There have also been numerous examples where vocational tutors have learnt to help the learners with language-related aspects. Some graduate from giving advice on simple aspects, such as punctuation, to more complex areas, such as commenting on the structure of a written assignment or talk. The impact of the vocational tutors paying attention to language can be profound because they are the people in authority and in possession of the vocational skills that the learners want to learn. Their focus on language raises not just its status; it also reinforces yours as the language teacher if you are seen to be sharing responsibility for such an important area.

One other aspect which you may be able to negotiate is whether team-teaching or separate language workshops best suit particular aspects of learning. Team-teaching can work well during practical sessions when the learners work individually or in small groups. For example, they may need to read instructions on how to carry out a task and complete a log, or they need to produce a report on a customer survey. These situations lend themselves well for both you and the mainstream tutor to move around the room and talk to the learners without interrupting each other. By contrast, team-teaching is not effective when the vocational tutor gives a presentation to the whole group, because language support cannot be given without disturbing the group or causing the language learners to be distracted from the vocational tutor's presentation. More effective is the approach where the vocational and support tutors work out aspects of the presentation which the learners are likely to have difficulties with. The language tutor can then set up a session to pre-teach the language which the learners will encounter during the presentation and follow up afterwards to revise and extend language and give support with any assignments. These support sessions can also be used to promote the learning of more general study skills as well as language-specific aspects, such as pronunciation, intonation, and using the right register to communicate with customers. Vocational tutors, learners, and employers often provide useful input on what aspects are most needed. Language support teachers can also use this information to design a programme which the learners can opt to attend, depending on their needs. This approach has been proved to work very well, with, for example, topics being offered on writing up an assignment or using social language.

Your organization may need to put the learners forward for the accreditation of their language skills to fund the language support, in which case you will need to use part of the support time to make sure that the learners cover those requirements, too. However, this can put language support tutors in a difficult position because the goal of supporting the learners in their aim to get a vocational qualification may not be the same as getting the learners ready to take a language qualification. The identification of language functions demonstrated in the vocational context against the national standards can help and often reassures that learning language in the vocational context also meets the targets set by government.

Learner intakes and their impact on achievement

TASK   The recruitment of a discrete ESOL group versus a mixed intake of first and second language speakers

Language support teachers may find that they have been allocated to a vocational course consisting of only second language speakers or a mixture of first and second language speakers.

- What in your view are the advantages and disadvantages for the learners of being in a mixed or ESOL-only group?
- How might you plan to overcome any disadvantages?

As a case study of two courses below shows, the composition of the groups of learners had an impact on achievement.

Two providers offered Information Technology courses to 15 people whose first language was not English. The learners on the two courses had comparable levels of language on entry to the course. Both organizations provided language support using qualified language tutors who worked alongside their vocational colleagues. The courses were similar in terms of accreditation and course design. However, there was one difference. One provider decided to open up an already established IT course to language learners. This meant that native English speakers and second language speakers were trained together. The other provider chose to set up a new course for which only second language speakers were recruited. This is how the two projects fared:

The two groups achieved similar pass-rates for the IT qualification, but the standard of work produced by the language learners who were in the mixed group was significantly higher. These learners also made more progress with their English. They were much more focused on the objectives of the course and aware of options for training and employment after the course finished. Follow-up three months after course completion showed that 25 per cent of the learners on the mixed-intake course had found a job and that others had continued their studies at the local college. By contrast, none of the ESOL-only group had found work.

It appears from this case study that the one factor that made a significant difference to the achievement of these learners was whether they formed part of a mixed intake or not. While working with a homogeneous intake makes it easier to plan for and deliver language support, this case study indicates that the disadvantages outweighed the advantages. Even if the learners in the mixed group did not always get instant support with their language needs, being with English-speaking peers created a much richer language environment. Secondly, in addition to relying on their tutors to learn how tasks should be done, they were provided by their peers with models of work. Thirdly, learners on the mixed course had found out from their peers what further learning and employment options were available. By contrast, the ESOL-only group were unaware of what to do next.

At the time of writing, groups consisting of language learners only are by far the most common. Yet this case study indicates that it may not be the most successful model of delivery and that there are significant benefits for the learners to learn in mixed groups. Recruiting ESOL-only groups can also leave the provision vulnerable, since a sufficient number of people needs to be found to run a viable course. Access to courses is much better if learners can be slotted into existing provision.

Since in reality language learners still find themselves on ESOL-only courses, here are some steps which can help language and vocational tutors overcome some of the disadvantages outlined above:

- use course work completed by first language speakers as models for language learners
- if parallel groups of first and second language speakers exist, see if there are occasions when timetables allow for them to work or be taught together
- reserve a specific time for learners from both types of intake to get support and work on their assignments together
- for the next intake of learners, suggest to the management that a pilot project should be set up with a mixed intake of learners and that this should be evaluated for impact on quality and success rates.

Some teachers have worried that first language speakers will get bored and fed up working alongside slower second language speakers. This is a real concern and calls for careful language assessment prior to the beginning of the course. On the other hand, many second language speakers already have vocational and professional skills. Many also have good study skills and a real desire to learn. For example, a course in refrigeration and air-conditioning attracted many learners who had been engineers in their country of origin. When they started a small group to work on the maths underpinning the vocational competences required for their NVQ, their English-speaking colleagues got interested and asked if they could join in. This more than anything else brought the two groups together and created respect for each other's strengths.

Monitoring and evaluation

As we have seen in this chapter, many variables contribute to the design and delivery of language support. This increases the need for close monitoring of the provision, especially if a new project is being established or significant changes are made to existing ones. Often problems can be sorted out if action is taken as soon as a difficulty arises. Since the relationship between mainstream and language support tutors is crucial, it is important to be alert to any misunderstandings or friction in the personal and professional sphere, too. Teams benefit from acknowledging to each other that the first phase of setting up language support can be challenging and that it is OK to discuss issues or get outside help if problems arise.

As the course progresses, it is advisable to review, in the light of the experience of actual delivery, the appropriateness of the planning for it. For example, you may find that the language level for initial assessment needs to be adjusted. The student record system provides a useful tool to monitor this, for example, if the results of initial assessment are compared with the progress of learners who have been identified as having language needs. The need for support may also change as the vocational tutor expands his or her ability to assist the learners with their language development. It is important to involve your mainstream colleagues, learners, and employers in any reviews that you carry out. For example, you could ask for feedback on aspects of language that may need further development. And last, once second language speakers get through the course successfully, you can use their work and reflections on their experience to refine your understanding of the course requirements further.

Summary

Equality of access is often mentioned as an important principle in state-funded education and training. At the same time, providers often face financial constraints which make it difficult to meet all the needs of individual learners. This chapter has provided an overview of steps that teachers can take to set up language support because it is a crucial tool to enable second language speakers to participate in mainstream learning. The key factor for success is to build a good relationship with vocational colleagues and to plan the delivery of the programme together. Language support teachers need to have sufficient time to get to know the vocational course and how it is delivered. Vocational and language teams should have regular opportunities to check if the delivery of the course is going to plan, review the progress of learners, and make adjustment where necessary.

We saw that the integration of first and second language learners can bring significant benefits. The last key factor also suffuses this book: the need to observe what the learners can already and not yet do and to create learning opportunities that enable them to develop their English language skills.

Further reading

Department for Education and Skills. 2004. *The Skills for Life Materials for Embedded Learning.* London: DfES Publications.
This series consists of materials packs on occupations such as trowel work, social care, horticulture, and communication for international nurses. While they contain some useful activities and the materials are well-produced, teachers should be aware that only the nurses' pack was produced to meet the needs of language learners hence adaptation is often required.

http://www.ukstandards.org.uk
This website consists of a directory of national occupational standards. It contains units of competence, performance criteria and knowledge requirements for just about any occupational standard you can think of. The website also has a full list of awarding bodies and links to their websites. These in turn provide information on resources, exam papers, etc. that can help plan language support activities.

http://www.lsc.gov.uk/National/Documents/ReadingRoom
This website provides access to all the documentation published by the Learning and Skills Council. The Reading Room is a useful source of policy documents such as on self-assessment reports, the funding of ESOL provision, etc.

http://www.scottish-enterprise.com
This website provides information on the services which Scottish Enterprise offers in terms of provision for people whose first language is not English. It also lists links to partner organizations and providers in Scotland.

8 REFLECTIVE PRACTICE

The teacher's ability to reflect on his or her own practice can be an important driving force to bring about change and improvement. For example, when teachers enter the classroom, they bring with them not just their teaching skills, but also their own experience, perceptions, and cultural assumptions of learning. This section explores the value of becoming aware of these and the possible impact they have on teaching. This includes the teacher's expectations of the learners and the impact of cultural assumptions on giving feedback. The skills of first and second language speaking teachers are explored. Attention is also paid to the potential tension between the strategies that teachers use to communicate with their learners in the classroom and the skills that are needed for language assessment. Classroom research can bring real insights into teaching and learning and the second part of this chapter is dedicated to approaches and techniques which can help the teacher engage in this activity.

The attitudes and skills of the teacher

TASK Perceptions of language learning

It is often said that our experiences as a learner shape our approach as teachers. Yet we may not be conscious of their impact on our perceptions and practice. That is why it is useful to focus on our own experiences of learning, and in particular of language learning.

1 Have you ever learnt a foreign language? What was good and not so good about the experience? Were there any activities and teaching approaches that you particularly liked and disliked?

2 Thinking about the activities which you liked and disliked, how do they compare to the activities you use in your own teaching?

3 Can you think of examples where your experience as a learner has influenced your teaching?

If your experience was positive, this is likely to have created positive attitudes to language learning. You will also have formed a view, consciously or unconsciously, of the language methods and activities used. For example, you may have enjoyed language drills and, as a consequence, adopt these with enthusiasm in your teaching. Equally, any negative learning experiences may also affect your teaching. If you disliked role-plays, you may not use them in your teaching as a consequence. Or you may never have had the benefit of help with pronunciation.

On the one hand, a teacher who is enthusiastic about an activity or teaching technique is more likely to inspire her students, so it makes sense to use activities she likes. On the other hand, teachers may not be aware that they avoid using an activity or technique because they did not like them as a learner. This is of concern if these would suit the needs of their learners. If you find that your likes and dislikes as a learner and as a teacher match each other, it is worth exploring why they overlap and experimenting with methods that you have not used so far. A good starting point is to take a group of students whose language skills you know well. Try to think of an activity which suits their needs and which you would not normally use. For example, if you do not use extended listening exercises or rarely get the students to write in class, you could try out such a task. Review its effectiveness and how you felt about doing it. You can also ask your students what they thought about the activities and how they felt it helped them learn. Another option is to use the course induction and mid-term reviews to find out what topics and learning methods the students like best. These can give you a valuable opportunity to 'think outside your own box' and inspire new ways of teaching.

For example, you could put these three headings on the board:

What English language skills would you like to learn?	What do you want to use the language for?	How would you like to learn?

Ask the learners to get into small groups and brainstorm ideas under these headings. Learners may write down under the 'language skills' heading: *grammar, past tense, vocabulary for reading an IT manual,* and *how to ask for a bus ticket.* They may put under the 'language use' heading: *how to read a letter from my daughter's school, understanding real English people,* or *finding out about politics in Britain.* You will see that the ideas under the first two headings overlap to a certain extent, but that is fine. This exercise is about creating ideas. Under 'how would you like to learn?', the learners may put: *talking to each other, writing lists of words, listening to tapes,* and *watching videos.* When all groups have contributed their ideas, you can work out together whether there are any sequences which fit well across the three headings. For example, in one year, some students mentioned that they would like to read English poetry, which the whole class agreed to try out. The teacher chose the poem *New Season* by Wendy Cope which was a great success as a reading activity, as a source for learning vocabulary, and for practising intonation and stress. The students loved its upbeat, optimistic tone and its sense that anything is possible. They also spent some time reading the poem aloud to each other, using the principles of stress and the linking of words, as they are explained in Chapter 5. The teacher had never used poetry until then and it is now part of her repertoire.

ESOL teachers' expectations of the learners

It is often said about learners in ESOL classes that their pace of learning and level of achievement is slow, particularly in comparison with learners of EFL. It is undoubtedly true that not all learners of ESOL make fast progress and often for good reason, such as a lack of education in their country of origin. At the same time, it cannot be true that all learners in ESOL classes are slow learners. Many are just as talented language learners as students in EFL classes. This poses the question whether ESOL teachers are always sufficiently ambitious for their learners. All professional communities acquire their own ethos over time. ESOL teachers have always offered their learners strong support, often providing their only sympathetic point of contact with English-speaking people. This is in itself not surprising as ESOL teachers have traditionally concentrated on the needs of people who arrive with little or no English. It is also important to remember that ESOL grew out of a desire to help people with a low level of formal education; especially women who were at home while their husbands went to work. As a consequence, ESOL has a tradition of dealing with the first stages of settlement, with the teacher acting in a support role.

Yet what if teachers do not always balance pastoral support for students with setting challenging targets and providing language-focused teaching? It is important that these questions are asked by individual teachers and within organizations. To help this process, it may be useful to explore how other countries such as Australia, New Zealand, and Canada deliver language teaching to migrants and refugees. For example, Australia has a history of offering intensive language and high-level vocational courses. Publications such as by Adriana VandenHeuvel and Mark Wooden (1999) for the Australian Department of Immigration and Multicultural Affairs document the success of migrant settlement there and the factors that contributed to it. The Centre for Canadian Language Benchmarks has published general benchmarks for English as a second language (Pawlikowska-Smith 2000) as well as specific standards to record the language demands of the nursing profession (2002). Closer to home, foreign language and EFL departments can also provide useful insights into different perspectives on language teaching.

The skills of first and second language speakers

English language teachers are likely to work as part of a team consisting of teachers who have a range of language backgrounds. Much has been written in the academic press about the differences between teachers who have English as their first language and teachers who have another language as their first language, but this has mostly been reported in an EFL rather than ESOL context.

TASK

Can you think of ways in which native English and non-native teachers bring different strengths and weaknesses into teaching?

Likely strengths and weaknesses of:

Teachers who have English as their first language	Teachers who have another language as their first language
provide consistently good models of language, especially of pronunciation	may have a foreign accent and / or some inaccuracies in language use
are able to say whether a word string or sentence is accurate or not	may not always be able to judge whether a word string or sentence is accurate
can identify inaccurate language but may not be able to say why it is wrong may lack an understanding of how the English language works and hence are less able to explain and help the learners reflect on their language use	are likely to have a good understanding of how the language works and to have knowledge of effective teaching techniques
have empathy with the learners but may have no direct experience of being a language learner or of settling in a new country	will have a real understanding through direct experience of what it is like to be a language learner, a migrant, or refugee

TASK

How can both types of teachers develop their skills?

The table above shows that the skills of the two types of teachers complement each other well. Where, for example, the native English speaker provides good models of language, the second language speaker may have a better understanding of the way the English language works. Teachers can make good use of each other's skills by setting up a 'buddy' system to learn from each other. Peer observations in mixed pairs of first and second language speakers can also provide valuable insights.

If you have never learnt another language or have not done so since you left school, there is one more way of exploring language learning: you should consider learning a language yourself. Many teachers report that they have gained new insights into what it is like to learn as an adult, especially if they manage to sustain it beyond the beginner level. For example, teachers have been surprised at how long it took them to learn a new language and how much repetition they needed. They have commented how they could use an aspect of the language well one day and not at all the next. These are all typical experiences of the language learner, which teachers can use to reflect critically on their use of teaching methodology.

The communication skills of language teachers

We now turn to the fourth and last aspect in this chapter, the communication skills and strategies which language teachers develop over time. Language teachers often find that their perception of their learners' language skills differs from other people who come into contact with second language speakers. The exercise below explores why this might be.

CASE STUDY

You will find below comments made by a language teacher, an IT tutor working in a college, and an employer. They are talking about the language skills of two language learners, a student who wants to take an IT course and another who wants to get a job.

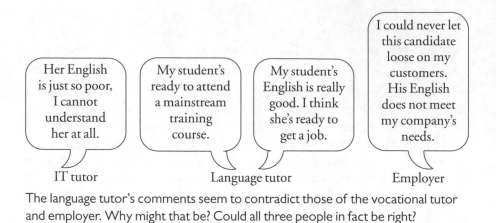

IT tutor   Language tutor   Employer

The language tutor's comments seem to contradict those of the vocational tutor and employer. Why might that be? Could all three people in fact be right?

Perceptions of language levels are often subjective and are made on the basis of personal experience. People who have had little contact with learners of English often find it hard to communicate with them. If you are an experienced language teacher, it may help to think back to the very early days of your teaching career to remember that feeling. It is likely that you found it hard to communicate with your students and that you had to concentrate hard on what they were saying. Over time, English language teachers develop both listening skills and strategies which enable them to maintain communication well beyond the capability of people who have little contact with second language speakers. Experienced teachers compensate for missing language, interpret any pronunciation errors, and create meaning where a less experienced person, such as the IT tutor or the employer, would have lost the thread of what was being said. So in a sense all three people in the case study above are right: the IT tutor and employer really do understand less than the language teacher.

Differences of opinion occur quite frequently between language tutors and others who come into contact with second language speakers. Understanding the reasons for this mismatch can be very useful, for example, when negotiating progression from language courses to further education or when advising a learner on whether she will need an interpreter during a doctor's appointment.

However, there is a second, important aspect to consider. On the one hand, the language teacher's skill in communicating with the learners is useful, indeed essential, particularly at beginner level. On the other hand, it is important to acknowledge that, having developed this specialist skill, language teachers are not representative of the English-speaking public. Since second language speakers learn English in order to communicate with people outside the classroom, the yardstick for language assessment should be whether the general public would be able to understand them. This is an important consideration when assessing the learners' language skills, especially when making a judgement on whether they are ready to progress to mainstream provision or employment. When in assessing mode, teachers need to ask themselves: 'Would a member of the general public, an employer, or a mainstream tutor be able to understand this person and vice versa? How much of the communication between me and the learner is achieved because I have got used to his or her language use?' This type of reflection is not just important during the final assessment process. If applied during initial and ongoing assessment, it can also inform the learning programme itself, by paying special attention to aspects such as pronunciation and use of grammar.

Reflecting on classroom practice

Research in the classroom has traditionally been carried out by academics. In addition, some teachers have also undertaken classroom research as part of an MA. However, in recent years the engagement of teachers as researchers has become increasingly popular. This started to a large degree with the encouragement of academic institutions which have an action research programme, for example, the National Research and Development Centre (NRDC) based in London or the National Centre for English Language Teaching and Research (NCELTR) at Macquarie University in Australia.

However, the realization has grown that classroom research can also usefully be undertaken by individual teachers who are interested in exploring a particular aspect of language teaching and learning. For example, they may want to evaluate the introduction of materials or a new approach to teaching. Also popular is the evaluation of the impact of the teacher's own practice on learning. These enquiries do not necessarily have to lead to improved teaching, although they may do so. They form part of a professional approach to teaching which enables the teacher to stand back and reflect on classroom practice. An important part of classroom research is the choosing of a line of enquiry. This section will focus on three methods which teachers can use to get started.

Critical incident analysis

The concept of the critical incident, formulated by the educational researcher David Tripp (1993), is based on the notion that events that go wrong or are out of the ordinary can form a good starting point for investigation. The case study below illustrates how this can be done.

CASE STUDY 1

A teacher has just started with a new group of learners. She has noticed that some of them do not participate fully in the lessons. She wants to find out why that might be. She is also keen to consider how she can engage these learners more effectively.

How could this teacher plan classroom research on this?

The realization that there may be a problem with student participation can be turned into a focus for enquiry. The teacher uses the 'when, why, and what' question framework to structure her line of investigation. These result in the following questions:

When do some of the learners not participate? Is there a pattern to their lack of engagement? What could be the reason(s) why the learners are not involved?

The teacher uses these questions to monitor classroom interaction. She realizes that, apart from one older woman, the non-participating learners concerned are all younger than the others in the class. She decides to talk to the younger learners. She finds out from them that they are all single and that they switch off when topics on home and family are addressed in class. The teacher suggests that the whole class should have a discussion on what topics are of most interest and make sure that there is a more balanced offer. Teacher and learners agree that they will try this out for a few weeks and then evaluate how well the new approach suits the learners in the group.

The teacher also talks to the older learner who participates hardly at all. This learner tells her that she is very shy and worried about making mistakes. While talking to her, the teacher realizes that the learner's language skills are quite good and that she has been placed in the right class. The teacher suggests to the student that she should to try to get involved more in small group work initially. Once the learner feels more at ease with this, she will also be drawn into whole group discussion. The teacher makes a mental note that, to build up this learner's confidence, she will initially ask the learner simple questions which she can be expected to be able to answer without difficulty.

CASE STUDY 2

Many of your learners arrive consistently late for the morning session, which is disruptive to you and the learners who are already present. You decide:

- to find out from the students what the reasons are for their lack of punctuality

- to monitor the impact of different methods of encouraging the learners to be on time.

When you discuss their lack of punctuality with the learners, you find out that some are late because they can only drop off their children at the crèche at nine o'clock, which is when your lesson starts. You decide to take this up with your manager to see if the crèche can be opened ten minutes before the lesson. In addition, there are two learners who tend to drift in later. You talk to the whole group about the need for punctuality, not just because the learners lose out on the start of the lesson, but also out of courtesy to the whole group. You explain that, if people are late, you will not interrupt the lesson but will continue with the activity you had started. Teachers may also want to alert the learners to the fact that it is a good idea to acquire the habit of being on time, as punctual arrival is expected for appointments, such as with doctors and children's teachers, as well as in the workplace.

Setting and exploring research questions

A second way to investigate a particular aspect of teaching and learning is to formulate one or more questions to guide your investigation. For example, you could frame questions such as:

- How do the learners view the benefits of learning grammar versus communicative activities, such as classroom talk and pair work?
- How effective is the practice of getting stronger and weaker learners to work together as a tool to manage the learners' individual learning needs?
- Does my teaching of the four skills of speaking, listening, reading, and writing reflect the needs of the learners?
- What do the learners think of the use of information and communication technology (ICT) in the classroom?

If we take the question on handling differentiated learning as an example, the teacher could collect data by observing what pairs of strong and weaker learners do while they are working on a task; or she could record them and analyse the data later. She could focus on aspects such as how the learners manage the task, what language is being produced, and what learning is taking place. She could evaluate the advantages and disadvantages of this paired approach, such as looking at what happens if the stronger learner produces inaccurate language.

Record material and then analyse

The two research methods mentioned so far have relied on drawing up questions to guide the research. The third method is to take classroom interaction as a starting point and to identify areas of interest during or after the analysis. Data collection can either be achieved by an external observer or by audio- or video-recording a lesson or part of a lesson. While this can feel a random process, it can throw up unexpected and illuminating information as well as useful prompts for further exploration. For example, having recorded yourself, you may find yourself reflecting on aspects such as:

- how you come across, for example, what your voice sounds like and whether it is pitched right so that you are easy to listen to
- whether your instructions are clear and pitched at the right level of language
- whether the sequence of activities that you had planned was coherent
- how you gave feedback to the learners, for example, how often, on what aspects, and at what points in the lesson.

These aspects show that recording yourself is a valuable tool not just to reflect on classroom interaction and major features of teaching but also on small, personal aspects and behaviour. This method of collecting and analysing data is called 'ethnographic' research. It was pioneered in anthropology where fieldwork was used to gather data which were subsequently analysed. It has since spread into areas such as the language classroom and the business environment.

Summary

In this chapter we have seen that reflection and self-awareness are powerful tools to review and improve the quality of teaching. Cultural assumptions and the teacher's own experience of learning can influence attitudes to teaching and affect his or her expectations of the learners. Experienced teachers may be unaware that the skill they have developed to communicate with language learners may cloud their judgements on the learners' language levels. Teams consisting of a mixture of teachers who have English as their first or other language can usefully draw on their relative strengths. In addition to reflecting on these aspects outside the classroom, teachers can also use classroom research to evaluate the effectiveness of their teaching practice. This can help improve both major teaching approaches as well as other aspects such as management and presentation skills.

Further reading

Pawlikowska-Smith, G. 2000. *Canadian Language Benchmarks: English as a Second Language—For adults.* Ottawa: Centre for Canadian Language Benchmarks.

Centre for Canadian Language Benchmarks. 2002. *Benchmarking the English Language Demands of the Nursing Professional across Canada.* Ottawa: Centre for Canadian Language Benchmarks.

http://www.immi.gov.au/living-in-australia/help-with-english/learn-english/
The Adult Migrant English Program (AMEP) is an Australian education and settlement programme for newly arrived migrants and refugees. The website provides an overview of reports and publications as well as access to national standards, etc.

http://www.nceltr.mq.edu.au/prospect/
AMEP also publishes *Prospect, an Australian Journal of TESOL,* which contains articles on research and professional issues in TESOL and applied linguistics.

http://www.langcanada.ca
This website provides information on resources which have been specially developed for the teaching of ESL in Canada.

GLOSSARY

ACTIVE VOICE: A way of expressing actions which focuses on who did what: e.g. *The dog bit the cat.*

AGENT: The doer of an action in a sentence; see ACTIVE VOICE.

ANTONYMS: Words which mean the opposite, such as *disappointed ≠ relieved, pleased*

ASYLUM SEEKERS: People who have had to flee their country of origin and whose application to remain in the new country has not yet been granted.

BOTTOM-UP PROCESSING: Building up meaning through focusing on small units of information. See also TOP-DOWN PROCESSING.

COLLOCATIONS: Words which habitually belong together, e.g. *fish and chips.*

COMPOUNDING: Forming a new word out of two or more existing words, a process which is common in English.

DECODING: The process of registering a text, identifying individual letters or sounds, and assembling these into syllables and words. See TOP-DOWN and BOTTOM-UP PROCESSING.

DISCOURSE MARKERS: Words that link ideas and events across paragraphs, e.g. *first, then, after that,* and *finally.* Discourse markers are used extensively in English and fulfill a wide range of functions. See also LINK WORDS.

FIRST LANGUAGE SPEAKERS: People who speak English as their first language and were brought up to speak English.

FOSSILIZATION: When learners get stuck at a basic level of language; they may need explicit feedback to improve (see also NOTICING).

FUNCTION: The purpose of the communication, e.g. asking for or providing information.

GRAMMAR: The way that language is organized. It refers to the collection of rules which are used to create words and sentences.

IMPERATIVE: The form of a verb used to give commands: e.g. *Give it to me!.* Can convey an impression of abruptness or rudeness in English.

INTERLANGUAGE: The emerging language produced by learners of a new language. Interlanguage is not static but changes as the learner develops from stage to stage. See also OVER-GENERALIZATION.

LANGUAGE AUDIT: (1) A process whereby tutors familiarize themselves with course content and the language requirements of MAINSTREAM PROVISION before they start offering LANGUAGE SUPPORT; (2) the process of gathering information on the language backgrounds of learners.

LANGUAGE COMPETENCE: Underlying knowledge of a language

LANGUAGE SUPPORT: A term used to refer to language tuition attached to vocational courses. See also MAINSTREAM PROVISION.

LEXICAL SEGMENTATION: The process of working out where words begin and end. Second language learners often find this hard to do. Even if they 'know' the written form, they may not recognize a word when they hear it in connected speech.

LEXIS: How learners use words as individual items and as strings of words which belong together.

LINK WORDS: Words that link events, objects, and ideas within sentences. For example, a link word such as *because* is used to explain why something has happened; and *either … or* to give alternative options. See also DISCOURSE MARKERS.

MAINSTREAM PROVISION: Programmes that have as their main goal an education or training qualification rather than language learning. See also LANGUAGE SUPPORT.

META-LANGUAGE: terminology to describe features of language or grammar.

MIGRANTS: People who have come to live in another country for economic reasons or for reasons of family reunion.

NOTICING: The concept of promoting learning by creating opportunities for learners to notice how they are using English and how they could improve.

OPAQUE SPELLING SYSTEM: Because of its mixture of regular and irregular spellings, English spelling cannot always be predicted from the pronunciation (and vice versa). See also TRANSPARENT.

OVER-GENERALIZATION: Applying an existing rule beyond the context in which it is normally used. Children often do this in the early stages of language learning, e.g. when they call all animals *dogs* or all men *daddy*. See also INTERLANGUAGE.

PASSIVE VOICE: Forms of verbs which indicate a focus on the process rather than the AGENT: e.g. *The factory was closed (by the owner).*

PAST TENSE: Forms of verbs which indicate that the action happened in the past.

PHONICS: A system of teaching learners to read by relating a particular letter to a particular sound. Because English spelling only partly reflects the pronunciation of words, it seems logical to use a multi-skilled approach when teaching reading and writing skills.

PRAGMATICS: How speakers express their attitude and intention through their choice of language.

PREFIX: A particle added to the front of a word, e.g. *un*happy. (See also SUFFIX.) Both are added to the ROOT of the word. These prefixes and suffixes give the English language tremendous flexibility.

PROVIDERS: Any organisation such as further and adult education colleges, training providers, prisons etc that deliver ESOL programmes.

REALIA: Using real objects such as *peppers, cutlery,* or *a bowl* to present new language.

REFUGEES: People who have had to flee their country of origin and whose application to remain in the new country has been granted.

REGISTER: A style of speaking and writing appropriate for a particular context, e.g. colloquial or formal.

ROOT: The part of a word which provides its core meaning: e.g. un*happi*ness.

SCANNING: In reading, searching a text for specific information, e.g. a name in a directory, a departure time in a timetable, or a specific detail in a manual. In a sense the opposite of SKIMMING.

SCHWA: The most common vowel sound in spoken English, although it is not represented in the alphabet. Represented as /ə/ in phonetic notation.

SECOND LANGUAGE SPEAKERS: People who speak other language(s) than English and are learning English as a second or additional language.

SKIMMING: In reading, getting the *gist* or general idea of a text, e.g. by flicking through a book, casting the eye over a text, looking at headings and opening and closing paragraphs. See also SCANNING.

SUFFIX: A particle added to the end of a word, e.g. happi*ness*.

SYNONYMS: Words which mean the same, for example, *disappointed = unhappy, not pleased.*

TOP-DOWN PROCESSING: Using knowledge of larger units to determine and confirm small units of information, by using knowledge of the language, the world, and the context. See also BOTTOM-UP PROCESSING.

TRANSPARENT SPELLING SYSTEM: A system which represents the pronunciation of words consistently, e.g. languages such as Spanish and Polish.

WASHBACK: The effect of an exam on classroom teaching. This can impact both positively and negatively on the content of lessons and on the perceptions of teachers and learners. Also known as 'backwash'.

WEAK FORMS: Unstressed variants of words, which occur frequently in fluent English speech and give it its characteristic rhythm. See also SCHWA.

BIBLIOGRAPHY

Acklam, R. and **A. Crace.** 2005. *Total English Pre-Intermediate.* Harlow: Pearson.

Aitken, R. 2002. *Teaching Tenses: Ideas for Presenting and Practising English Tenses.* London: Longman.

Alderson, J. C., C. Clapham, and **D. Wall.** 2006. *Language Test Construction and Evaluation.* Cambridge: Cambridge University Press.

Ammar, A. and **N. Spada.** 2006. 'One size fits all? Recasts, prompts, and learners' learning'. *Studies in Second Language Acquisition.* 28/4: 543–74.

Carter, R. and **M. McCarthy.** 1997. *Exploring Spoken English.* Cambridge: Cambridge University Press.

Carter, R. and **M. McCarthy.** 2006. *Cambridge Grammar of English: A Comprehensive Guide to Spoken and Written English Grammar and Usage.* Cambridge: Cambridge University Press.

Centre for Canadian Language Benchmarks. 2002. *Benchmarking the English Language Demands of the Nursing Professional across Canada.* Ottawa: Centre for Canadian Language Benchmarks.

Cliff, P. and **T. Bradbury.** 2005. *Skills for Life Exam Preparation Pack.* Oxford: Oxford University Press.

Coffield, F., D. Moseley, E. Hall, and **K. Ecclestone.** 2004a. *Learning Styles and Pedagogy in post-16 Learning.* London: Learning and Skills Development Centre.

Coffield, F., D. Moseley, E. Hall, and **K. Ecclestone.** 2004b. *Should We Be Using Learning Styles? What Research Has to Say to Practice.* London: Learning and Skills Development Centre.

Crystal, D. 2004. *Rediscover Grammar.* London: Longman.

Cunningham, S. and **P. Moor.** 2005. *New Cutting Edge.* London: Longman.

Cunningham, S. and **P. Moor** with **F. Eales.** 2005. *New Cutting Edge Elementary.* London: Longman.

Cutler, A. 1990. 'Exploiting prosodic possibilities in speech segmentation' in G. Altmann (ed.): *Cognitive Models of Processing.* Cambridge, Mass.: MIT.

Davis, P. and **M. Rinvolucri.** 2000. *Dictation.* Cambridge: Cambridge University Press.

Department for Education and Skills. 2000. *National Standards for Adult Literacy and Numeracy.* London: DfES Publications.

Department for Education and Skills. 2001. *The Adult ESOL Core Curriculum.* London: DfES Publications.

Department for Education and Skills. 2003a. *Pathways to Proficiency: The Alignment of Language Proficiency Scales for Assessing Competence in English Language.* London: DfES Publications.

Department for Education and Skills. 2003b. *Skills for Life Learner Materials Packs for ESOL at Entry 1, 2, and 3; and Levels 1 and 2.* London: DfES Publications.

Department for Education and Skills. 2003c. *Working with Refugees and Asylum Seekers: Support Materials for ESOL Providers.* London: DfES Publications.

Department for Education and Skills. 2004a. *ESOL Exemplars for Speaking and Listening, Reading, Writing.* London: DfES Publications.

Department for Education and Skills. 2004b. *The Skills for Life Materials for Embedded Learning.* London: DfES Publications.

Department for Education and Skills/Home Office. 2005. *Citizenship Materials for ESOL Learners.* London: DfES Publications.

Derwing, T., M. Munro, and **G. Wiebe.** 1998. 'Evidence in favor of a broad framework for pronunciation instruction.' *Language Learning* 48: 393–410.

Derwing, T. and **M. Rossiter.** 2003: 'The effects of pronunciation instruction on the accuracy, fluency, and complexity of L2 accented speech.' *Applied Language Learning* 13: 1–17.

Ellis, N. 2007. 'Cognitive perspectives on SLA: the associative-cognitive creed.' *AILA Review vol 19*

Field, J. 2003a. 'Promoting perception: lexical segmentation in L2 listening.' *English Language Teaching Journal* 57/3: 325–43.

Field, J. 2003b. *Psycholinguistics.* London: Routledge.

Foley, M. and **D. Hall.** 2005. *Total English Elementary.* London: Longman.

Graham, C. 1978. *Jazz Chants.* Oxford: Oxford University Press.

Grellet, F. 1996. *Writing for Advanced Learners of English.* Cambridge: Cambridge University Press.

Hancock, M. 2003. *English Pronunciation in Use: Intermediate.* Cambridge: Cambridge University Press.

Hattie, J. 1999. *Influences on Student Learning.* Inaugural lecture. University of Auckland.

Hedge, T. 2001. *Teaching and Learning in the Language Classroom.* Oxford: Oxford University Press.

Home Office. 2003. *The New and the Old.* The report of the 'Life in the United Kingdom' Advisory Group. London: Home Office. Available to download from http://www.ind.homeoffice.gov.uk/aboutus/reports/new_old (accessed 8 December 2006).

Howatt, A. with **H. Widdowson.** 2004. *A History of English Language Teaching.* Oxford: Oxford University Press.

Hughes, A. 2002. *Testing for Language Teachers.* Cambridge: Cambridge University Press.

Karlsen, L. 2005. *The ESOL Literacy Resource Pack.* Second edition. www.esolliteracy.co.uk

Kempton, J., R. Haque, C. Dustmann, and **M. Shields.** 2002. *Migrants in the UK: Their Characteristics and Labour Market Outcomes and Impacts.* London: Home Office RDS Occasional Paper 82.

Kenworthy, J. 1987. *Teaching English Pronunciation.* London: Longman.

Krashen, S. 1985. *The Input Hypothesis: Issues and Implications.* London: Longman.

Krashen, S. and **T. D. Terrell.** 1983. *The Natural Approach.* Oxford: Pergamon.

Laufer, B. 1992. 'How much lexis is necessary for reading comprehension?' in Arnaud, P. and H. Béjoint. (eds): *Vocabulary and Applied Linguistics.* Oxford: Macmillan.

Leech, G., P. Rayson, and **A. Wilson.** 2001. *Word Frequencies in Written and Spoken English.* Harlow: Pearson.

Lewis, M. 1993. *The Lexical Approach.* Hove: Language Teaching Publications.

Lewis, M. 1997. *Implementing the Lexical Approach: Putting Theory into Practice.* Hove: Language Teaching Publications.

Lightbown, P. and **N. Spada.** 2006. *How Languages are Learned,* 3rd edn. Oxford: Oxford University Press.

McCarter, S. 1998. *A Book on Writing.* Woodlands: Intelligene.

McCarter, S. 2006. *Tips for IELTS.* Oxford: Macmillan.

McCarthy, M. and **F. O'Dell.** 1999. *English Vocabulary in Use.* Cambridge: Cambridge University Press.

McCarthy, M. and **F. O'Dell.** 2004. *Test Your Vocabulary in Use Elementary.* Cambridge: Cambridge University Press.

McGovern, E. and **G. Smith.** 2006. *New English File ESOL Teachers' Resource Book.* Oxford: Oxford University Press.

Mennim, P. 2003. 'Rehearsed oral L2 output and reactive focus on form.' *English Language Teaching Journal* 57/2: 130–38.

Millar, R. and **C. Klein.** 2002. *Making Sense of Spelling – A Guide to Teaching and Learning How to Spell.* London: SENJIT/Institute of Education.

Murphy, R. 2004. *English Grammar in Use.* Cambridge: Cambridge University Press.

Nation, I. S. P. 2001. *Learning Vocabulary in Another Language.* Cambridge: Cambridge University Press.

National Center for ESL Literacy Education. 2003. *Adult English Language Instruction in the 21st Century.* Washington, DC: Center for Applied Linguistics.

Northedge, A. 2005. *The Good Study Guide.* Buckingham: Open University Press.

Oberg, K. 1960. 'Cultural shock: Adjustment to new cultural environments.' *Practical Anthropology* 7: 177–82.

Oxenden, C., C. Latham-Koenig, and **P. Seligson.** 2004. *New English File Pre-Intermediate.* Oxford: Oxford University Press.

Oxford Collocations Dictionary for Students of English. 2002. Oxford: Oxford University Press.

Oxford Wordpower Dictionary. 2006. Oxford: Oxford University Press.

Pawlikowska-Smith, G. 2000. *Canadian Language Benchmarks: English as a Second Language – for Adults.* Ottawa: Centre for Canadian Language Benchmarks.

Rinvolucri, M. 1985. *Grammar Games.* Cambridge: Cambridge University Press.

Rogerson, P. and **J. Gilbert.** 1990. *Speaking Clearly.* Cambridge: Cambridge University Press.

Schellekens, P. 2001. *English as a Barrier to Employment, Education, and Training.* DfES Publications.

Schellekens, P. 2004. 'Advanced learners' in Roberts, C., Chopra, P., Hodge, R., Baynham, M., Cooke, M., Pitt, K., Schellekens, P., Wallace, C., and Whitfield, S.: *ESOL: Case Studies Of Provision, Learners' Needs and Resources.* London: National Research and Development Centre: 114–28. Available to download from http://www.nrdc.org.uk/publications_details.asp?ID=19 (accessed 8 December 2006).

Schmidt. R. 1990. 'The role of consciousness in second language learning.' *Applied Linguistics* 11/1: 17–46.

Schmidt. R. 2001. 'Attention' in P. Robinson (ed.): *Cognition and Second Language Instruction*. Cambridge: Cambridge University Press.

Selinker, L. 1972. 'Interlanguage.' *International Review of Applied Linguistics* 10/2: 209–31.

Setter, J. and J. Jenkins. 2005. 'State-of-the-art review article' *Language Teaching* 38: 1–17.

Spiegel, M. and H. Sunderland. 2006. *Teaching Basic Literacy to ESOL Learners*. London: LLU+.

Swan, M. 2005. *Practical English Usage*. Oxford: Oxford University Press.

Swan, M. and B. Smith (eds.). 2001. *Learner English*. Cambridge: Cambridge University Press.

Swan, M. and C. Walter. 2001. *The Good Grammar Book*. Oxford: Oxford University Press.

Thornbury, S. 1999a. *About Language: Tasks for Teachers of English*. Cambridge: Cambridge University Press.

Thornbury, S. 1999b. *How to Teach Grammar*. London: Longman.

Thornbury, S. 2002. *How to Teach Vocabulary*. London: Longman.

Tripp, D. 1993. *Critical Incidents in Teaching: Developing Professional Judgement*. London: Routledge.

Ur, P. 1988. *Grammar Practice Activities: A Practical Guide for Teachers*. Cambridge: Cambridge University Press.

VandenHeuvel, A. and M. Wooden. 1999. *New Settlers Have Their Say: How Immigrants Fare over the Early Years of Settlement*. Canberra: Department of Immigration and Multicultural Affairs.

Vaughan-Rees, M. 1994. *Rhymes and Rhythm*. Oxford: Macmillan.

Watcyn-Jones, P. 1981. *Pair Work*. Harlow: Penguin English.

Weir, C. 2005. *Language Testing and Validation*. Basingstoke: Palgrave MacMillan.

Welsh Assembly. 2005. *Words Talk – Numbers Count*. Cardiff: National Assembly for Wales Circular no. 15.

West, C. 1996. *Recycling Your English*. St Helier: Georgian Press.

Wilkins, D. 1972. *Linguistics in Language Teaching.* London: Edward Arnold.

Windsor, V. and **C. Healey.** 2006. *Developing ESOL, Supporting Achievement.* Leicester: NIACE.

Wolderufael, H. 1998. 'The emotional and psychological impact of displacement on the education of Somali students.' Unpublished report for Tower Hamlets College.

Wray, A. 2002. *Formulaic Language and the Lexicon.* Cambridge: Cambridge University Press.

Websites

The Further Reading sections at the end of each chapter provide references to numerous online resources. A few more general sites are listed below. The information provided is up-to-date at the time of going to press. Inclusion in these lists does not necessarily mean that the author or publishers of this book endorse these sites or their content.

http://www.qca.org.uk
The Qualifications and Curriculum Authority (QCA) website provides sample national literacy tests as well as details of the test specification.

http://www.ind.homeoffice.gov.uk/aboutus/reports/accession_monitoring _report
The Home Office publishes regular monitoring reports on the number of people who have come to work in the UK since ten new countries, for example, Poland, Lithuania, and Slovakia, joined the EU in 2004. The reports provide data on their job roles as well as regional distribution in the UK.

http://www.statistics.gov.uk/census and www.nomisweb.co.uk provide access to Census data on country of birth by ward, borough, and nation for England and Wales. www.gro-scotland.gov.uk does the same for Scotland; and www.nisra.gov.uk for Northern Ireland.

http://www.nln.ac.uk/
The National Learning Network provides useful online materials to support learning in areas such as construction, media, and IT. Like the Skills for Life embedded materials, the NLN materials are not specifically aimed at learners whose first language is not English. Organizations engaged in teaching and learning can download the materials and make them available locally to teachers and learners.

INDEX